INDIAN MINIATURES

The Ehrenfeld Collection

BY

DANIEL J. EHNBOM

with Essays by

Robert Skelton and Pramod Chandra

HUDSON HILLS PRESS

NEW YORK

in Association with

the American Federation of Arts

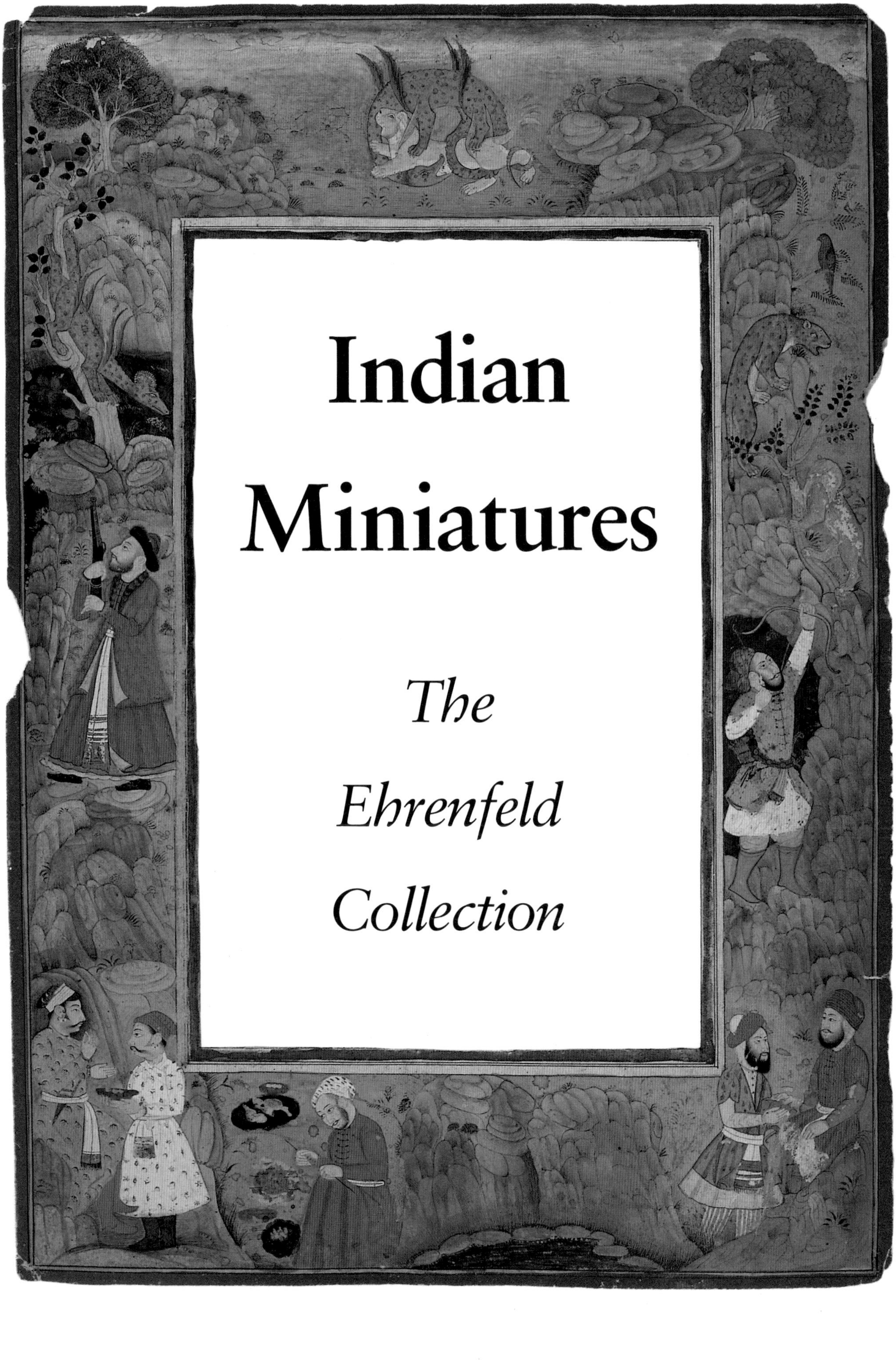

Indian Miniatures

The Ehrenfeld Collection

FIRST EDITION

Published in the United States by Hudson Hills Press, Inc., Suite 301,
220 Fifth Avenue, New York, NY 10001.

Distributed in the United States by Viking Penguin Inc.
Distributed in Canada by Irwin Publishing Inc.
Distributed in the United Kingdom, Eire, Europe, Israel, and the Middle East by Phaidon Press Limited.
Distributed in Japan by Yohan (Western Publications Distribution Agency).

Editor and Publisher: Paul Anbinder
Copy editor: Irene Gordon
Designer: Philip Grushkin
Composition: Trufont Typographers
Manufactured in Japan by Toppan Printing Company

Library of Congress Cataloguing in Publication Data

Ehnbom, Daniel J. (Daniel James), 1950–
Indian miniatures.
"Published in conjunction with the exhibition... organized by the American Federation of Arts. AFA Exhibition 84-5, circulated September 1985–November 1987"—T.p. verso.
Bibliography: p.
Includes index.
1. Illumination of books and manuscripts, Indic—Exhibitions. 2. Miniature painting, Indic—Exhibitions. 3. Ehrenfeld, William K., 1934– —Art collections—Exhibitions. 4. Illumination of books and manuscripts—Private collections—California—San Francisco Bay Area—Exhibitions. 5. Miniature painting, Private collections—California—San Francisco Bay Area—Exhibitions. I. Skelton, Robert. II. Chandra, Pramod. III. Ehrenfeld, William K., 1934– IV. American Federation of Arts. V. Title.
ND3247.E36 1985 745.6'7'0954074013 85-14310
ISBN 0-933920-29-6 (alk. paper)

This book has been published in conjunction with the exhibition *Indian Miniatures from the Ehrenfeld Collection,* organized by the American Federation of Arts.

AFA Exhibition 84-5
Circulated September 1985–November 1987

Title-page illustration: Catalogue number 51. Miniature border: A royal hunting party in a fantastic landscape. See page 118.

Cover illustration: Catalogue number 87. Leaf from a *Devī* series: Brahmā, Śiva, and Viṣṇu worship the goddess Indrākṣī. See page 182.

CONTENTS

FOREWORD

The American Federation of Arts is pleased to be the organizer of this exhibition of Indian miniatures from the collection of Dr. and Mrs. William K. Ehrenfeld of the San Francisco Bay Area. This comparatively young collection, assembled during the past eight years, contains exceptional examples of Indian painting that extend in time from the sixteenth to the mid-nineteenth century. This unusual breadth in both chronological range and stylistic scope reveals the high standards that have guided the formation of the collection.

Dr. Ehrenfeld, a professor of surgery at the University of California, San Francisco, studied art for many years with the intent of becoming a medical illustrator. Mrs. Ehrenfeld has had a lifelong interest in the arts and studied Asian art and Indian painting at Mills College, California. She is presently the manager of an art gallery in San Francisco. Together they have immersed themselves in the history of Indian miniature painting, bringing an acute eye and a keen intellect to the formation of a collection that is a highly personal statement and contains significant works from nearly all the major schools of Indian painting. We are deeply indebted to the Ehrenfelds for their generosity in lending these works for a lengthy tour, and also for their cooperation in the development of the exhibition and this publication.

We are also grateful to Robert Flynn Johnson, Curator in Charge, Achenbach Foundation for Graphic Arts, Fine Arts Museums of San Francisco, who first brought the collection to our attention four years ago. Mr. Johnson has also been instrumental in arranging for the opening presentation at the California Palace of the Legion of Honor, a distinguished and appropriate setting for this premiere viewing.

Daniel J. Ehnbom, a noted young scholar who has recently received his Ph.D. in South Asian art history from the University of Chicago, selected the miniatures included in the exhibition and wrote the catalogue entries as well as an introductory essay. Essays on special aspects of Indian miniature painting have been contributed by two eminent scholars who have written extensively in the field of Indian art: Robert Skelton, Keeper of the Indian Section, Victoria and Albert Museum, London, and Pramod Chandra, George P. Bickford Professor of Indian and South Asian Art, Harvard University. Irene Gordon has been a sensitive and dedicated editor; Philip Grushkin has designed the handsome book; Paul Anbinder, President, Hudson Hills Press, has brought his customary care to making this an excellent publication. To all, we express our gratitude for producing a book which we hope will be of permanent significance in the field.

For their assistance in the care and preparation of the miniatures for display, we thank members of the staff of the Achenbach Foundation: Judith C. Eurich, Curatorial Assistant; Robert Futernick, Conservator; and Niccolo Caldararo, Preparator. To Paul Waring of Biomed Arts Associates, Inc., we express our appreciation for his fine photography of the miniatures included in the catalogue.

The participation of members of the staff of the American Federation of Arts who were most closely associated with this project must be acknowledged: Jane S. Tai, Associate Director and Director, Exhibition Program; Amy V. McEwen, Coordinator, Scheduling, who, as the coordinator for the exhibition, supervised the numerous organizational and administrative details; and Fran Falkin, Exhibition Assistant, who provided the necessary attention to the preparation of materials for the exhibition. Other AFA staff members who have made significant contributions include Jeffery Pavelka, Assistant Director, Exhibition Program, and Sandra Gilbert, Public Information Director. We have also benefited from the varied skills and support of Mary Ann Monet, Konrad G. Kuchel, Carolyn Lasar, Teri Roiger, and Lindsay South.

We acknowledge with thanks the Society for Asian Art, San Francisco, for its support of the exhibition while it is on view in that city, as well as for the symposium that is to accompany the presentation there.

The trustees and staff of the AFA are proud that this exhibition has been designated a part of the official program of the Festival of India, a series of artistic events taking place throughout the United States during the years 1985 and 1986 which aim at illuminating the history and culture of India.

Wilder Green
Director
The American Federation of Arts

ACKNOWLEDGMENTS

MANY PEOPLE HAVE HELPED make this catalogue possible. First, I should like to thank Dr. William K. Ehrenfeld, whose vision and energy assembled the collection, and Robert Johnson of the Achenbach Foundation, whose enthusiasm and efforts did so much to make the exhibition a reality.

I should also like to express my thanks to Pramod Chandra and Robert Skelton, not only for their valuable contributions to this catalogue, but also for their continuing generosity of spirit and constant encouragement. B. N. Goswamy, too, was a great help, directly by his interest in the project and indirectly by the example set by his scholarship. Edwin Binney, 3rd, gave untiringly of his knowledge and time and opened up his collection to me, for which I can never thank him enough. And I also extend my thanks to the many collectors, scholars, and museum staff members who so generously shared with me whatever I needed, especially Mildred Archer, Stuart Cary Welch, Robert Brown, John Seyller, and Andrew Topsfield.

Every scholar knows the difficulties of the many languages and scripts that must be considered when cataloguing a collection of this range, and I thank all who helped me. Mohammad A. Khadim, Mohammad Ghanoonparvar, C. M. Naim, Abdulaziz A. Sachedina, Mohammed Sawaie, Laurel Steele, and Muhammad S. Yusuf read the Persian, Urdu, and Avadhī texts for me, and Simon Digby and John Roberts were of great assistance in discussing and interpreting the Hindi and Sanskrit texts and notations. It was only through the assistance, examples, and encouragement of Robert Skelton and B. N. Goswamy that I dared to tackle the thorny *ṭākarī* script of the inscriptions and captions on many of the Pahāṛī pictures.

My former colleagues at the University of Virginia in Charlottesville were of assistance in many ways. I should particularly like to thank Marjorie Balge, Richard Crozier, Marcy Edelstein, JoAnne Paradise, and David Sensabaugh.

Finally, I must give special thanks to the American Federation of Arts for its tireless efforts on behalf of the exhibition and catalogue, especially to Amy V. McEwen, Jane S. Tai, and Wilder Green.

DANIEL J. EHNBOM

Note

A.H. The era A.H. (anno hegirae) is reckoned from A.D. 622, the year of Mohammed's flight from Mecca.

V.S. The era V.S. (Vikramāditya saṃvat), generally used in northern India, is reckoned from 57 B.C.

Collecting Indian Miniatures

by Robert Skelton

No one has calculated how many Indian miniatures survive today, but clearly the total is very considerable. A vast number have undoubtedly been lost, but the tens of thousands that remain owe their continuing existence to a disparate group of men whose attitudes toward these fragile treasures have ranged from casual neglect to passionate absorption.

Connoisseurship as it is known in Europe or the Far East is alien to the Indian tradition. Despite some early evidence of codification, Indian taste in the visual arts appears, in general, to be instinctive rather than studied. If literary sources are to be our guide, the *rasika* (who applied discrimination in his appreciation of the arts) centered his interest on performance and poetry rather than on the artifact, or on the more curious productions of nature. Before the maharajas and princes of commerce adopted the style of the English gentry there was no indigenous parallel to the European *Wunderkammer* (cabinet of curiosities), even though the popular Indian term for a museum, *ʿajāʾīb ghar* (house of wonders), has the same meaning.

However, the activities of one man must be excluded from this generalization. Jahāngīr, emperor of India (r. 1605–27), fourth of the Mughal dynasty, shared with his contemporary Rudolf II, Holy Roman Emperor (1576–1612) and Europe's archetypal collector, the mania for acquiring *naturalia* and *artificialia*, which to some extent may be attributed to his Timurid, i.e., non-Indian, ancestry, which included Tamerlane and Genghis Khan. This Turco-Persian heritage was reinforced by contact with European men of education and the exotica they brought with them, but Jahāngīr never aspired to the singular erudition of the Hapsburg monarch, and his acquisitive curiosity and connoisseurship barely outlived him. As for the modern descendants of the *Wunderkammer*, it is true that the Indian Museum in Calcutta (founded 1814) outranks many august Western institutions in seniority of foundation, but it was an imposition from the Western Age of Reason; a visit to Calcutta today will confirm that such foreign bodies are prone to suffer gradual rejection.

We know so little about the motivation behind early Indian collecting that it should be no matter for surprise that we can question whether any positive impulse indeed existed. Was the survival of paintings due only to benign indifference? In the extreme physical environment of India this was not at all enough to account for what still remains. In view of the ravages of monsoon, termites, and other hazards, one wonders at the pristine condition of so many miniatures, particularly those from the libraries of the Rājput dynasties (though these were among the main defenders of India's ancient values in later times). These pictures could not have survived as we see them today without a sound empirical tradition of conservation practice that implies both the will to preserve and the organization required to achieve this. In the bureaucracy of the Hindu court, modified as it was by the emulation of imperial Mughal administrative practice, there was an undisturbed niche for the humble *lekhnias* (clerks) and *bhanḍārīs* (storekeepers), who formed the lower ranks of the *mutṣaddī* (administrative class). In their custody the pictures were kept superlatively well in their cloth bundles protected by pest-deterrent leaves.

If we inquire how works of art came into the stewardship of these devoted functionaries we shall find art historians frenetically combing the dynastic histories for those all too-elusive passages that suggest, or can be made to suggest, that a particular ruler actually cared about the arts or actively patronized artists. It is true that some maharajas were undoubtedly keen and, to various degrees, discerning patrons who raised the output and sometimes the quality of the works commissioned for them. Our main evidence for this is the pictures themselves. Almost no one reveals himself to us so compellingly as does the mid-eighteenth-century prince of the Punjab Hills whom we know from inscriptions as Rājā Balwant Siṅgh (cat. no. 111). Anyone familiar with the pictures can only see Balwant Siṅgh as a lovable personal acquaintance, yet controversy still continues as to his exact identity and we are still not certain which royal family he belonged to.

If such rulers as Balwant Siṅgh were clearly active and discriminating in their patronage of painting, we still have practically no evidence that they seriously sought to acquire works from the past or from other places. True, there is ample evidence that Indian royal collections contained earlier or imported pictures, but these are usually explained by writers on the subject as spoils of war, part of a dowry, or perhaps the exchange of diplomatic gifts. It would strain our credulity to believe that a Balwant Siṅgh was interested only in pictures that reflected his own life-style; yet at one very important level we must accept that art patronage in India merely satisfied a set of socio-economic relations whereby members of one class provided regular services in exchange for the means of subsistence supplied by those at the summit of the hierarchy.

When the collection of the Mahārājā of Bikaner was dispersed some years ago there appeared on the market a batch of paintings all of which depicted that heroic, legendary combat in which the goddess Durgā overcame Mahiṣa, the buffalo demon. There are standard compositional models for the depiction of such mythological subjects and among the dozens of versions held by the Bikaner *poṭhikhāna* (manuscript library) there was little freshness of invention or evidence of inspirational engagement with the theme. If these routinely executed pictures had any interest, it was confined to the librarian's contemporary annotations on the reverse of each, which recorded in repetitive detail the name of the artist and date of presentation. These pictures were painted over a period of several generations, but the dates in the inscriptions had one thing in common. In whatever year they were painted, the pictures were always presented to the maharaja on the tenth day of the autumn month of Asoj, when the artists came into the city from the villages whose rents were assigned to them, to attend the royal celebration of the Dusehra festival when the goddess is worshiped. It was a basic ritual of Indian court life that courtiers and officials should make a suitable gift (*nazrāna*) to the ruler at the durbar held for any major festival, whether religious and seasonal, or the celebration of some domestic felicity, such as a birth or a marriage. The Dusehra was thus only one of a number of religious festivals whose celebration demanded the gift of paintings with subject matter related to the occasion.

Although Rajput patronage and collecting continued into the present century, there has been no serious investigation of even such a distorted mirror of ancient Indian attitudes and practice. It is with some relief, therefore, that one turns to the Mughal dynasty, whose historians and memorialists do sometimes reveal nuggets of information on this topic. As already remarked, some degree of connoisseurship was in the imperial blood. Several of Timur's grandsons were outstanding patrons of the illustrated book, and the greatest of all Persian masters, Bihzād, worked for a later member of the dynasty in Herat. After visiting that city, the first of the Mughals, Bābur (1483–1530), recorded in his memoirs (*Bābur-nāma*) some of the earliest known remarks on the stylistic qualities of that great master's work. We know also that Bābur possessed at least one illustrated manuscript and would doubtless have become more securely remembered as a connoisseur had the circumstances of his short life permitted it.

With this parental background it is hardly surprising that Bābur's son Humāyūn (r. 1530–40, 1555–56) actually studied painting under the leading Persian masters whom he brought to India and that Humāyūn's son Akbar (r. 1556–1605) was also instructed in the art. In his history of Akbar's reign, the great emperor's friend and minister Abū'l Faẓl recounts a curious anecdote about his master's boyhood. "One day this cyclopaedia of Divine things was in the library of H. M. Jahanbānī [i.e., his father, Humāyūn] and in order to sharpen his mind was employing himself in drawing. He drew with inspired pencil the figure of a man with all his limbs separated. One of the courtiers saw that strange picture and asked the meaning of it. H. M. with mystery-explaining tongue said that it represented Hemū. At that time the name and note of Hemū were unknown, and so the listeners did not comprehend the matter and refrained from further enquiry" (*Akbarnama*, vol. 2, p. 67). Following the defeat and death of Hemū, soon after the young prince became emperor, Akbar's responsibilities must have left him little time to indulge himself with the skills of the brush. He did, however, enlarge the small coterie of artists employed by his father into an establishment of more than a hundred miniature painters, and there is no doubt, both from the quality of their prodigious output and his own recorded observations on the art, that his patronage was of a very particular and informed nature. Under his direction the imperial library was expanded to a total of twenty-four thousand volumes, many of which were richly illustrated with paintings. Also, we know that by the end of his reign the imperial collection contained the work of masters from outside India and that the styles of Europe and the Middle Eastern lands of Islam were known, appreciated, and copied.

It was in this atmosphere that the empire's most distinguished collector-patron grew up. Although it has long been known that the father and grandfather of Jahāngīr took lessons in painting, it is not generally realized that there is at least one surviving painting that is his own work. The words *shāhzādaye ʿālamiyān*, listed without remark by one modern scholar as the name of a painter in the Jaipur manuscript of the *Razm-nāma*, actually mean "the Crown Prince," indicating that the coloring of this composition by the master draftsman La'l is an example from the royal hand. Jahāngīr's participation in the illustration of this great manuscript is scarcely remarkable when we recall that his close school companion Muḥammad Sharīf was a son of one of the founders of the royal painting studio and was himself an artist who occupied some sort of supervisory role in the production of the manuscript.

This evidence of the future emperor working alongside the artists in his father's atelier enables us to give more serious credence to the boast in his memoirs that: "As regards myself, my liking for painting and my practice in judging it have arrived at such a point that when any work is brought before me, either of deceased artists or of those of the present day, without the names being told me, I say on the spur of the moment that it is the work of such and such a man. And if there be a picture containing many portraits, and each face be the work of a different master, I can discover which face is the work of each of them" (*Tūzuk*, vol. 2, pp. 20–21). His concluding assertion, "If any other person has put in the eye and eyebrow of a face, I can perceive whose work the original face is, and who has painted the eye and eyebrows," does appear to represent the excessive self-congratulation that sometimes accompanied regality in the age of absolutism. Whatever the degree of exaggeration here, the emperor need have had no fear for his future reputation as a connoisseur, since that is securely established. Many critics regard his reign as marking the high point of Mughal pictorial achievement, and there is also ample testimony in his memoirs, in inscribed works of all kinds that he owned, and in the statements of others, such as Sir Thomas Roe (1581?–1644), the English ambassador to the court of Jahāngīr from 1615 to 1619, that he made every effort to secure whatever was rare, curious, or beautiful both within and outside his realm.

From Jahāngīr's reign onward the possession of a royal picture collection was an essential attribute of Mughal kingship and even his austere grandson Aurangzīb (r. 1658–1707) did nothing to disturb this heritage. Only in the eighteenth century was it gradually broken up, firstly with the sack of Delhi in 1739, by Nādir Shāh who carried many paintings off to Persia, and ultimately through the pathetic dependence of the impoverished and blind Shāh ʿAlam upon whatever military power held him and his crown in its sway. The ultimate legatees were the British, and as the puppet emperor conferred high-sounding titles and real executive power upon the officials of the East India Company the collecting of Indian painting entered a new phase.

Indian paintings had, of course, been collected by Europeans long before Britain emerged as the dominant power in India. During the reign of Jahāngīr's son Shāh Jahān (r. 1628–58) both Charles I of England and Archbishop William Laud (1573–1645) had Indian miniatures in their possession. The Dutch painter Rembrandt (1606–1669) collected them and made copies in his search for authenticity in the representation of Oriental costume. The Venetian traveler Niccolao Manucci (1639–1717) commissioned pictures to illustrate his travels before leaving India in 1686 and boasted that "So far as I know, no one has yet imparted such portraits to the public, or if any ingenious person has so done, this collection of mine has nothing in common with such, mine being the veritable, which the others cannot be. Meanwhile, to get them I have spared no expense, and have given many presents; and the whole was carried out under great difficulties, it being incumbent on me to observe profound secrecy as to my having the copies" (vol. 1, p. liv).

Despite his claims, Manucci was not the only Italian to possess authentic portraits and other Indian pictures in the early eighteenth century. One outstanding, though nearly forgotten, collector of Oriental objects and pictures was Conte Abate Giovanni Antoni Baldini (1654–1725) of Piacenza. A varied selection of Baldini's Indian miniatures was engraved by B. Picart for H. A. Châtelain's *Atlas historique* and published in Amsterdam in 1719. It was, in fact, during his temporary residence in this city frequented by merchants trading in the Indies that Baldini assembled a large part of his collection. Another contemporary collector of Indian paintings was Amsterdam's burgomaster Nicholas Witsen, who possibly acquired some of Rembrandt's Indian collection. In 1728, a few years after his death, no fewer than three hundred and seventy of Witsen's Indian paintings were auctioned, and some of these found their way via the Van Buren auction of 1808 to the Rijksprentenkabinet of Amsterdam and the Musée Napoléon in Paris.

While Indian paintings were contributing some sort of visual substance to the writings of seventeenth-century travelers whose accounts of Mughal splendor made such a deep impression in Europe, a new generation of visitors to the Indies was being bred in the intellectual climate of the Enlightenment. Their arrival coincided with the collapse of Mughal power, and their employment by the East India Company or by Indian warlords placed them in situations of responsibility with unparalleled opportunities for making acquisitions. It was essential that they acquire Oriental languages such as Arabic, Persian, and Sanskrit, and the illustrated manuscripts and paintings becoming so readily available in the turmoil of changing fortunes were perfect grist for their appetite for knowledge.

Robert Clive (1724–1774), who arrived in India in 1744, was perhaps the first of this new breed of collector, but, unlike most of his immediate successors, he was a man of action rather than scholarly inclination. His victory in 1757 over the young Nawāb of Bengal totally changed the situation of the Company in northern India and set the stage for the advancement of British rule. Clive's diplomatic transactions with the Mughal nobility, with their consequent exactions and exchanges of presents, contributed not only to his great wealth, but also to the collection of luxurious artifacts, which he brought home. In this collection there were three albums of Indian miniatures together with a number of loose album leaves that had not been bound up.

Although he possessed fine Mughal paintings there is no evidence that Clive collected them systematically, and his role in this field was in no way as significant as that of another great empire-builder, who became Governor-General in 1774, the year of Clive's death. Warren Hastings (1732–1818) was a man of very different caliber, who actively promoted Oriental studies and gave encouragement to a number of distinguished scholars. He mastered Urdu and gained a knowledge of Persian soon after his arrival in India in 1750, was the founder of the Calcutta madrasah (Mohammedan college) in 1780, and helped to set up the Asiatic Society of Bengal, founded in 1784 by his friend Sir William Jones (1746–1794). Like Clive, Hastings also owned albums and separate Indian miniatures; however, these have now been dispersed and we do not know the full extent of his collection other than stray miniatures and an album bought at the 1853 Daylesford sale by the bibliophile Sir Thomas Phillips (1792–1872), also now dispersed. The real importance of Hastings was the leadership he gave to his contemporaries, among whom there were several outstanding collectors.

One of the best known of these, whose collection fortunately remains intact in the India Office Library, London, was Richard Johnson, who went to India in 1770 as Writer in the Bengal Civil Service and two years later became Hastings's assistant after the latter's appointment as Governor of Bengal. His advancement in the Company's service was rapid, and his interest in Indian languages and culture prompted him to collect manuscripts and paintings and to patronize scholars, scribes, and artists. After ten years in Calcutta he was posted as head assistant to the Resident at the court of the Nawāb of Oudh in Lucknow, which was then one of the principal centers of Mughal painting. Here, during the years 1780–82, he enjoyed the society of several kindred spirits, including the Nawāb's architect and engineer, Colonel Antoine Louis Henri Polier (1741–1795), a Swiss of French extraction, who used his time in Lucknow to pursue an interest in Indian historical and literary studies. Polier's own large collection of Mughal paintings included many that were commissioned by him from Lucknow artists and as a result it is less varied in scope than that of Johnson, who went on to collect in Hyderabad, where he served during 1784–85. Johnson returned to England in 1790; by 1807, the year of his death, he had fallen into financial difficulties and sold his large and valuable collection to the newly founded library of the East India Company for three thousand guineas. The collection of his friend Polier also came to England after its purchase by the collector and eccentric William Beckford (1760–1844). Eventually, as part of the duke of Hamilton's manuscript collection, Polier's Indian albums were purchased for the Prussian state and are now in the Staatsbibliothek in Berlin.

Johnson and Polier were the outstanding collectors of their time and their acquisitions remain largely intact. There were also others motivated by similar interests, of whose activities there is still some trace. Shortly before either Polier or Johnson went to Lucknow, the court of the Oudh nawabs was at Faizabad, where the French officer Colonel Jean Baptiste Joseph Gentil (1726–1799) occupied an honored status as an employee of the Nawāb Shujāʾ al-daula (r. 1754–75). Like Polier, Gentil was a keen student of Indian history and culture who collected and commissioned manuscripts and paintings. He employed local artists to illustrate his own historical writings and researches in which he attempted to assemble encyclopedic data on life and events in the waning years of Mughal rule. Most of his collection is now in the Bibliothèque Nationale, Paris.

The year 1775, when Shujāʾ al-daula's death ended Gentil's employment in Oudh, is also the year engraved on the seal of Sir Elijah Impey (1732–1809), often found on Indian miniatures, which he must have had made soon after his arrival in Bengal in late 1774 as the first chief justice. Impey's Indian paintings appear largely to have been of Hindu subject matter such as *Rāgamālā* miniatures and *Rāmāyaṇa* illustrations executed in local Bengal styles of painting. However, he and his wife, Lady Mary, were also among the early patrons of what later came to be known as "Company painting," for which Indian artists learned to adapt themselves to European pictorial taste. Among the notable examples the Impeys commissioned was a series of splendid natural-history paintings and two charming impressions of Anglo-Indian domestic life.

At the turn of the century there were others whose collecting embraced both traditional Indian paintings and works designed for Europeans. One of these was Richard Colley Wellesley (1760–1842), who—like the Impeys—employed Indian artists to make natural-history paintings, but also had a number of Mughal pictures in his possession. As Governor-General in Bengal, the Marquess Wellesley accelerated the pace of British interference in Indian politics and paved the way for a new era in which the British, as rulers, began to distance themselves from Indian life. In the 1760s a man like Surgeon William Fullarton (d. 1805) collected Indian miniatures as part of a life-style that emulated that of a cultivated Indian gentleman. In the nineteenth century, however, it was the Indian nobility who increasingly adopted the life-style of the British, and while this introduced new concepts of collecting and connoisseurship to the subcontinent, it resulted in a barren epoch so far as the collecting of Indian miniatures was concerned.

Of course, this trend did not develop overnight. At the beginning of the century there were still Europeans who adopted elements of an Indian way of life and patronized Indian painters to record their fascination for things Indian. William Fraser (1784–1832), apprenticed as secretary to the Indianized Resident of Delhi, Sir David Ochterlony (1758–1825), became so intimate with Indians as to be described by the French traveler and botanist Victor Jacquemont (1801–1832) as "half Asiatic in his habits" (p. 254), and it is hardly surprising that he engaged Delhi artists to produce portraits of his Indian associates and contemporaries. He also owned high-quality copies of early-seventeenth-century miniatures from the royal albums of Jahāngīr and S͟hāh Jahān. Another patron of Delhi painters at this time was Colonel James Skinner (1778–1841), who was indeed "half Asiatic," since his mother was a Rājput lady. Skinner was the author of several works in Persian, which he wrote more easily than English, and he delighted in having these transcribed and illustrated for his English friends for whom he wrote dedicatory verses in Persian on the flyleaves.

Men such as these fought a final rearguard action

before the imposition of Victorian values closed a chapter in British relations with Indian culture. It should not be forgotten, however, that the great Queen was not herself arrogant in her attitude to Indians, and although she never visited India, she had a great enthusiasm for things Indian, surrounded herself with Indian servants, and took the trouble to learn a certain amount of Urdu. There were, of course, illustrated Indian manuscripts and album paintings in the Royal Library during Victoria's reign, but the prevailing attitude was such that even a lover of India and its handicrafts like Sir George Birdwood (1832–1917) could write in 1880 that "the monstrous shapes of the Puranic deities are unsuitable for the higher forms of artistic representation; and this is possibly why sculpture and painting are unknown, as fine arts, in India" (p. 125). With such a view of the Indian fine arts it is hardly surprising that the collecting of Indian paintings had reached a low ebb. However, this tide was soon to turn.

To some extent a more favorable reaction to Indian painting and sculpture was sparked off by some injudicious remarks by Birdwood after a lecture delivered at the Royal Society of Arts in 1910 by E. B. Havell, who had served as principal of the Government School of Art and Keeper of the Art Gallery in Calcutta. At once a number of artists and intellectuals wrote in support and admiration of Indian art in a famous letter to the *Times* (February 28, 1910), which led to the founding of the Royal India Society. Even before this, however, Havell's own enthusiastic appraisal of Indian art had already been published in 1908 in his *Indian Sculpture and Painting*, and from then on the collecting of Indian paintings received a fresh impetus.

One important signatory of the 1910 letter was the artist William Rothenstein (1872–1945), principal of the Royal College of Art, London, whose interest in Indian miniatures was being aroused by his friend Ananda Coomaraswamy (1877–1947). Although partly Indian, of Sinhalese birth, Coomaraswamy was educated in England and visited India for the first time in 1910 when he also published *Indian Drawings*, a book concerned mainly with the Mughal school. During this visit he avidly collected Indian paintings and became particularly excited by Rājput paintings. Early in the following year Rothenstein joined him in India and started building his own collection with Coomaraswamy's assistance. At that time Mughal miniatures were already being collected and studied as an offshoot of Persian painting, but the Rājput schools were virtually unknown apart from the portraits of rulers which T. H. Hendley (1847–1917), the Residency Surgeon in Jaipur, had got copied and published in 1897. To Coomaraswamy the Rājput schools of painting were a revelation worthy of comparison with the work of fifteenth-century Italian masters such as Botticelli, and in a letter to Rothenstein he confessed, "I have been spending more than all my possessions on pictures" (Archer 1973, p. xxvii). In 1912, on his return to England, he published the first account of Rājput painting in the *Burlington Magazine*, and four years later, drawing on the collections formed by himself and enthusiasts such as Rothenstein, he published *Rajput Painting*, his pioneer book on the subject.

In India itself the advance of the nationalist movement went hand in hand with a growing pride in the nation's artistic heritage and this led to a revival of collecting and connoisseurship. The Tagore family formed a collection of miniatures containing works from sets divided also between Coomaraswamy and Rothenstein and took inspiration from them in their own paintings. In Patna, the lawyer P. C. Manuk was forming an important collection with a heavy emphasis on works from the Punjab Hills, and in Banaras (Varanasi), Rai Krishna Das was expanding his ancestral collection so that it would eventually pass to Banaras Hindu University as one of India's greatest museums, the Bharat Kala Bhavan. Among those inspired by these pioneers were N. C. Mehta, W. G. Archer of the Indian Civil Service and subsequently Keeper of the Indian Section of the Victoria and Albert Museum, London, and Sri Gopi Krishna Kanoria, a cultivated businessman of Patna. Meanwhile important collections were being formed in Bombay by A. C. Ardeshir, Sir Cowasji Jehangir, Dr. Alma Latifi, and Karl Khandalavala.

When India became independent in 1947 it was from collections such as these that loans were selected for the great exhibition of Indian art held in the winter of 1947/48 at the Royal Academy of Arts in London. Basil Gray's contribution to the commemorative catalogue of this exhibition, edited by Leigh Ashton, was a landmark in the study of Indian painting and marked the beginning of an intensive period of scholarship that has lasted until the present time. Yet, despite the exhibition, the appreciation of Indian painting in the aftermath of Indian independence was restricted to a comparatively small circle centered in the Royal India Society, and the only collectors were men like J. C. French, who had served in the Indian Civil Service; W. B. Manley, a lawyer who had been in the Indian Police and finally took up medicine; and F. B. P. Lory of the Indian Educational Service. Another collector of this period was Colonel T. G. Gayer-Anderson, who was introduced to Indian paintings by his twin brother, Major R. G. Gayer-Anderson, Pasha, stationed in Cairo. On posting to India in 1926, Colonel Gayer-Anderson began to form a collection of Indian paintings, and especially drawings, which is now divided between the Victoria and Albert Museum, London, and the National Library in Canberra. In the preface to the catalogue he compiled in 1952 he touched on this lifelong interest. "With increased experience and knowledge," he wrote, "my preference for Indian paintings and drawings has become ever more marked and they now have for me an almost obsessive attraction and give me a subtle pleasure which I get from no other form of visual art!" (manuscript in the Victoria and Albert Museum).

Although the subject of Indian art was being popularized by the writings of W. G. Archer, British interest in India was waning. Those who had served in India were gradually passing away, and eventually the Royal India Society died with them. By the end of the 1950s the urge to collect Indian paintings had largely moved across the Atlantic.

Perhaps collectors in the United States had never been hampered by the colonialist attitudes that hindered the appreciation of Indian art among people in Britain. Even so, American interest was fairly slow in developing. As early as 1907 Charles Lang Freer (1856–1919) had bought a collection of Mughal paintings that had been assembled in India by Colonel H. B. Hanna, who had hoped, in vain, that the London National Gallery would acquire them, but they are now among the holdings of the Freer Gallery of Art, Washington, D.C. At about the same time as Freer was making his first Indian purchases that catholic collector Henry Walters (1848–1931) was also obtaining fine Mughal miniatures which were becoming available through the activities of Armenian dealers active in Paris. A third, but less discriminating, collector was J. F. Lewis (1860–1932), who exhibited his Persian and Indian paintings and drawings in the winter of 1923/24 at the Pennsylvania Academy of the Fine Arts, of which he was president. At the other extreme during the early years of this century was the most impressive Mughal collection of all, which was beginning to be formed by an expatriate American, the mining engineer and millionaire Alfred Chester Beatty (1875–1968), who had moved to England in 1911. Beatty started collecting Islamic and Indian manuscripts and miniatures after World War I, when it became his habit to spend the winters in Egypt. Soon, with the aid of several distinguished experts, he built up the greatest private library of Oriental manuscripts in the world; after World War II he took it with him to Dublin, where it now belongs to the Irish nation.

Almost without exception the first collectors of Indian paintings in America concentrated on Mughal miniatures, as did Dr. Denman Ross (1853–1935), a trustee of the Boston Museum of Fine Arts for over forty years, who became a pioneer collector of Indian art when it was known to only a handful of European scholars, collectors, and dealers. By 1913 exhibitions containing the Indian miniatures he had collected provided the first examples to be presented in any significant numbers to the American public. Not long afterward he acquired the collection of Indian art formed by Ananda Coomaraswamy, who, primarily through Ross's influence, joined the staff of the museum as Keeper of the Indian collections. One of Coomaraswamy's accomplishments in this capacity was the publication of a comprehensive catalogue of the Indian collections; the three volumes devoted to Indian paintings are still essential works of reference and models of their genre.

When this great scholar died in 1947 India was in the process of gaining independence and was about to emerge as a leading third-world power. Among the fundamental changes of the postwar epoch have been the breakup of the old princely collections and the growth of international tourism. The world has become a smaller place and a generation of collectors has grown up in the New World with all the energy, opportunities, and dedication that marked their most distinguished predecessors. A particular feature of this new collecting trend has been the tendency for owners to bring their pictures before a wider public through exhibitions, and the resulting catalogues have proved an invaluable resource for scholarship in the field. The Ehrenfeld Collection maintains this practice and thus makes it quite clear that the impulse to collect Indian paintings is still alive and well.

Notes on the Study of Indian Miniatures

by Pramod Chandra

THE MAJORITY of those Indian paintings that have survived are of small size, being, essentially, illustrations to books. These range from the innumerable miniatures in manuscripts of the Western Indian school, many of them mechanical workshop products, to the sumptuous and refined paintings in the most elaborate books produced for the Mughal court, most notably for the emperor Akbar (r. 1556–1605). The traditions of book painting seem to have thrived at one time or another at sites in Rajasthan and Gujarat, the vast regions of central India, the erstwhile Himalayan Hill states, the remote eastern provinces of Orissa and Assam, and in the Deccan as well. Sets, or series, of pictures, sometimes lacking a continuous text, were based on popular themes that did not require exposition. These might be literary, legendary, romantic, historical, or religious in content, or the conventional visual representation of the musical modes.

As the books themselves and the paintings they contained were fragile and easily transportable, their destruction and dispersion in the course of India's checkered history is not too surprising. The great libraries of the Mughal kingdom were scattered to the winds during the disintegration of the empire. Economic and political circumstances of the twentieth century led first to the dispersal of Pahāṛī miniatures from their homes in the Himalayan states, and then to the scattering of those from Rajasthan. Nevertheless, while paintings were being dispersed, they were also being carefully collected, particularly during this century. The part played by public collections is well known, but private collections have not been far behind and, indeed, have often taken the lead in matters of research and publication. The A. Chester Beatty Library in Dublin and the collections of Motichand Khajanchi in India and Edwin Binney, 3rd, in the United States are just such examples (see *Beatty*; Khandalavala, Chandra, and Chandra; Archer and Binney; and Binney 1973). Important works such as this exhibition and catalogue, which summarize and present in a skillful and scholarly manner our present knowledge of Indian miniature painting, prompt one to take a look at the history of the scholarship of the subject and to reflect upon where we are and how we got here—a process that not only commends itself to scholars, but may also be useful to educated museum visitors, allowing them to see works of art in a broader intellectual context. As we do this, what is immediately apparent (and this in contrast to studies of Indian architecture and sculpture) is the relatively short period of time that has been devoted to the study of Indian painting. Nevertheless, progress has been rapid, so that it is no exaggeration to say that a greater sophistication has been achieved in the approach to Indian painting than in the study of either architecture or sculpture, although the situation is showing signs of change.

Mughal painting was the first to receive serious attention from British scholars, who had begun to take an interest in the history, antiquities, and art of India as a part of their imperial duties. Vincent A. Smith (1911), a historian and a member of the ruling bureaucracy, was one of the most prominent of these men who, despite vested interests in the perpetuation of British rule and European notions of general supremacy, managed to give a short and straightforward account of Mughal painting; however, the heavy emphasis he laid on the European and Persian sources of the style reveals his bias against the possibility of Indian originality. Percy Brown (1924) filled out the sketchy outline of Smith, providing us with a wealth of knowledge regarding the painters, the artists, and the sources of the style, on the basis of which he was able to demonstrate that though Persian influence was undeniably present, the name "Indo-Persian" preferred by Smith for the Mughal style was clearly untenable because of the manner in which what had been received was transformed. Brown also set up a basic chronology of some value, though it was not backed up by sensitive visual examination. He was often inclined to date paintings according to the date of the events portrayed in them, a method that did not take stock of the possibility of copies and thus led him to grave error.

The evolution of Mughal painting was, quite rightly, one of the main concerns of these earlier scholars. The principal contribution of the time was made by Hermann Goetz (1924), who, by successfully dating the kinds of dress worn during a particular time in the Mughal period, proceeded to date a painting on the basis of details of costume worn by the figures depicted therein. The method looked promising and became a popular one, Karl Khandalavala (1950; 1958) applying it both to Rājasthānī and Pahāṛī painting with a certain measure of success. Though once useful, this method of dating has proved to have serious limitations, for it fails to address itself to the essentials of style and does not distinguish between superficial pattern and significant form.

The basic work on Mughal painting was a landmark when it first appeared in 1929 and remains such to this day: Ivan Stchoukine's *La Peinture indienne à l'époque des Grands Moghols*. Here the author subjected Mughal painting to close analysis, paying careful attention to form, movement, color, and composition. These, together with a comparative assessment of the treatment of man, animals, and nature, allowed him to throw basic light on the nature of Mughal painting, its sources and its development. He was thus successfully able to demonstrate the vital place of Mughal painting in the mainstream of Indian painting, regarding it as a renaissance after a long interval of decay on one hand, and as a vital source of inspiration to other schools of Indian painting on the other. My own researches (1976), based on a large number of miniatures not available earlier, strongly support Stchoukine's earlier position.

Recent studies of Mughal painting have sought to tackle problems of connoisseurship, important contributions being those made by Stuart Cary Welch (1961) and Milo Cleveland Beach (1978). Not only has the evolution of Mughal painting become fairly clear, but it has also become possible to make serious studies of individual artists and their works. Robert Skelton (1957) has carried out such investigations in which, in addition to keen observation, he displays an ability to place successfully Mughal painters and their work in the context of their times.

In summary, what is known of Mughal painting is that the style essentially came into being some time in the 1560s during the reign of the emperor Akbar (1556–1605) and lasted well into the nineteenth century, giving way, ultimately, to the so-called Company Style, a hybrid of Mughal and European elements. Its various phases have been divided according to regnal period: thus, the Akbar period, the Jahāngīr period (1605–28), the S̱hāh Jahān period (1628–58), the Aurangzīb period (1658–1707), and the period of the Later Mughals, to which work done after the period of Aurangzīb has been broadly assigned. It should be noticed that this classification has emphasized the part played by patronage in the evolution of the style. While this appears to be considerable in the case of Akbar and Jahāngīr, recent research tends to suggest that even their roles may have been exaggerated, the nature of the Mughal style at a particular stage being dependent upon a variety of other factors as well, notably the skill and inclination of the artists themselves. It is also true that while the earlier phase of the Mughal style has been intensively studied, a great deal remains to be done on painting from the mid-seventeenth century onward. Thus, the stage has been set for new kinds of research that seek to understand Mughal painting in a variety of contexts, notably the nature of its relationship to the society in which it flourished or decayed, and the precise processes of artistic and cultural interaction that are a part of its growth and determine its relationship with other contemporary schools of Indian painting, such as those flourishing in Rajasthan and the Himalayan foothills.

Miniatures belonging to the styles that have come to be called Rājasthānī and Pahāṛī were known; but, in comparison to those of the Mughal style, not much attention was paid to their collection and study until the appearance of Ananda Coomaraswamy's work that appeared in 1916. There Coomaraswamy posited the existence of a style patronized by Rajput rulers—as opposed to Mughal—which in some way represented a continuation of the classical traditions of ancient Indian painting of the type seen at Ajanta of the fifth century A.D., the relationship between the two being the same as that of the North Indian vernacular languages to classical Sanskrit literature. The history of this style, he speculated, might be traced back to the early thirteenth century and extended to approximately the mid-nineteenth, when it came to an end due to the much vulgarized taste of its patrons, who began to prefer hybrid and debased works of a Europeanized character. According to Coomaraswamy, Rajput painting was a separate development from the Mughal school and relatively free from its influences, emphasizing as it did the abstract and the ideal rather than the naturalistic and academic throughout its history. He divided the style into two broad groups, one represented by work produced in Rajasthan (Rājasthānī), and the other by that produced in the Himalayan Hill states (Pahāṛī). This distinction survives to the present day, though the overarching unity between the two styles envisaged by Coomaraswamy has been somewhat obscured.

What Coomaraswamy accomplished, basically, was to establish successfully a theoretical framework for the study of Rājasthānī and Pahāṛī painting. In the course of this he made many insightful observations that were often based not on material facts, which in any case were woefully inadequate, but on deeply felt intuition. It is truly astonishing to observe how many of his broad speculations, long forgotten, are now proving essentially correct through the mature and thoughtful scholarship directed to the abundant materials discovered since the publication of his important book.

Coomaraswamy's real concern, however, was the explication of the themes of Rajput painting and this he did with both knowledge and poetic skill. He was not very successful in setting up a proper apparatus of names and dates, nor was he able to identify and chart the detailed progress of the various sub-styles. However, he can hardly be blamed for this, as the materials with which he was working were hardly sufficient, and adequate materials would continue to be scarce until the late forties and early fifties of this century. Great collections, both public and private, were formed then which made detailed and careful studies possible. Paintings with firm dates and provenances began to be discovered; and the existence, as well as the development, of a variety of individual schools began gradually to emerge. The methods employed were simple but a great improvement on what had gone before. The treatment of costume, jewelry, of man and nature, as well as color and composition were all studied in the manner of Goetz and Stchoukine to determine the evolution of individual styles.

As a result of much painstaking work we now have a fairly good idea of the schools of Mewar, Bundi, Marwar, Amber/Jaipur, Bikaner, Kishangarh, and Sirohi in Rajasthan proper, and also of Gujarat and Malwa. Of these, our understanding of the schools of Mewar and Bundi is the most comprehensive, while many gaps remain in our knowledge of the others. Thus, the origins of the Bikaner style, and its history during the first half of the seventeenth century, are not known and this is also largely true of the school of Marwar. The school of Malwa is well documented for most of the seventeenth century, but its subsequent history remains unclear, nor are we certain whether the provenance is confined to Malwa or spreads farther inland. The course of painting at Amber/Jaipur is only known in patches, and this is also the case with Kishangarh and Sirohi.

The advance in our knowledge has been considerable, but a large mass of floating material, not fitting easily into any of the known schools, still awaits proper classification. The basic facts of the Rājasthānī styles are hardly set out as clearly as those of the Mughal. Among the problems that remain is the satisfactory resolution of the origin and development of the Rājasthānī style, despite the attention it has received and the considerable new materials that have become available for study. Two principal points of view have developed. One affirms that there was no Rājasthānī style before the existence of the Mughal style and that the Rājasthānī style was essentially the result of Mughal influence on the Western Indian style. The other point of view insists on the opposite, asserting that the Rājasthānī style existed before the Mughal school and was actually instrumental in its formulation. Often the matter seems to be one of quibbling over definitions, for it is now a matter of general agreement (except for a diehard or so) that there did indeed exist some kind of "proto-Rājasthānī" style before the development of the Mughal style, whether it was centered in the Mathura region, Malwa, or Rajasthan, or flourished in the area that included all these regions. These "proto-Rājasthānī" paintings were a natural product of the so-called Western Indian style, which in turn was clearly derived from classical Indian painting of the fifth century A.D. And Coomaraswamy's intuition regarding the continuity of the Indian tradition we now know was essentially correct.

Studies on the Pahāṛī style were initially ahead of those concerned with Rājasthānī work for the simple reason that more Pahāṛī miniatures were accessible. Coomaraswamy himself had more to say about the provenance and chronology of Pahāṛī painting, though his conclusions in this instance are clearly out of date. Still, his work initiated further studies, culminating in that of Karl Khandalavala (1958). In a considerable advance over previous investigations Khandalavala sought to establish the existence of three phases. The first, which he called the Basohli school, lasted from the end of the seventeenth century to approximately the mid-eighteenth and was characterized by works of vibrant color and great power. This initial phase was followed by a transitional stage called "pre-Kangra" that extended into the 1780s, culminating finally in the delicate and lyrical Kangra style that survived beyond the mid-nineteenth century. While Khandalavala's basic pattern largely holds, William G. Archer, in his great work published in 1973, chose to replace it with a classification based on the large number of individual princely states that existed in the area till fairly recent times. B. N. Goswamy's emphasis on the family as a basis for style (1968) has thrown new light on the history of Pahāṛī painting and has provided us with a valuable approach that cannot be ignored.

The tendency to take relatively recent political units as the basis for individual schools, in the manner of Archer, should be treated with caution. With regard to Rājasthānī painting, for example, let us take the so-called styles of Bundi and Kota. Till their merger in the Indian Union these two small princely states were a part of one culturally integrated territory that is still called Hāḍautī. Kota was separated from Bundi at the order of S͟hāh Jahān in the seventeenth century. Nonetheless, in spite of this history and the facts that the area is still culturally homogeneous, that the centers of Bundi and Kota are located at no great distance from one another, and that the paintings produced at them are very similar, two distinct schools—one of Bundi and one of Kota—have been posited. This rests, I suppose, on the unstated assumption that each Rājasthānī state, irrespective of its broader geographic and cultural affiliations, had ipso facto its own style of painting. This premise has quite recently been extended to vassal states as well, so that we hear of schools of Deogarh, Indragarh, Delwada, and so on. This may or may not be the case; but the adjudicating factor, I believe, must be the nature of the materials themselves and not the condition of political units that sometimes coincide, and sometimes do not, with well-defined cultural and linguistic regions.

This type of emphasis on political entities is also at the basis of the division of a Rajput style, whether Rājasthānī or Pahāṛī, according to the regnal periods of the various rulers, a procedure no doubt inspired by a corresponding one adopted for Mughal painting. Once again, the implications of such a system have not been fully understood, for it is being taken for granted that the style of painting changed from one reign to the other and was heavily dependent on the patronage of individual kings. Both of these assumptions could conceivably be true, but before this method of constructing the phases of a style according to the reigns of kings can be countenanced, the assumptions must be *proved to be true* on the basis of the materials available. Continued use of dynastic terminology hardly seems tenable considering what we know at present, or are likely to know in the future. Surely, there must have been rulers whose tastes affected the work of the painters they employed, but, then, there seem also to have been many who let the art of painting follow its own course. Prolonged absence from their homes of Rajput rulers in the imperial service must have further weakened the ties between patron and artist, as must the nature of the art itself which on the whole, like most Indian art, shows little effect of individual idiosyncrasy.

The themes of Indian painting have not been studied with any intensity for quite some time, unlike the study of Indian sculpture where a great deal of attention has been paid to the elucidation of subject matter and iconography. This is not surprising, for the intellectual equipment needed is varied and demanding. Many of the scholars responsible for significant advances in the field have nevertheless been handicapped by a lack of knowledge of Indian language and, particularly, literature, which is inextricably related to the painting. There are, however, signs that this is beginning to change, and significant studies relating miniatures to text are beginning to take place in Rajput as well as Mughal painting.

All this is part of the general problem of relating art to its context, which has been of increasing concern to historians not only in India, but also in the West. True, the corpus of materials, and the depth and extent of their study, are much more advanced in Western art, so that studies along these lines have been fruitful and convincing. Nevertheless, with adequate preparation this kind of study can also be attempted for Indian painting, even though the outlines of basic knowledge have just begun to emerge and its study, compared with Western art, is in its infancy. One has to admit that preparations for these studies will have to be arduous if they are to carry any conviction at all. This would involve a knowledge of language and literature, an erudition in history far beyond the nineteenth-century romantic fantasies of James Tod, a clear understanding of the cultural environment, and training in the use of valuable archival materials now becoming available for study. But the results are also likely to be deeply satisfying. It is my hope that this careful catalogue of the Ehrenfeld Collection will be among the first of a whole series of new studies that will extend and deepen our understanding of a very precious part of the Indian cultural heritage.

Indian Painting from the Sixteenth to the Nineteenth Century

by Daniel J. Ehnbom

THE SIXTEENTH CENTURY saw a profound change in Indian painting, a revolution that challenged a full millennium of stylistic development in just a few decades. From the time of the rich textures and sensuous rhythms of the wall paintings of about the fifth century A.D. in the Ajanta caves near the city of Aurangabad in western India, Indian painting had evolved in a direction favoring flat planes of vivid color, angular movement, and wiry linearity. The dominant style that emerged is called the Western Indian style, though in fact it was practiced far beyond those geographic limits. Like other expressions of Indian art before and since, this style, fully developed by about the eleventh century, filled a variety of religious and secular functions and served patrons of different sects and social classes.

By the fifteenth century the Western Indian style had become for the most part stiff and hard; but a few progressive sub-styles showed signs of significant and vigorous change, and by the beginning of the sixteenth century a new style had come into being. As yet scholars have given it no permanent name, but call its examples the *Caurapañcāśikā* (or CPS) group after the text—a brief but beautiful poem written in Sanskrit in the eleventh century whose title translates into "Fifty Stanzas of a Thief"—illustrated by the first pictures that became known in the style. This idiom, still only dimly understood, was certainly practiced in north India around Delhi and Agra. Like the Western Indian style, it may have been much more widely spread. Paintings in the CPS group illustrate poetical and religious works from Hindu, Jain, and Muslim traditions. One of the group's finest series of paintings depicts the life of Kṛṣṇa, the ever-popular blue god, at once child, lover, hero, and teacher (cat. nos. 1 and 2). The color is bright, the line bold and full of vigor. At about the same time, Persian influence softened both the line and the palette of traditional Indian painting, to produce a style that is even less well understood. Only three manuscripts illustrated in this style are known, two of them devoted to the *Candāyana*, a mystic romance written by a Muslim divine in the last quarter of the fourteenth century (cat. no. 3). Both these styles—as well as other Indian styles of the time—draw on the rich blend of indigenous Indian and imported Persian elements and are evolutionary rather than revolutionary in character. But they help set the stage for a startling development that was to alter significantly the nature of subsequent Indian painting.

Akbar, third and greatest of the Mughal dynasty that conquered India in 1526, came to the throne in 1556 as a boy of fourteen. When he died in 1605 he left the empire at its peak of strength and grandeur. A brilliant monarch and an administrative genius, he had also been trained as a painter. Artists schooled in the court workshop of Persia had already come to India in the service of his father, Humāyūn (r. 1530–40, 1555–56), who retook India after a long and arduous exile only to die shortly after his return to Delhi. Akbar created a workshop of painters from Persia and artists trained in Indian styles. Together, by about 1560–65, they developed an entirely new expression of Indian painting. It is already highly sophisticated in its earliest examples (cat. nos. 4 and 5) and embraces a naturalism and three-dimensionality alien to any of its parent idioms. Indian painting was deeply and fundamentally affected by this Mughal style, not only by that practiced in the imperial workshop, but also through more modest examples prepared in lesser circumstances for patrons less exalted than the emperor (cat. nos. 14–18).

When Jahāngīr (r. 1605–27) came to the throne his artists built on the accomplishments of the workshop of his father's reign. Gradually the special characteristics of painting of the Jahāngīr period began to assert themselves. Portraiture became a major concern of the style, and Mughal painting reached heights of penetrating observation and illusionism (cat. nos. 21 and 22). Though manuscript illumination did not cease entirely, it took second place to the preparation of grand imperial albums which contained separate studies by individual artists rather than the collaborative textual illustrations so typical of the Akbar period (cat. no. 7). For a moment, rare in Indian art, the course of stylistic development is revealed through individualistic works by known artists.

The soft refinement of the early seventeenth century began to stiffen in the reign of S͟hāh Jahān (r. 1628–58). Painting exchanged psychological penetration for surface elegance and extreme richness of materials and technique. Continuing a trend that manifested itself under Jahāngīr, artists of the imperial workshop turned out fewer works than their counterparts had during the reign of Akbar, no doubt in part due to the hyperrefinement and meticulous craftsmanship necessary to produce the icy, polished jewels that are S͟hāh Jahān period paintings.

Later in the seventeenth century, and in the eighteenth, Mughal painting moved closer to the values of flatness and abstraction that characterize more conservative Indian painting (cat. nos. 30–33). Works of quality were produced, but most of the output is world-weary, heavy, and overtly sensual, the art of a culture that looked back with longing and ahead with uncertainty.

During the eighteenth century the steadily weakening empire reeled under shock after shock, teetering toward the events of 1857–58 that were to sweep away even the remnants of greatness. The refined grace of the Mughal style was pressed into service by India's new masters, the British. An offshoot of Mughal painting, known as the Company Style—after the East India Company, which sought and won control of the subcontinent—specialized in depictions of the great monuments of India (cat. nos. 82 and 83) and scenes of an everyday life far different from that of the British Isles (cat. no. 84).

Other dynasties challenged Mughal hegemony during its long rule, among them those of the Deccan, a vast plateau extending far to the south. The richly mannered and intensely colored paintings of the Deccani states have hardly begun to yield their secrets to scholars and connoisseurs. There is a wide stylistic range in the art of the Deccan, from highly refined paintings of the central Muslim courts (cat. nos. 35–38), which may reflect Persian and Ottoman as well as Mughal and other Indian sources, to boldly stated pictures whose flatness and bright color (cat. nos. 43 and 44) recall much earlier Indian styles. These idioms never completely relinquished their distinctive characters, not even late in the seventeenth century when the Deccan at last fell to the Mughals, and Mughal taste as well as Mughal political might was triumphant from Kabul in the far north to the Kaveri River near the very tip of India. The Mughal empire had never been bigger, but the long slow decline had begun.

The profound influence of Mughal painting is readily apparent in the schools of Rajasthan and its contiguous regions and the Punjab Hills. Some of these styles emerged directly from the Mughal workshop (see cat. nos. 58–64) while others preserve the abstract vision of catalogue numbers 1 and 2 (see cat. nos. 45–49 and 87–90). It is in large part the interplay between these two stylistic strains, ends of a continuum rather than diametric opposites, that makes Rājasthānī and Pahāṛī painting so richly expressive and brilliantly realized.

There is much we do not know about Indian painting and much confusion about what we do know. In the present catalogue, I have generally followed traditional classifications, fully aware that they are at times uncertain, even misleading and inaccurate. This is particularly true of the Pahāṛī schools (cat. nos. 86–127), where two broad stylistic groups—one boldly expressive and the other coolly reserved—were produced in many different painting centers. This catalogue adheres to the geographical system of classification so brilliantly articulated by the late W. G. Archer, former Keeper of the Indian Section of the Victoria and Albert Museum, London. At the same time, the continuing research of B. N. Goswamy and others makes clear that geography is only part of the question, and the fullest interpretations of Hill painting are those that take into consideration the personal and family styles of related artists who moved throughout the Hill regions, spreading and absorbing influences as they moved. Another problem is the so-called Malwa style, a "Rājasthānī" idiom practiced outside Rajasthan, though we are still not certain exactly where. The Bundi school (cat. nos. 58–63) presents a different question, for scholarship has sought to assign different strains within the style exclusively to one or another of the political divisions within the region. This is a classification system that requires careful re-examination, for a place of production does not necessarily define a school.

Much remains to be done on the technical aspects of Indian painting. Most is on paper, ranging from the finest quality to rough village products. A few surviving examples are on cloth (see cat. nos. 4 and 34), and there must have been many more processional banners and painted hangings than remain to us. Until the advent of European technology, colors were natural mineral, vegetable, and even animal pigments prepared according to formulas passed down from master to pupil. The clear enamel-like surfaces of many Indian paintings were achieved through turning a miniature over onto a flat, hard surface and rubbing it from the back with a burnisher. This compacted the dried pigment. The more layers of burnished paint, the richer the effect. Miniatures were further enriched by application of gold, either paint or leaf or both, for different effects. The Basohli idiom (cat. nos. 87–92) frequently embellished miniatures with tiny jewels made from the iridescent wing cases of beetles. The art of the miniature suffered greatly in the nineteenth century when British influence introduced chemical dyes that replaced the mellow colors of previous generations and disrupted patronage patterns that had sustained Indian painting for centuries.

A few general observations on Indian miniatures may help the museum visitor and the reader understand these pictures better. Indian painting as we know it is an intimate art. Gone are most of the wall paintings that once adorned Indian palaces, temples, and mansions. What remains to us—and even this only a small percentage of what must have been produced—is essentially an art of manuscripts (either bound in the Islamic manner or unbound in the traditional Indian fashion), albums, and illustrated series that were meant to be held and examined at close range. Their subject matter is varied. The Mughals commissioned illustrated histories, literary works (including Persian translations of Indian classics), and portraits. Mughal subject matter extended to other schools as well. Most traditional subjects were religious in origin. The life of Kṛṣṇa was popular in virtually every school and period. The ideal child, lover, hero, and religious teacher of the *Bhāgavata Purāṇa* (ca. ninth–tenth century) and the *Gīta Govinda* of the poet Jayadeva (twelfth century) was also the model for masculine behavior in later rhetorical texts that enumerate the characteristics of heroes and heroines. The ancient epics—the *Mahābhārata* and especially the *Ramāyaṇa*—were rich sources. The many illustrated *Ramāyaṇas* that exist attest to the popularity of its hero Rāma, the embodiment of nobility and kingly virtue. Another very popular subject is the *Rāgamālā*—The Garland of Melody—that consists of personifications of musical modes. These modes are presented in families, most often as a set of six male melodies (*rāgas*) with five wives (*rāginīs*) each. The earliest surviving illustrated melodies date from the fifteenth century; by the sixteenth century the basic iconographic forms common to most of India were set. Iconographic variations were sometimes regional and usually reflected different textual traditions. The Hill schools followed different iconographic standards from those used elsewhere, and their *Rāgamālā* sets include melodies personified as sons (*rāgaputras*) and daughters-in-law (*rāgaputrīs*).

It is not possible to sum up the painting of India in a few words, but a unifying concern that underlies the various styles is the timeless value of abstract statement over the passing nature of literal physical description.

Important Sites and Schools of Indian Painting: 16th–19th Centuries

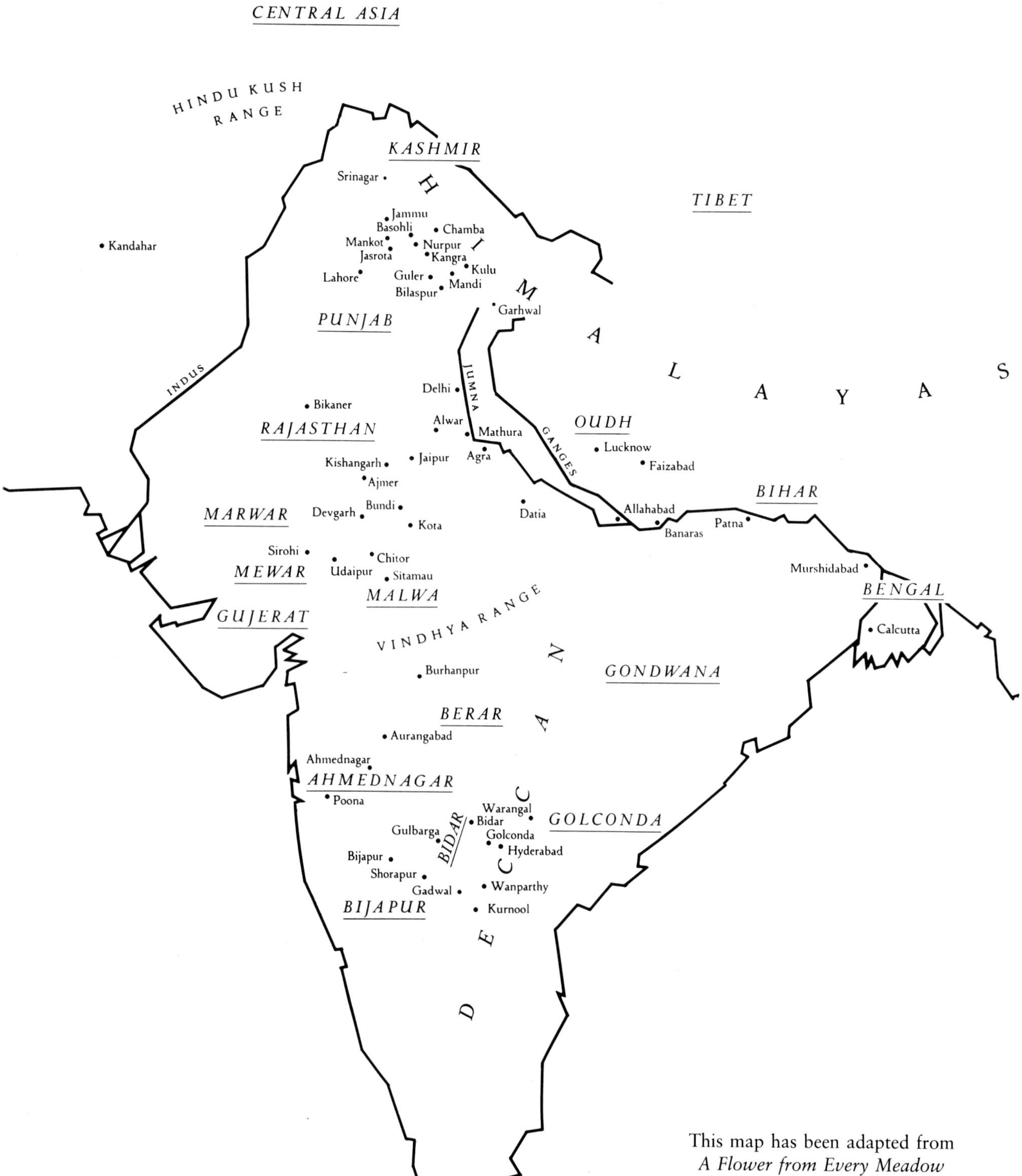

This map has been adapted from
A Flower from Every Meadow
with the permission of the Asia Society.

INDIAN MINIATURES

The Ehrenfeld Collection

❀ I ❀ 2 ❀

Two leaves from a *Bhāgavata Purāṇa* series

PROBABLY DELHI-AGRA REGION, ca. 1520–30

1. Distraught *gopīs* (cowherd women) search in vain for the vanished Kṛṣṇa

Image 6¼ × 8⅝ in. (159 × 220 mm); sheet 6⅞ × 9¼ in. (175 × 235 mm), irregular

The cowherd women of Kṛṣṇa's home have become arrogant as a result of their constant association with him, so he has disappeared to teach them a lesson. It is night. A full moon illuminates the sky as the distraught women search the forest for their lover. At the top left three of them ask a shrub if it has seen the vanished lord. In the middle panel another woman asks the same question of a female deer, while to the right two more ask a tree. In the lower register the women, bewildered by their fruitless search, begin to imitate the exploits of their lover. One takes the role of a demoness while another plays Kṛṣṇa sucking the life from the creature's breast. In the center a cowherd holds up a knotted cloth representing Mount Govardhana (see cat. no. 73) as another kneels in homage. Still other women dance and play the flute in emulation of their beloved. The flat background panels of red, blue, and green are typical of the style.

At the top left corner is the nearly illegible name "S[ā]——," and the name "Hīrabāī" is in the lower right corner. The precise significance of these names is unknown. In the upper margin an abraded inscription runs from the middle across the border. A damaged number is in the lower left. The text on the reverse is *Bhāgavata Purāṇa* 10.30.9–20. The leaf is published in Ehnbom 1982, pp. 17, 94.

A similar illustration is in a private collection in London. The leaf illustrating Kṛṣṇa's reappearance among the delighted *gopīs* is in the Brooklyn Museum.

2. Kṛṣṇa and Arjuna hunt animals suitable for sacrifice

Sheet 7 × 9¼ in. (178 × 235 mm), irregular

Tigers, rabbits, boar, cobras, antelope, a mongoose, and a rhinoceros flee the deadly onslaught of the hero Arjuna's arrows. The terrified animals run against black, yellow, and green grounds. Kṛṣṇa drives the chariot, prefiguring his role as Arjuna's charioteer in the decisive battles of the *Mahābhārata*, the national epic of ancient India, where he reveals his divinity to the astonished hero and discourses on the path to salvation. The brilliant yellow and red of the chariot glow against the dark, shrubbery-filled ground. Below, two attendants carry away a black buck, its tied legs and tightly curled body presenting a vivid contrast to the free movement of the animals who struggle to escape the relentless hunters. In a pavilion to the left sits Kālindī, whom Kṛṣṇa will marry. The vessels under the bed, fabric patterns, and black-and-white tassels are common motifs of the style.

The text on the back is *Bhāgavata Purāṇa* 10.58.13–16 (first line). The miniature is published in Hutchins, pp. 59 and 120–21, no. 15.

The life of Kṛṣṇa is a major source of subjects for Indian painting. The tenth book of the *Bhāgavata Purāṇa* (ca. ninth–tenth centuries) is the standard Sanskrit text of his exploits. Countless illustrated versions of it were prepared in all parts of India (see cat. nos. 17, 18, 45, 46, 49, 68, 85, 99–101, 106, 107, 112, 113, 121). These two leaves are from the earliest known series to survive, a stylistic and iconographic prototype that was of profound significance to subsequent Indian painting. The series is known for its vigorous movement and inventive compositions. It is widely dispersed among public and private collections in India, the United States, England, Continental Europe, and Australia, a fact that has delayed its detailed study until recently and obscured its central importance to a clear understanding of early-sixteenth-century painting. The original number of leaves may have been as great as three hundred sixty, but it is not certain that the series was ever finished. About three hundred leaves are known to have been completed. Around two hundred of these survive.

Because of its wide dispersal many individual leaves of this series have been published; for a consideration of this *Bhāgavata* in its entirety, see Ehnbom, in press.

❀ 3 ❀

Folio from a manuscript of the *Candāyana* of Dā'ūd

PERHAPS DELHI-AGRA REGION, ca. FIRST HALF OF 16TH CENTURY

Image 7½ × 6⅜ in. (191 × 162 mm); sheet 10 × 7¾ in. (255 × 197 mm)

Loraka mourns the death of his beloved Cānda killed by snakebite

Loraka and Cānda have fled his shrewish wife and her one-eyed, crippled, impotent husband. The adulterous lovers have taken refuge in a grove of trees. That night, as they sleep, a snake bites and kills the unfortunate Cānda. Loraka mourns extravagantly, cursing the very tree that sheltered the serpent. In his grief he prepares a funeral pyre for his lover. Luckily, a female snake charmer happens by and is able to raise Cānda from the dead. Cānda has a great deal of trouble with snakes in the story, and this is not the only time she dies of their venom and is brought back to life.

The refined line and pale color of this picture are in marked contrast to the boldness and brightness of catalogue numbers 1 and 2, yet figure types and decorative motifs are similar, and both styles contributed significantly to the inception of Mughal painting. The high horizon, pink ground, and delicate arabesque designs are typical of the *Candāyana* group style, a Persianized Indian idiom known from only three manuscripts, two of this same text. Written in the late fourteenth century, this romance with mystic dimensions was tremendously popular in north India, but Dā'ūd's text was lost totally to modern readers until recently. No complete version is known to survive. For the Avadhī (Eastern Hindi) verses written in Arabic script on the reverse, see Gupta, sec. 348, pp. 275–76.

The bulk of this manuscript is in the Prince of Wales Museum of Western India, Bombay. Detached leaves are in the Asian Art Museum, San Francisco; the Goenka Academy of Art and Music, New Delhi; the J. P. Goenka Collection, Bombay; Collection of Edwin Binney, 3rd, San Diego; a private collection in Cambridge, Massachusetts; and a private collection in London. For the Binney and Cambridge pages, see Chandra and Ehnbom, pp. 28–29, nos. 20–22, pl. 7; and Binney 1973, no. 6. The Bombay portion is published in part in Khandalavala and Chandra 1969, pp. 94–103, pl. 24, figs. 156–175; see pl. 25 and figs. 176–177 for another manuscript of the *Candāyana*, related in style but rougher in execution, which is preserved in the John Rylands Library, Manchester.

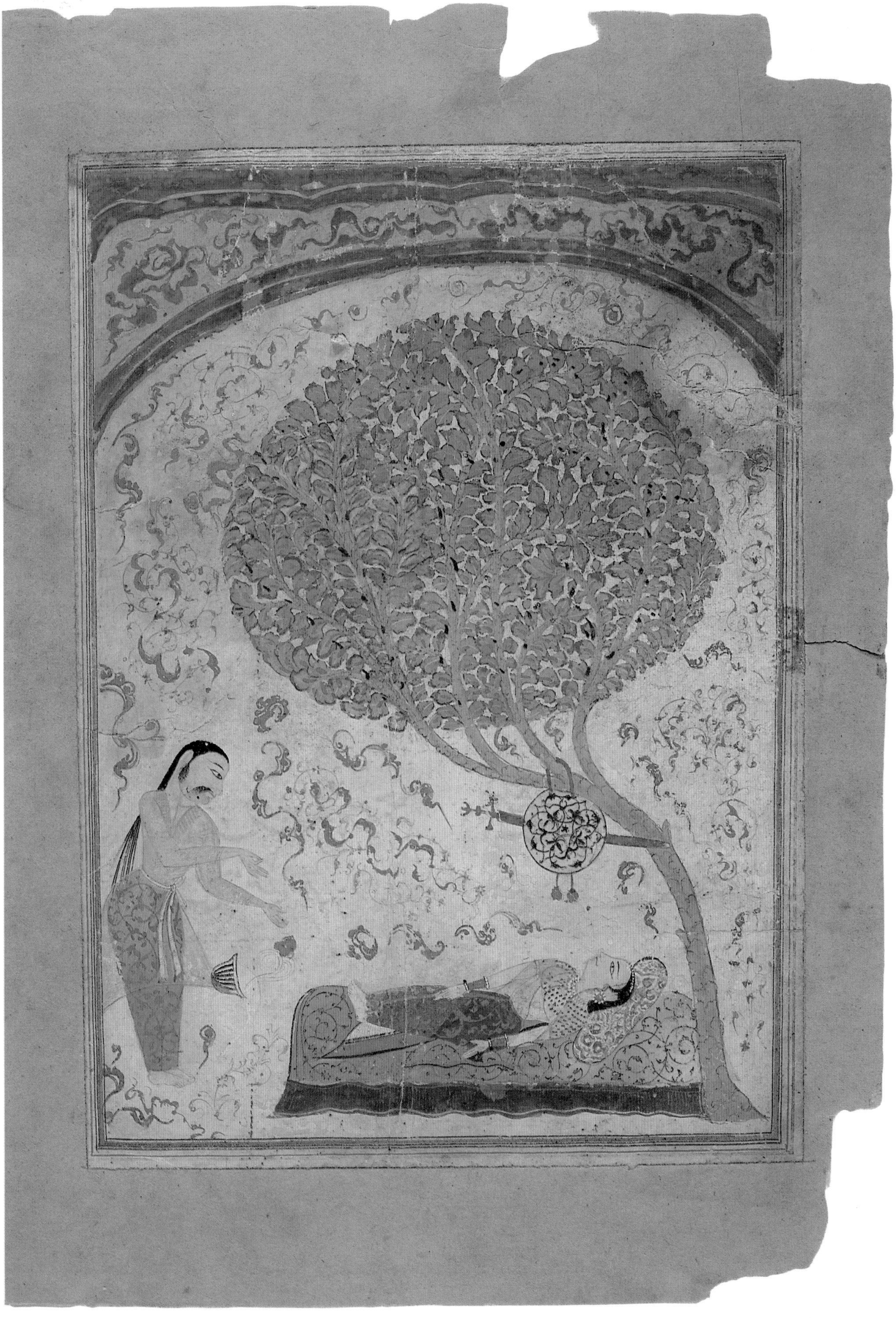

❀ 4 ❀

Folio from a manuscript of the *Ḥamza-nāma*

MUGHAL, AKBAR PERIOD, ca. 1562–77

Sheet 25 3/8 × 21 7/8 in. (645 × 556 mm)

The Fine Arts Museums of San Francisco, Achenbach Foundation for Graphic Arts, Gift of Dr. William K. Ehrenfeld

A battle among Ḥamza's forces, demons, and fairies

The battle is ferocious. Ḥamza and a human ally attack giant demons while other demons fight with Ḥamza against the fairies. In the upper left a fairy princess shoots arrows from a flying litter supported by horned demons. Her winged forces and their demon allies descend on the foe. The fantastic demons are both ferocious and amusing. In the center a green creature with an enormous head crosses his eyes as Ḥamza slices open his chest. To the right a huge spotted demon raises his boulder-mace as his enemy's sword rips into his soft potbelly. A gigantic orange demon warrior in the lower right corner has been cut completely in half. In the upper left paint loss has revealed sensitive underdrawing in a group of fairies.

Though most of the surviving leaves of the manuscript originally bore texts on paper glued to their backs, this leaf may belong to the small group that carried front text panels, which are now lost. The leaf has been trimmed somewhat, yet little or nothing is missing from the illustration. With the text lacking, it is difficult to identify the exact scene depicted. It is probably an incident from Ḥamza's visit to a mythical land identified with the Caucasus region of Asia. His foster brother Rāʿd, driven from his throne by a wicked uncle, asked him to join in the fight to regain his birthright. The campaign was successful, but then Rāʿd was killed in battle by a fairy princess. First she hated Ḥamza, but then she came to love him. After a while he loved her in return, and they lived together in a marvelous palace where she bore him a child.

The *Ḥamza-nāma* was the most ambitious undertaking of the fledgling Mughal workshop. It was the earliest known Mughal manuscript until the discovery of the Cleveland *Ṭūṭī-nāma* (cat. no. 5). Always called the *Qiṣṣa-i Amīr Ḥamza* in contemporary sources, the manuscript contained fourteen hundred paintings on cloth and took fifteen years to complete. Its fourteen volumes chronicle the fabulous adventures of the uncle of the Prophet (Mohammed). Only about one-tenth of the illustrations survive, mostly in the Museum für angewandte Kunst, Vienna, and the Victoria and Albert Museum, London.

This leaf belongs to the group of *Ḥamza* illustrations that show strong Persian influence. The winged fairies and the elongated, small-headed figure type derive from Safawi painting. Persian painters accompanied Humāyūn, the second Mughal emperor (r. 1530–40, 1555–56), back to India from exile in Iran, and these masters supervised the *Ḥamza* project illustrated during the reign of his son and successor, Akbar (r. 1556–1605). Nevertheless, the gory violence, vigorous movement, and emphatic diagonals are typically and characteristically early Mughal. Fortunately, the picture has escaped the iconoclastic effacement and maladroit retouching that mar so many leaves of this great and important manuscript.

For textually and stylistically related leaves, see the classic monumental study of the manuscript, Glück, pl. 4, figs. 8, 9; and the ongoing publication that will reproduce in three volumes all known leaves, *Ḥamza-nāma*; vol. 1, no. V.6, vol. 2, no. V&A.3. Two more related leaves are published in Skelton 1976b, p. 236, no. V.2, pl. 29; and Skelton 1976a, p. 268, fig. 1. Other leaves are in private and public collections in India, England, Ireland, Continental Europe, and the United States.

❀ 5 ❀

Folio 286 from the Cleveland *Ṭūṭī-nāma (Tales of a Parrot)* of Ziyā' al-Dīn Nakhshabī

MUGHAL, AKBAR PERIOD, ca. 1560–65

Image 3¾ × 3⅞ in. (95 × 99 mm); sheet 8 × 5 in. (204 × 127 mm)

Khujasta and the parrot at the beginning of the forty-fifth night (recto)

Khujasta stands within an intensely colored, patterned pavilion set in a tiled courtyard. A garden and a flat, deep-blue sky are in the background. The woman's ornaments recall those of the women in catalogue numbers 1 and 2, but the delicacy of the line is more akin to that of catalogue number 3, and the movement toward three dimensions in the treatment of the exterior and interior of the pavilion and the bird cage is entirely Mughal. The bold juxtapositions of pattern and color relate to the fervor of *Ḥamza* illustrations (cat. no. 4), but are handled here on a more intimate scale. Khujasta pauses to listen to the parrot, whose goal is to keep her from an adulterous affair while her husband is away on a business trip. Night after night he tells her fabulous tales of vice and virtue. The bird accomplishes its purpose, but the husband slays Khujasta on his return for even considering infidelity and then becomes a wandering religious.

Though the *Ḥamza-nāma* was the most ambitious undertaking of the Mughal workshop that began under Akbar's patronage, the manuscript from which this leaf comes is stylistically the earliest. It documents the formative process in which artists from all over the Indian empire were brought together under Persian masters and formed a revolutionary new style. Painters whose early training was in the flat, abstract idioms of catalogue numbers 1–3 embraced a new standard of refined naturalism. At times halting and uneven, early Mughal painting quickly coalesced into a brilliant expression quite unlike any of its parent styles.

This leaf was formerly in the Collection of Edwin Binney, 3rd, San Diego; see Binney 1973, p. 28, no. 12a. The manuscript originally consisted of three hundred forty-one folios. Of these (some text leaves of which are later replacements), three hundred twenty-eight are in the Cleveland Museum of Art, six in private collections, and seven are missing. The entire extant manuscript has been published in color facsimile with an accompanying analysis and description which clarify its central place in the study of early Mughal painting; see Chandra 1976.

The miniature discussed in catalogue number 6 is from a *Ṭūṭī-nāma* manuscript produced later in the Akbar period.

بجام بر طوطی رفت و گفت ای مستمند جگر از کباب جر بسند و خون جگر

از دامن گذشت   وهل لی علی حتفی بقصد مکشوف   قال علی حدی در ملاء مجمع

من خود را مست در کوچه افکند بی امر و بهر حیله بر دست رفتنی طوطی دید که مست

سید
قلق و از شبهاء دیگر غالب تر است و اضطرار او از سایر اوقات غالب تر

نباید که همچنان کند و خود را در آن کوچه افکند و محنت چند بن شبه

مر ضایع گرداند گفت ای کدبانو تو مثل این کلمات و نی گویی که مرا در

❀ 6 ❀

Folio from the Beatty *Ṭūṭī-nāma (Tales of a Parrot)*

MUGHAL, AKBAR PERIOD, ca. 1580

Image 6¾ × 5 in. (172 × 127 mm); sheet 10 × 7⅛ in. (255 × 181 mm)

The twenty-seventh night. The story of Zarīr the garment weaver who leaves home to seek his fortune

Zarīr the garment weaver excels at his trade but, to his despair, he does not prosper. He leaves his home in Iraq and goes to the town of Nishapur in Iran where he indeed earns a great deal of money. Twice he begins his journey home to share his bounty with his loved ones, and each time he is the victim of thieves. When he finally arrives home, empty-handed and dejected, he is greeted by his wife's admonition that there is no point in a man's exerting himself since he will never achieve what fate has not intended him to. In this scene, which takes place in a green-tiled courtyard bounded by a wall of brown brick, Zarīr's sons touch his feet and his women bid him farewell as he sets out to find his fortune.

By the time this manuscript was painted the disparate stylistic elements of early Mughal painting had coalesced into a consistent and uniform style. Vigorous movement and penetrating color give way to greater calmness and a cool, coordinated palette. Some memory of the striking patterning found in catalogue numbers 4 and 5 survives in this illustration, but gone are the dizzying juxtapositions and startling contrasts we see at the inception of the style.

For a translation of the text on this folio, see Simsar 1978, pp. 175–76. Another leaf from the same story is published in *Indian Heritage*, p. 32, no. 23. These incidents in the story of Zarīr either were not illustrated in the Cleveland version of the *Ṭūṭī-nāma* or have not survived. Two Cleveland pages dealing with the twenty-seventh night (fols. 187–88) appear to be nineteenth-century replacements.

The manuscript from which this folio comes is called the "Beatty *Ṭūṭī-nāma*" because most of its miniatures are preserved in the Chester Beatty Library, Dublin (MS. 21). Detached leaves are in many public and private collections, including the National Museum of India, New Delhi; the Bharat Kala Bhavan, Banaras (Varanasi); the Andhra Pradesh State Archaeological Museum, Hyderabad; the Museum of Fine Arts, Boston; the Los Angeles County Museum of Art; and the Collection of Edwin Binney, 3rd, San Diego (see Binney 1973, p. 33, no. 14). For a general discussion of the manuscript and its relationship to the Cleveland *Ṭūṭī-nāma*, see Chandra 1976, p. 82, pls. 47–61.

The manuscript was brought to France from India by General Jean-François Allard (1785–1839), a mercenary who served the maharaja of Lahore. It was purchased by Félix Feuillet (later Baron F. S. Feuillet de Conches), a distinguished collector of manuscripts and documents. Not long after its arrival in France the literary critic J. Garcin de Tassey (vol. 1, p. 85) noted the manuscript as "a very handsome specimen embellished with curious drawings and perfectly finished." Though leaves may have been extracted before the manuscript arrived in France, it seems that most of the separate leaves were removed after it was sold during the dispersal of the Feuillet de Conches collection later in the century. See also Losty 1982, pp. 88–89, no. 60, pl. XXII. A portrait of Allard painted in Lahore in 1838 is published in S. C. Welch 1978, pp. 124–25, no. 55.

داستان زریرشعار باف و رفتن او و بتحصیل مال و خایب و خاسر باز
آمدن و حکایت اسب و شکال شب بیست هفتم

جون نساج فلک نسیج زرین آفتاب در طلیه مغرب رفت و شعری
سپهر حریر سپیده ماه از کارگاه مشرق پرون آورد خجسته
جامها چمن و زیبائی پوشیده و جامها طنز و رعنایی نوشیده
خورم و خندان و خوشدل و شادان از برای دستوری بر طوطی رفت

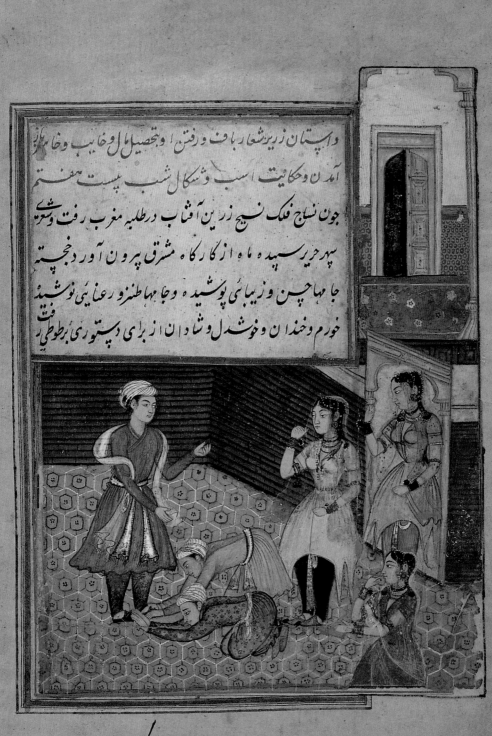

طوطی گفت

❀ 7 ❀

Folio from the Victoria and Albert *Bābar-nāma*

Three Indian trees

Ascribed to Tulasī the Younger (design) and Banavārī the Elder (coloring)

MUGHAL, AKBAR PERIOD, ca. 1589

Sheet 10½ × 6⅛ in. (260 × 156 mm)

The jackfruit tree

Image 4½ × 3⅜ in. (115 × 86 mm)

Recto. The tree is shown growing against a yellow and blue sky in a gently rolling green landscape. A text panel cuts through the tree's dense foliage. In red letters on the right margin is the scribal ascription *ṭarḥ tulsī khurd ʿamal banwārī kalān* (design by Tulasī the Younger, coloring by Banavārī the Elder). The illustration is numbered 156.

The monkey-jack and the lotefruit trees

Image 9⅝ × 4⅞ in. (244 × 124 mm)

Verso. Two trees are shown in a manner similar to that of the recto except that the landscape of the monkey-jack is filled with flowering plants. Of the monkey-jack tree Bābar wrote, "Unripe it is a singularly tasteless and empty thing," and of the lotefruit, "Most of them are not very good" (Beveridge, vol. 2, p. 507). The illustrations are numbered 157 and 158 respectively.

Zahīr al-Dīn Muḥammad Bābar (1483–1530) was the first Mughal emperor of India (r. 1526–30). He was a vigorous and cultivated prince who left behind an extraordinary journal written in Turki, the mother tongue of the Mughals. But Persian was the language of the court, and in the 1580s Bābar's revealing memoir was translated. On November 24, 1589, it was presented to his grandson Akbar (1542–1605) by ʿAbd al-Rahīm Khān, himself a patron of art and literature (see cat. no. 14). The manuscript from which this leaf comes was probably the presentation copy, now known as the "Victoria and Albert *Bābar-nāma*" from the twenty-one pages in that museum.

Though Bābar found India an uncongenial land and never ceased to yearn for his native Central Asia, he was fascinated by the flora and fauna of his newly conquered territory. He carefully noted the animals and plants that he saw, an early indication of the Mughal love of natural history so evident during the reign of his great-grandson Jahāngīr (1569–1627; see cat. no. 22). The jackfruit he found especially interesting: "This is a fruit of singular form and flavour; it looks like a sheep's stomach stuffed and made into a haggis (*gīpa*); and it is sickeningly-sweet." He goes on to note a curious characteristic of the fruit: "It is heard of also as growing, not only on the branches of its tree, but on trunk and root too. One would say that the tree was all hung round with haggises." The tree depicted here fits Bābar's description perfectly. For a translation of the original text, see Beveridge, vol. 2, p. 506.

Collaboration by two or more artists on a single painting was common in the Mughal production of historical and epical manuscripts during the closing decades of the sixteenth century. Generally, senior artists were responsible for the design and junior artists for the coloring, but sometimes a master would rework a page and imprint his individual style. Chandra 1976, pp. 56–57, discusses this process. Tulasī the Younger is best known as a colorist, but careful study of paintings ascribed to him, to Tulasī the Elder, and simply to Tulasī may reveal more about his work. Banavārī the Elder is fairly well known as a somewhat conservative painter who probably began his career in the imperial workshop as early as about 1560–65. For a brief but detailed consideration of his style, see Chandra 1976, p. 97.

There are at least four sixteenth-century copies of the *Bābar-nāma*, the subsequent three copies probably having been prepared as gifts. The next in date (ca. 1591) is in the British Library, London (Or. 3714). Folio 399 of that copy, painted by Manī, corresponds to the page published here (the verso is published in Suleiman, pl. 78). Tulasī the Younger painted folio 398 of the British Library copy unassisted (see Suleiman, pl. 77); Banavārī the Elder painted folio 253r (see Suleiman, pl. 34). The third manuscript (ca. 1593) is divided between the State Museum of Oriental Cultures, Moscow, and the Walters Art Gallery, Baltimore. The fourth (dated 1597–98), in the National Museum of India, New Delhi, is the most complete of the group. See Smart 1973, pp. 54–58; Smart 1978, pp. 111–32; and Beach 1981, pp. 77, 81, no. 7 and pp. 83, 85, no. 8. See also Binney 1973, pp. 36–37, no. 15.

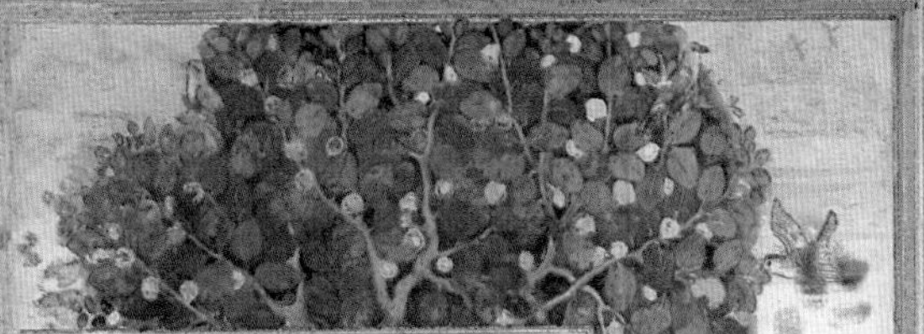

بدهل است کلانی او برابر سیب بوده باشد بویش بد نیست

غریب پست و بیمزه چیزیست یک دیگر برابر است در فارسی

او را اچار می کنند این انواع می شود از آلوچه یک چیزی کلانتر است
یک نوع دیگر می شود اندام انگور حسینی اکثر آن بسیار خوب

184

18

کدهل است این غریب بدهیأت و بدمزه میوه ایست

186

بعینه شکنبهٔ گوسفندیست که مثل گیپا درون او را بیرون کرده
باشند مزهٔ او شیرین دل آشوریست در درون او مثل فندق
دانها می باشند بجز ما فی الجمله شباهتی دارد دانهای این گرد است
دراز می شود این دانها از خرما نرم تر گوشتی دارند این را می خورند
خیلی چسپنده است از جهت چسپندگی او بعضی بدستها و
دهن روغن مالیده می خورده اند هم در شاخ درخت می شود
هم در تنهٔ درخت می شود هم در بیخ درخت می شود گویا از
درخت گیپاها را آویخته آویخته مانده اند دیگر

سوادی

❀ 8 ❀

An album page

MUGHAL, AKBAR PERIOD, ca. 1590

Image 6½ × 4¾ in. (165 × 121 mm); sheet 14¾ × 10 in. (375 × 255 mm)

Fantastic birds

Three brilliantly colored birds are in a cool green landscape filled with flowers. To the left a red-crested heron stands on a riverbank watching as a fantastic jungle fowl (right) and a fancifully plumed mythical bird (top) square off to fight. The bird at the top is especially noteworthy. Fiercely reptilian in aspect, it coils its long neck around to face its foe as its serpentine red, green, and white tail feathers spotted with black spread aggressively behind. If the jungle fowl crows a challenge, its mysterious enemy certainly hisses in reply, its tongue flicking to the very point of its razor-sharp beak. The gently undulating ground and brightly colored flowers dotting it serve to frame the birds and subtly reinforce their movements.

The picture has been trimmed and remounted in a later border. A strip from the left has been used to enlarge the picture at the top. Hindi and Persian captions on the back relate the top bird to the mythical *sīmurgh* of Persian literature.

Natural history studies are commonly associated with the reign of Jahāngīr (1605–27; see cat. no. 22), but more generalized animal pictures are not uncommon in the Akbar period. Some were used as illustrations in the various copies of the memoirs of Bābar (cat. no. 7), but others, such as this one, probably served no direct literary purpose, being painted instead as independent studies.

This picture is closely related in subject, date, and style to a composition in the Musée Guimet, Paris (3619, Q,a), published in W. G. Archer 1956, pl. 4, but is probably by a different artist.

❀ 9 ❀

An album page

MUGHAL, AKBAR PERIOD, LATE 16TH CENTURY

Image 4½ × 5⅜ in. (115 × 137 mm); sheet 10¾ × 15¼ in. (273 × 388 mm)

Composite elephant

Two demons ride an elephant through a hilly landscape—and what an elephant it is! Its body is an ingeniously interwoven welter of a lion, a tiger, a blue-skinned demon, a leopard, a fish, a vulture, foxes, and other animals. Its legs are formed of rabbits, foxes, deer, antelope, a tortoise, a bear, and a buffalo with splendidly curving horns. The elephant's head is an intricate interlace of a man whose flaring lower garment forms an ear, various beasts, a mythical crocodilian creature whose long body and tail form the trunk, and fish that form the tusks. A demonic handler carries an elephant goad made of a cobra and a curving fish tied on with a tiny snake. The demon rider behind him blows an undulating animal-head trumpet. The fierceness of these creatures is lightened by the golden bells that dangle incongruously from their horns. The fabulous elephant, threatened at each foot by rearing cobras, natural enemies of these enormous beasts, seizes and overturns a demon swordsman to the right. The figures are lightly tinted and highlighted here and there with gold. The landscape is subtly modeled. In the distance are trees painted in soft washes, a small shrine on a loaf-shaped hill, and a multitowered city nestled beside the mountain that rises to the right.

Though the picture carries no ascription, its superb quality leaves no doubt that it is a product of one of the masters of Akbar's workshop. Certain aspects of the style suggest that it may be from the hand of the painter Miskīn, whose elegantly shaded animal pictures are among the most delightful Mughal pictures of the last decade of the sixteenth century. However, the apparent delight in soft, fleshy forms and the characteristic rendering of trees and landscape indicate a more likely attribution to Dharma Dāsa, a still little-understood painter of great skill and vision who was active from about 1580 to the opening years of the seventeenth century. This composite elephant is very close to his work of the 1590s. For examples, see his contributions to the *Akbar-nāma* of about 1590 in the Victoria and Albert Museum, London (I.S.2-1896.24/117), and the *Khamsa* of Niẓāmī of 1595 in the British Library, London (Or. 12208, fols. 40v, 52v, 102r, 195r, 254r). An excellent brief survey of Dharma Dāsa's style is in Beach 1981, pp. 105–7.

Though we enjoy composite animals primarily for their wit and ingenuity, these studies are a common theme in the painting of the Islamic world and probably have symbolic significance that is still obscure. Composite pictures were especially popular in India, though few compare in liveliness or in early date with this painting. For other roughly contemporary examples, one of which is in the Collection of Edwin Binney, 3rd, San Diego, see Binney 1973, p. 56, no. 31; Welch and Welch, pp. 184–88, no. 62. The Binney page is published with references to possible Indian and Persian prototypes in S. C. Welch 1976, pp. 40–41, no. 11.

❀ 10 ❀ 11 ❀

Two illustrations from a Persian translation of the *Kathāsaritsāgara* of Somadeva

MUGHAL, AKBAR PERIOD, ca. 1585–90

10. Indīvarasena, his wives Khaḍgadaṃṣṭrā and Madanaṃṣṭrā, and his younger brother Anicchasena travel magically to the city of Irāvatī

Sheet 3½ × 5⅜ in. (89 × 137 mm)

Astonished city dwellers watch from the left as the hero and his retinue approach in a flying pavilion powered by a magic sword. At the left a man in red "bites the finger of amazement," a convention for expressing wonder in Indian and Persian painting. The city is a complex mass of buildings depicted from different vantage points. Heavy shading gives the picture a somewhat sooty, almost somber tonality, though the subject is a joyful return after many tribulations. The miraculous pavilion is surrounded by opalescent clouds that drift over the tree-filled landscape.

For a translation of Somadeva's version of the story, see Penzer, vol. 3, pp. 273–75. The text on the back of this picture (probably the recto of the original folio) is the portion in Penzer, p. 273.

11. A king slays a mendicant as a god observes from the sky

Sheet 3½ × 6¾ in. (89 × 172 mm)

The composition is simpler than that of the previous illustration, the color clearer, and the work finer. From a lotus seat resting on a cushion of clouds a god looks down. A sword-bearing king has just beheaded a prostrate mendicant in a rocky landscape outside a city wall. Blood gushes from the mendicant's neck. Before him on the ground lie his water pot, two manuscripts, and a soft broom for sweeping his path clean lest he inadvertently crush an insect too small to be seen. The broom suggests that the man was a member of the Jain religion, a sect that developed about the time of the Buddha and is still influential, especially in western India.

It is difficult to identify precisely the story from the bits of text on the back, but it may be the incident at the end of the tale of King Trivikramasena and the demon who had the power to enter and animate human corpses. If so, the god represented is Śiva, though he lacks his usual attributes; see Penzer, vol. 7, pp. 122–25.

The rich narrative tradition of India is the ultimate source for many of the world's most revered fables and stories. The *Kathāsaritsāgara* (literally, The Ocean of the Streams of Story) by the eleventh-century Kashmiri poet Somadeva draws on the same material that provided the basis for cycles as disparate as the fables of Aesop and the tales of the *Ṭūṭī-nāma* (cat. nos. 5 and 6). Akbar (1542–1605) was interested in the traditions of his Indian subjects and ordered many of their texts translated into Persian for imperial edification. The manuscript from which these two illustrations were cut is known only from brutally trimmed fragments. Most of them seem to have been formerly in the Ardeshir Collection, dispersed in 1964. There are examples now in the Los Angeles County Museum of Art; the Collection of Edwin Binney, 3rd, San Diego; and other private collections. Many fragments were formerly in the Pan-Asian Collection, now dispersed. For published examples, see Binney 1973, p. 50, no. 26; and *Heeramaneck Collection*, no. 197. The Heeramaneck Collection is now in the Los Angeles County Museum of Art.

❀ 12 ❀

Folio from a history of the Barmakids

MUGHAL, AKBAR PERIOD, ca. 1595–1600

Image 8⅝ × 5 in. (219 × 127 mm); sheet 15⅝ × 10⅞ in. (398 × 277 mm)

An errant son begs forgiveness from his father

In a courtyard overlooking cypress trees in a garden a man in green kneels in supplication before his father. The father, dressed in pink and yellow, has two attendants, one holding a sword in a scabbard, the other waving a flywhisk. Other retainers observe the scene.

The text of this page describes a son pleading for the forgiveness of his father, but does not give sufficient information for a more precise identification of the incident depicted. The verses on the other side treat the theme of filial remorse and paternal forgiveness. It was common in Persian literature to intersperse prose narratives with interludes of related poetry.

The Barmakids were a distinguished Iranian family of ministers who served the ʿAbbāsid caliphs. They traced their ancestry from Buddhists who converted to Islam, but were transformed by later legend into the descendants of a Zoroastrian priest. Nearly as powerful as the rulers they served, they lost their position in a single night of execution and imprisonment in January 803.

The illustrations from this dispersed manuscript are relatively simple, suggesting that it may have been prepared for a patron other than the emperor. On the other hand, recent research seems to indicate that the imperial workshop itself was capable of turning out more modest productions than scholars had previously suspected, and this manuscript may number among them (see cat. no. 13).

This leaf was formerly in the Collection of Edwin Binney, 3rd, San Diego; see Binney 1973, p. 39, no. 18b.

تقصیر کرده ام و یقین میدانم که آن بر خاطر مبارک تو گران آمده در مدت عمر همین چند چیز معذور فرموده من در ان اهمال و تقصیر کردم
هرآینه آن نیز علامت عقوبت خود میدانم و نیکو دریافتم که ظهور این سپید بها اثر رنج خاطر عاطر تست تا تو بکلی از من خشنود
نشوی من ازین رنج خلاص نیابم این بگفت و با هزار عذرخواهی در پای پدر افتاد

و چندان بگریست که نزدیک بود قالب تهی بکند بعد از آن سوگند خورد که من ترا چنان دوست که اگر وقتی سخنی گفتی
یا سخنی از موعظت و پند من نشنیدی در خاطر من کدورت نمانده و این زمان تا ترا باری تعالی ازین رنج خلاص ندهد و صحت کلی

❀ 13 ❀

A folio from a manuscript of the *Razm-nāma*

Ascribed to Kānhā

MUGHAL, AKBAR PERIOD, DATED 1598–99

Image 7 3/8 × 4 1/4 in. (187 × 107 mm); sheet 11 7/8 × 6 7/8 in. (302 × 174 mm)

A *brāhmaṇa* and his son Medhāvin discourse on the path to salvation

A *brāhmaṇa* sits in a courtyard conversing with his son Medhāvin (literally, "intelligent"), who tells his father of the necessity of breaking all worldly attachments. At the left two men sit talking. In the foreground two young students with writing boards and pots of ink are having a disagreement. The smug boy on the left has done something to anger the lad on the right, who gestures decisively. The green and tan ground is softly modeled. In the background trees rise above the rooftops. Birds wheel through the cloudy sky.

The *Razm-nāma* is a Persian translation of the *Mahābhārata*, an Indian epic of great importance and influence, prepared for Akbar (r. 1556–1605) between 1582 and 1584. Around that time the Mughal workshop began a splendidly illustrated version of the story, a project finished about 1586, which is now preserved in the Maharaja Sawai Man Singh II Museum, Jaipur. Subsequently other versions of the story were prepared and illustrated, though not as sumptuously as the Jaipur copy. This leaf is from a copy dated A.H. 1007/A.D. 1598–99 which is dispersed, though significant portions are now in the British Library, London (Or. 12076), the Baroda Museum and Picture Gallery, and the Victoria and Albert Museum, London.

The ascription in the lower margin reads *kanhara*, a variant of the more usual Kānhā, the name of a painter of the imperial workshop who contributed to several major manuscripts of the 1580s and 1590s. He seems to have specialized in animal studies. Here his work is simpler and less finished than is typical of first-quality imperial manuscripts, a characteristic that applies to this 1598–99 *Razm-nāma* in general, which has led scholars to suggest that it may have been prepared for a patron other than Akbar. But the number of imperial painters who worked on it confirms that it was painted in the imperial studio. Perhaps the likeliest explanation is that it was prepared as a gift. We know that Akbar ordered illustrated versions of the story to be presented to grandees of the realm.

This page was formerly in the Collection of Edwin Binney, 3rd, San Diego; see Binney 1973, pp. 48–49, no. 25a. For a meticulous reconstruction of the manuscript and a thorough analysis, see Seyller, where this folio is cited in Appendix A, no. 92. Two more 1598–99 *Razm-nāma* pages by Kānhā are in the Prince of Wales Museum of Western India, Bombay (26.4705; Seyller, Appendix A, no. 117), and in the British Library, London (Or. 12076, fol. 83v; Seyller, Appendix A, no. 145). Seyller, to whom I am grateful for providing me with information for this, and the next, entry, has traced one hundred sixty-one illustrations to the manuscript. See also Losty 1982, pp. 123–24, no. 88 (the British Library portion bears the date); and Gangoly, pp. 10–14, no. 198/1–32. There is a brief survey of Kānhā in Beach 1981, p. 81. For the Jaipur manuscript, see Hendley 1883, vol. 4; and Skelton 1970, pp. 41–54.

The Sanskrit text of the *Mahābhārata* is enormous. For the critical edition, see *Mahābhārata*, 27 volumes (including indices and supplements). The text of this incident is *Mahābhārata* 12.169.1–37. For an English summary, see Sörenson, p. 481, XII, 175. There is a complete English prose translation of the text in twelve volumes; for this story, see Roy, vol. 9, pp. 6–8.

تصویر برهمن عالم دو پسرش را زیاده از پدر در فن علم و عمل آن [illegible]

کنهر

❀ 14 ❀

A leaf from a manuscript of the *Razm-nāma*

Painted for ʿAbd al-Rahīm Khān, Khān-i Khānān

SUB-IMPERIAL MUGHAL, DATED 1616–17 AND 1617

Image 12¾ × 8½ in. (324 × 216 mm), irregular; sheet 13 × 8⅞ in. (330 × 226 mm)

Karṇa slays Ghaṭokaca with a dart given to him by Indra, King of the Gods

The hero Karṇa slays the powerful Ghaṭokaca with Indra's dart after most others have fled the field of battle. The background with its archaistically high horizon line is in modeled green, tan, and pink. The lively figures of the fighters are arranged across the middle of the page. Karṇa's fatal thrust is emphasized by the diagonal placement of his brightly colored chariot in relation to Ghaṭokaca's elephant. The victim's dark face is contorted as the dart penetrates his body and he falls lifeless from his mount. His elephant handler vainly shoots an arrow at the victorious Karṇa, who will be slain in the next section of the epic (*Mahābhārata* 8). The forces of the Pāṇḍavas are temporarily disheartened by Ghaṭokaca's death, but Kṛṣṇa, Arjuna's charioteer (cat. no. 2), is pleased. The weapon given by Indra can be used but once, and Arjuna and his brothers have been spared its fatal fury. For the text, see *Mahābhārata* 7.154.1–63; Sörenson, p. 306, VII, 179; and Roy, vol. 6, pp. 451–55.

ʿAbd al-Rahīm Khān was a valued member of the courts of Akbar (r. 1556–1605) and Jahāngīr (r. 1605–27), attaining the elevated status of Khān-i Khānān. He was himself a great patron of literature and painting (see cat. no. 7), though to judge from works known to have been produced under his patronage, his taste was conservative. The Khān-i Khānān's workshop could not compete with the imperial studio in quality and refinement. Indeed, if this manuscript were not securely dated, we would certainly place it in the Akbar period rather than with the superbly and subtly finished works painted for his successor, Jahāngīr (see cat. nos. 21 and 22).

Many *Razm-nāma* leaves bear the names of artists, but this leaf has lost its borders and any ascription it may have had. This manuscript, unfortunately dispersed, is closely related in style to another product of the Khān-i Khānān's workshop, a *Khamsa* of the poet Amīr Khusrau Dihlawī now in the Deutsche Staatsbibliothek, Berlin.

Seyller has traced sixty-eight leaves of this manuscript and cites this leaf in Appendix B, no. 11. It was long thought that the manuscript bore only one date (A.H. 1025/A.D. 1616–17), on a leaf in the Victoria and Albert Museum, London (see Seyller, fig. 1), but Seyller publishes another leaf (figs. 2 and 3), now in the Free Library of Philadelphia, which is dated A.H. 1026/A.D. 1617. For a detailed treatment of the manuscript and complete references to known pages, see Seyller. For more references to Mughal versions of the *Razm-nāma*, see the entry for catalogue number 13. Catalogue number 43 illustrates an incident from the *Mahābhārata* in a style that is antithetical to the Mughal sense of refinement. Beach 1981, pp. 128–55, no. 15a–q, publishes a *Rāmāyana* painted for ʿAbd al-Rahīm Khān.

که ایندر افسونی بمن آموخته آنرا بر نیزه دوسیتی خوانده حواله کهروکه می کنم و او را می کشم
بس کرن آنرا بدست گرفت و از تاثیر آن نیزه تعبیه دغابازی کهروکه همه باطل شد
و تنها بجنگ کرن ماند عاقبت کرن آن نیزه ایندر را بر کروکه انداخت آن نیزه بر سینه
کروکه خورده از پشتش در گذشت و کروکه از بالای فیل سرنگون بر زمین افتاد

و کوروان خوشحال و پاندوان ازین قضیه غمگین شدند بعد از آنکه کهروکه کشته شد کشن
بخندید و با پاندوان گفت که طرفه چیزی ست امروز بلایی که بر ارجن خواست
نازل شد بر کهروکه افتاد شما از مردن کهروکه بدحال مباشید ایشان پرسیدند که سر
این معنی را روشن تر بیان بکنید کشن گفت چون کرن زره پوشیده و حلقه در گوش
انداخته در عالم وجود آمد از تاثیر آن زره و حلقه هیچکس نمی توانست او را کشت
غایتش ایندر کاری کرد که آنها را بمکری و حیله از کرن گرفت چنانچه بالا مذکور شده
و در وقت وداع کرن از ایندر آن افسون نیزه دسیتی بقصد جان ارجن گرفته بود تا
آنکه امروز آنرا بر کهروکه انداخت و او را کشت شما شکرانه حق سبحانه و تعالی
بجای آرید که ارجن بسلامت ماند و چنانچه من برای خاطر شما جراسنده و ششپال
و ایکلب را کشتم درین نزدیکی کرن را هم می کشتم چیزی که او داشت آن زره و این افسون
ایندر بود زره خود بیشتر ازین رفته بود و افسون حالا رفت و کرن بی سلاح مانده است
حالا مردانه باشید و جنگ کرده او را بکشید و از کشته شدن کهروکه غم و افسوس مخورید
که اگر ارجن بسلامت است باز نعم البدل پیدا خواهد شد سخن چون بدینجا رسید در تراست

❀ 15 ❀

Folio from a manuscript of the *Rāmāyaṇa*

SUB-IMPERIAL MUGHAL, ca. 1600

Sheet 11⅜ × 7 in. (289 × 178 mm)

Lakṣmaṇa, seeing Bharata's approach, tells Rāma that he intends to slay their brother

As Bharata's army pauses in the foreground, he and his brother Śatrughna approach the forest retreat of their brother Rāma. Bharata is seeking to convince Rāma that he should return to rule in Ayodhya rather than remain in exile. Lakṣmaṇa, seeing their brother approach, misapprehends his intention and reveals that he intends to kill him and to reinstate Rāma. Rāma rebukes him. He will receive Bharata but refuse to end his exile. Rāma, at the upper left, listens as Lakṣmaṇa gestures angrily toward the approaching Bharata. The artist skillfully sets the brothers Rāma and Lakṣmaṇa apart. They see all, but are unseen. Bharata turns as if sensing his brothers' presence, but his sight is blocked by a line of trees. The army is hemmed in by rocky ridges, indicating that it poses no threat to the divine brothers.

This picture is an example of painting in the Mughal style produced for a patron well versed in the Sanskrit classics. The rich, deep color, the naturalistic rendering of trees, rocks, and humans, the lively movement, and the unified composition indicate derivation from the imperial style, but the workmanship does not attain the high level of refinement characteristic of even relatively modest imperial productions. The work is nonetheless clear and attractive. The elephants, depicted with stately rhythm and ponderous grace, are especially well done. More than one artist and at least two scribes produced the work. Like other folios from this manuscript, this one is damaged by fire, particularly the figure of Rāma.

The *Rāmāyaṇa* is an epic of enormous popularity in India. There are many illustrated versions of it (see cat. nos. 95–97, 102, 103, 116–118). The classic version of the story is the one traditionally assigned to the poet Vālmīki; for the critical edition, published in seven volumes, see *Vālmīki Rāmāyaṇa*. The Sanskrit verses on the reverse of this page (see Appendix, p. 254) are a variant version of chapter 90 of the *Ayodhyākāṇḍa* (Book 2) of the epic.

This folio was formerly in the Collection of Edwin Binney, 3rd, San Diego; see Binney 1973, p. 60, no. 34. Other pages are in the Prince of Wales Museum of Western India, Bombay; the Bharat Kala Bhavan, Banaras (Varanasi); the National Museum of India, New Delhi; the J. P. Goenka Collection, Bombay; the Los Angeles County Museum of Art; the Collection of Edwin Binney, 3rd, San Diego; and formerly in the Pan-Asian Collection, now dispersed. See Chandra 1960, pl. x, fig. 16; and Chandra 1957–59, pp. 64–70, frontispiece, and figs. 18–27.

❀ 16 ❀

Leaf number 33 from a *Rāgamālā* series

SUB-IMPERIAL MUGHAL, DATED V.S. 1662/A.D. 1605

Image 6⅞ × 4⅝ in. (175 × 118 mm); sheet 8⅝ × 5⅞ in. (219 × 150 mm)

Malāra Rāgiṇī

A woman transformed into a male ascetic by the agony of separation from her lover sits outside a domed shrine under a rain-filled sky. She has smeared herself with ashes, and so, the Sanskrit text above tells us, she is white like the night lotus and the moon. Some of her hair is gathered into a bun resembling a conch shell on the top of her head, the rest falls around her shoulders. Bearded and wearing a coral-pink loincloth, she kneels on a tiger skin and grasps a necklace of beads with her right hand. Her left hand rests on a spouted water pot. The distracted ascetic stares to the right. Her few belongings are wrapped in a bundle at the left. The brooding intensity of the strange figure is emphasized by the subdued rose-pink of the tiled foreground, the mauve wall of the shrine, and the gray-green background. A dark tree shelters the scene. The margins are yellow.

The series from which this leaf comes is closely related in style to the famous *Rāgamālā* of the W. B. Manley Collection now in the British Museum, London (1973, 9–17). Both are part of an early group of *rāgamālā*s that provide iconographic and textual models for subsequent illustrations of musical modes in many parts of India. See Ebeling, pp. 118–28 and 161–62, no. 8.

This leaf and another (present location unknown) are published in Christie's 1979, lots 192 and 193. The colophon of this important series is in the Museum für indische Kunst, Berlin (I.5681); see Waldschmidt and Waldschmidt 1975, p. 286, fig. 109. There are three more leaves in the same museum (I.5501, 5679, and 5680). Other leaves are in the J. P. Goenka Collection, Bombay; the Collection of Edwin Binney, 3rd, San Diego (see Binney 1973, p. 59, no. 33a); and the Paul Walter Collection, New York. See Pal 1978, pp. 56–57, no. 5. For a version of the Sanskrit text at the top of the leaf and an English translation, see Dahmen-Dallapiccola, p. 377, no. 33.7.

॥शंखावदात ... लबकाराकमुदंडवर्णः॥ कौपीनवासा
सुविद्दारखारी॥ मल्हाररागः कथितस्तपस्वी॥३३॥ मलाररागिणी॥
सुय
३३

❀ 17 ❀ 18 ❀

Two leaves from a *Bhāgavata Purāṇa* series

SUB-IMPERIAL MUGHAL, ca. 1600

17. Brahmā kidnaps cows and cowherds

Image 6¾ × 9¾ in. (171 × 248 mm); sheet 9⅝ × 11⅞ in. (245 × 302 mm)

Cowherds tend their cows against a shaded green ground as four-headed Brahmā approaches from the right. The boys wear pointed hats to protect themselves from rain that threatens from a cloudy sky. Trees dot the horizon; a gently undulating river is at the bottom.

Powerful Brahmā, one of the three major gods of Hinduism, kidnapped Kṛṣṇa's friends and their cows in order to see what he would do (*Bhāgavata Purāṇa* 10.13). To Brahmā's astonishment, Kṛṣṇa assumed the forms of the missing beings for an entire year, whereupon the four-headed god acknowledged the greatness of the divine child.

A descriptive Hindi caption and the Bikaner stamp are on the reverse.

18. Kṛṣṇa and Balarāma slay the washerman of the king

Image 6⅝ × 9½ in. (168 × 242 mm); sheet 9⅝ × 11⅝ in. (245 × 295 mm), irregular

Kṛṣṇa, blue as usual, has just beheaded an arrogant washerman with only his hand. Balarāma, white-skinned, accompanies his brother as the dead man's assistants scramble to snatch drying clothes from a line stretched across the top of the picture. In the confusion Kṛṣṇa and Balarāma are able to pick out the appropriate clothes to wear in Mathura (*Bhāgavata Purāṇa* 10.41. 32–39), where they have come to kill Kṛṣṇa's wicked uncle, the king. The background is Indian yellow with only the slightest indication of sky at the top. Below, in the river that flows across the bottom of the leaf, stands a sloping washboard, still a familiar sight along the banks of Indian rivers and lakes.

A descriptive caption and the Bikaner stamp are on the reverse. The painting is published in Spink & Son 1976, p. 14, no. 44.

The series from which these two miniatures come attests to the nonsectarian nature of Indian painting. Though the style is clearly a simple expression of the Mughal idiom, the subject of the series is the story of Kṛṣṇa, one of the most popular and frequently painted of Hindu divinities (see cat. no. 2). Originally in the collection of the Rājasthānī state of Bikaner, this *Bhāgavata Purāṇa* is now dispersed. Leaves are in the J. P. Goenka Collection, Bombay, and the Goenka Academy of Art and Music, New Delhi; the Suresh Neotia Collection, Calcutta; the Paul Walter Collection, New York; the Collection of Edwin Binney, 3rd, San Diego; and other public and private collections. The noted German scholar Hermann Goetz (1950, p. 100 and fig. 91) assigned the miniatures to Amber (Jaipur), circa 1580. Pal 1978, pp. 54–55, no. 4, assigns them to "early Bikaner painting" of circa 1600. Documented examples of Bikaner painting date from circa 1650 and later (see cat. nos. 66–69). Before its unfortunate dispersal, the Bikaner collection included many different styles of painting, including Mughal, sub-imperial Mughal, Mewar, and even Persian. These pictures are readily identifiable by the Bikaner stamp on their backs.

❀ 19 ❀

Recto and verso of a folio from a manuscript of the *Dīwān* of Ḥāfiẓ

BORDER: MUGHAL, ca. 1605. TEXT: PERSIAN, LATE 15TH CENTURY

Image 6 × 3⅛ in. (152 × 79 mm); sheet 9⅝ × 6¾ in. (245 × 171 mm)

The margins are adorned with gold cartouches enclosing animals and flowers. The recto has an interesting double-mouthed vase at the left filled with flowers at both top and bottom. The birds that decorate it are upside-down in relation to the text.

This superbly remargined leaf is from a collection of the works of the mystic Persian poet Ḥāfiẓ of Shiraz (d. 1389). The verses deal with seemingly secular subjects of wine, human love, and conversation between a flower and a bird, but these themes are merely vehicles for the poet's profoundly mystical vision of the divine. The Mughal emperors were especially fond of Ḥāfiẓ and had several illustrated versions of his works prepared, including some so tiny that they fit comfortably in a single hand. Jahāngīr (r. 1605–27) frequently took omens from the odes. Once when the fate of a rebel was unclear, he learned to his satisfaction from a verse chosen by chance that the man was dead, a fact that was not confirmed for several days. Another time, impatient for news of a battle in the Deccani campaign, he satisfied himself that the imperial forces were victorious nearly a month before news of the victory reached court. See *Tūzuk*, vol. 1, pp. 214–15 and 381, where Jahāngīr goes on to say, "In many of my desires I have resorted to the Khwāja's diwan, and (generally) the result has coincided with what I found there. It is seldom that the opposite has happened." An unillustrated copy that Jahāngīr used for this purpose, which once belonged to his grandfather Humāyūn (r. 1530–40, 1555–56), is preserved in the Khuda Baksh Library in Patna.

The manuscript from which this folio has been detached was formerly in the collection of the marquess of Bute and is now in the British Library (Or. 14139). Some of the leaves in the British Library portion contain human figures as well as animals and flowers and have color added to the gold. The manuscript lacks a colophon, but bears a note by Jahāngīr recording his ownership of the manuscript in the year of his accession (1605–6) and another by Shāh Jahān (r. 1628–58), who attributes the calligraphy to the pen of Sulṭān ʿAlī (active ca. 1442–1519), who worked in Herat and Mashhad. In addition, Losty 1983 has noticed a previously overlooked date of A.H. 1014/A.D. 1605–6 on folio 58r, presumably a workshop note, which helps us fix the date of the decorative remargining to the very end of Akbar's reign or the first year of Jahāngīr's.

For the British Library portion of the manuscript, see Losty 1983, pp. 13–14; and *Indian Heritage*, pp. 34–35, no. 33. For a folio in the Keir Collection, Pontresina (Switz.), see Skelton 1976b, p. 251. For illustrated Mughal manuscripts of the Persian poet, see Losty 1982, pp. 94–96, nos. 73, 76 and pls. XXVIII, XXIX.

مخمور جام عشقم ساقی بده شرابی
پر کن قدح که بی می مجلس ندارد آبی

شوخ چو ماهش در پرده راست ناید
مطرب بزن نوایی ساقی بده شرابی

شد حلقه قامت من تا بعد ازین رقیبت
زین در دگر نراند ما را بهیچ بابی

در انتظار رویت ما و امیدواری
در عشوه وصالت ما و خیال و خوابی

مخمور آن دو چشمم آیا کجاست جامی
بیمار آن دو لعلم آخر کم از جوابی

حافظ چه می نهی تو دل در خیال خوبان
کی تشنه سیر گردد از لمعه سرابی

می خواه و گل افشان کن از دهر چه میجویی
این گفت سحر گه گل بلبل تو چه میگویی

ال به چه که بستانی معشوقه و ساقی را
لب گیری و می نوشی رخ بینی و گل بویی

غنچه خندانت ایزد بکه خواهد داد
ای شاخ گل رعنا از بهر که می رویی

شمشاد خرامان کن و آهنگ گلستان کن
تا سرو بیاموزد از قد تو دلجویی

چون شمع نکورویی بر رهگذر باد است
طرف هنری بربند از مایه نیکویی

آن طره که هر جعدش صد نافه چین ارزد
خوش بودی اگر بودی بویش خوش خویی

هر مرغ بدستانی در مجلس شاه آید
بلبل بنواسازی حافظ بدعاگویی

عجب از وفای جانان که تفقدی نفرمود
نه بخامه سلامی نه بنامه پیامی

سر خدمت تو دارم بخرم بلطف و مفروش
که چو بنده کمتر افتد بمبارکی غلامی

بکجا برم شکایت بکه گویم این حکایت
که لبت دوای ما بود و نداشتی دوامی

اگر این شراب خامست وگر آن حریف پخته
بهزار بار بهتر ز هزار پخته خامی

بگشای تیر مژگان و بریز خون حافظ
که چنان کشنده را نکند کس انتقامی

لبش می بوسم و در می کشم می
بآب زندگانی برده ام پی

نه رازش می توانم گفت با کس
نه کس را می توانم دید با وی

لبش می بوسد و خون میخورد جام
رخش می بیند و گل میکند خوی

گل از خلوت بباغ آورد مسند
بساط زهد را چون غنچه کن طی

بده جام می و از جم مکن یاد
که میداند که جم کی بود و کی کی

بزن در چنگ چنگ ای ماه مطرب
رگش بخراش تا بخروشم از وی

چو چشمش مست را مخمور مگذار
بیاد لعلش ای ساقی بده می

نجوید جان از آن قالب جدایی
که باشد خون جامش در رگ و پی

زبانت درکش ای حافظ زمانی
زبان بی زبانان بشنو از نی

❀ 20 ❀

An album page

Sheet 15⅜ × 10 in. (391 × 254 mm)

A lion attacks the elephant of a prince; mounted in a border showing animals in a forest landscape

MUGHAL, IMAGE PROBABLY EARLY 17TH CENTURY, BORDER ca. 1670–80

Image 7¾ × 5⅛ in. (197 × 130 mm)

Recto. A prince, whose generalized features suggest those of both Akbar (r. 1556–1605) and Jahāngīr (r. 1605–27), raises his sword to smite a lion assaulting his elephant as a retainer rides to the attack. Another lion has jumped the horse of a hunter in the lower right who turns coolly and prepares to stab it. Barking dogs leap about while a fox flees and two antelope, temporarily spared the hunters' attentions, watch curiously from above. Members of the prince's retinue shoot arrows into the fray or simply watch from the safety of distance. A hunting cheetah, an animal now extinct, is on a cart in the upper right. Rocks are in the upper middle, a city is in the background. The scene is mounted in a figured border of animals in a landscape. The thin pigment, simplified forms, and rectilinear arrangement of the elements suggest a date late in the seventeenth century. Verse panels are at top and bottom. A spurious ascription to the artist Manṣūr is in the right margin.

Calligraphic panel mounted in a floral border

MUGHAL, BORDER ca. 1670–80

Image 9⅜ × 4⅞ in. (244 × 122 mm)

Verso. The panel records the opening lines of Saᶜdī's celebrated poem from the *Gulistān* which describe a conversation between a lover and a "lump of fragrant clay" received from his beloved in the bath. The tightly wound floral arabesques surrounding the panel confirm a late-seventeenth-century date for the margins.

Hunting scenes like the one on this album page belong to a stylistically diffuse group of pictures produced from the late sixteenth century in the imperial workshops and in the painting studio maintained by Jahāngīr when he stayed in Allahabad, from 1599/1600 to late in 1604, in rebellion against his father.

Skelton (1969, pp. 33–48) has deftly analyzed Mughal hunt scenes. He publishes another version of this same composition (fig. 8) prepared around the middle of the seventeenth century (Bodleian Library, Oxford University, MS. Douce Or.a.1, fol. 33r) after an earlier original.

The lightly tinted drawing technique of this page is ultimately derived from Persian models. It proved very popular in Mughal painting and extended its influence to other Indian styles (see cat. no. 50).

Other leaves from this same album are in the Collection of Edwin Binney, 3rd, San Diego, and in the Collection of Prince Sadruddin Aga Khan. See Binney 1973, pp. 90–91, no. 65; and A. Welch, pp. 191–92, no. 83.

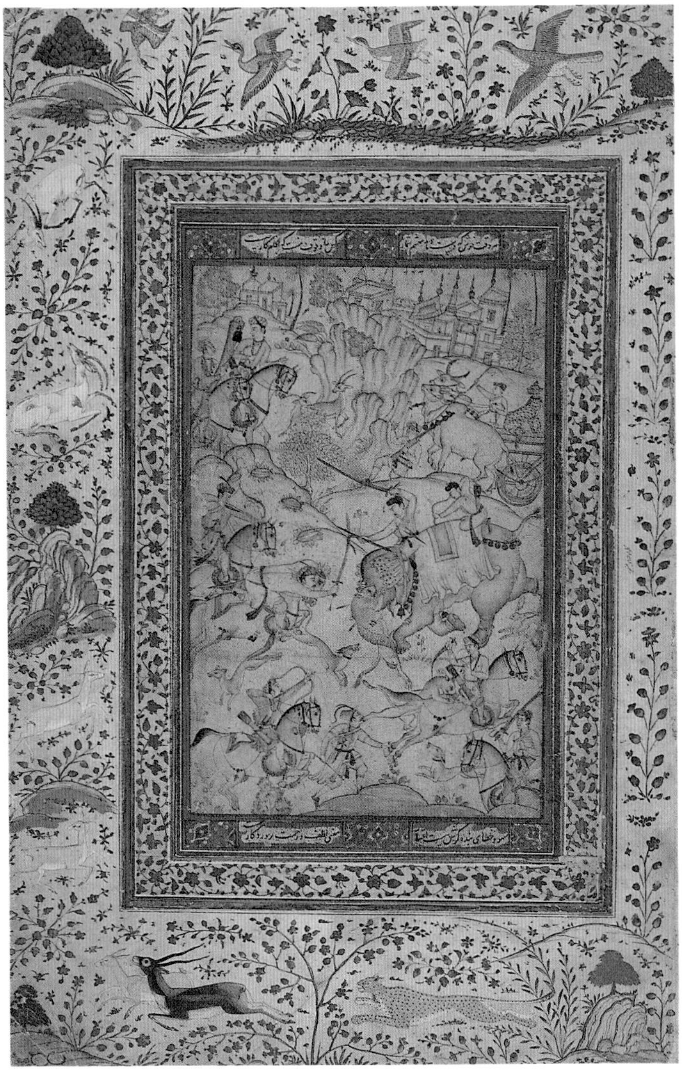

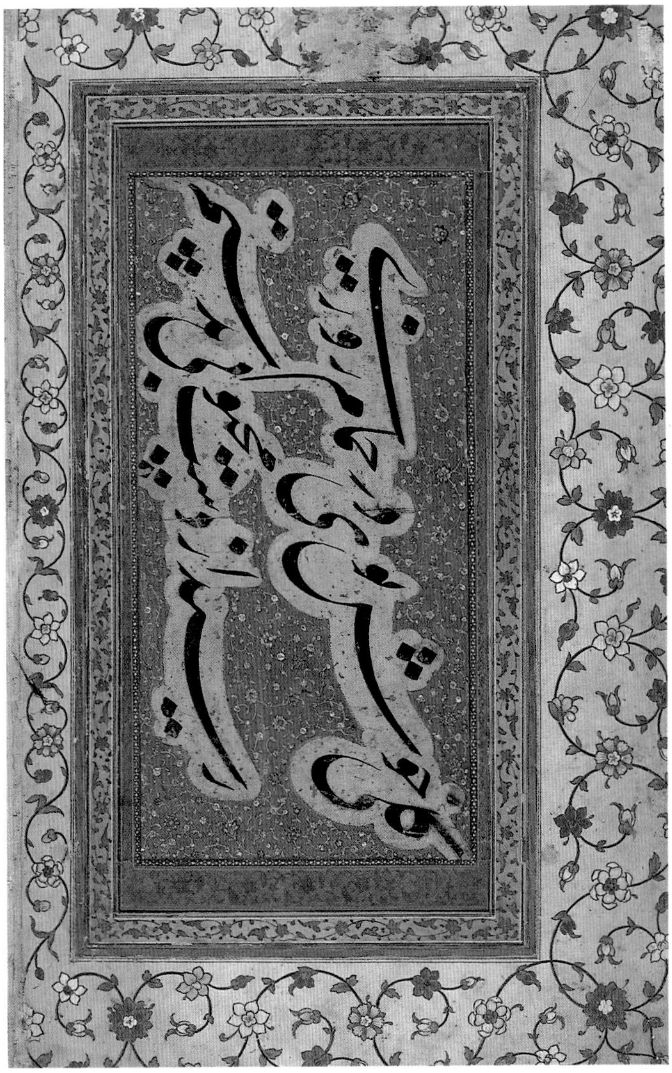

❀ 21 ❀

Double portrait

Signed by Manohara

MUGHAL, JAHĀNGĪR PERIOD, ca. 1610

Image 7½ × 4⅜ in. (191 × 111 mm); sheet 13 × 8½ in. (331 × 216 mm)

Akbar handing Jahāngīr a falcon

Jahāngīr (r. 1605–27) stands before his father, Akbar (r. 1556–1605), who presents him with a falcon. Both are nimbated. Jahāngīr wears a chocolate brown *jāmā* (full-skirted coat), his father is dressed in deep pink. The plain, green background typical of portraits of the period has here been incorporated into a landscape. Tufts of grass and flowers are below, rocks and a cloudy sky above. Blank gold cartouches are below the figures. Between the two is a diminutive inscription in Persian which reads *band dargāh manohar pīr ghulām* (the slave of the threshold Manohara, the old servant). The small size, placement, and humility of the inscription suggest that it is an actual signature instead of being merely a scribal ascription. The image is mounted in a sumptuous border of gold flowers on red and blue. That the border may have originally served some other purpose is suggested by the trimmed verse panel in the upper left.

The falcon seems to be associated in Mughal iconography with political power and its transmission (see cat. no. 23). Jahāngīr spent several years in open rebellion against his father (1599/1600–1604), but after his own accession he sought in his memoirs to explain his actions and expressed his affection for his extraordinary parent (*Tūzuk*, vol. 1, pp. 24–26, 33–45). This double portrait thus reveals the subjects as men as well as monarchs. A rebel as a prince, Jahāngīr in turn became the target of a plot by one of his sons to seize the throne in 1606.

Manohara was the son of Basāvana, a pre-eminent artist of the Akbar period, and he practiced a linearized version of the emphatically plastic style of his father. He was skilled in portraiture, a major concern of Mughal painting in the reign of Jahāngīr. His earliest known work is a self-portrait in a manuscript dated 1581 in the Royal Asiatic Society, London. See Ashton, p. 143, no. 642 and pl. 121; and A. Welch, p. 12 and p. 176, no. 76. He continued to paint at least until late in the reign of Jahāngīr. Lowry offers a brief but penetrating analysis of Manohara's style in Beach 1978, pp. 130–32.

There is another version of this composition, similarly inscribed, now in the Academy of the Socialist Republic of Romania, Bucharest. The Romanian picture is probably slightly earlier than this one; its movement is freer and its workmanship smoother. See Oprescu, no. 106. Though the version in the Ehrenfeld leaf is harder in style, it is probably a roughly contemporary copy and there is no reason to doubt the inscription. Also, it is close stylistically to an equestrian portrait by Manohara in the Victoria and Albert Museum, London (I.M. 12–1925) of approximately the same date except for the central faces, which were repainted by a later artist. Both pictures share similar broadly worked landscape forms; see W. G. Archer 1957, pl. 5. Perhaps this portrait was prepared to be given as an imperial gift.

❀ 22 ❀

Animal study

Attributed to Govardhana

MUGHAL, JAHĀNGĪR PERIOD, ca. 1616

Sheet 6 × 7⅞ in. (152 × 200 mm)

A young African elephant

The young elephant is shown in a profile view which permits the best display of his tail, big ears, and long trunk with its double protuberances, a feature that sets him apart from his Asian relatives who bear only one. He is represented as an individual animal, not merely a type. His front legs are restrained by a chain pegged to the ground, but he casually crosses his back legs as he reaches out with his trunk toward some choice bit of food invisible to the viewer. The mouth and eye are especially well rendered. The artist's love of subtle shading and textured surfaces is revealed in his delineation of the creature's hide, each wrinkle, bump, and roll of flesh carefully depicted. Though the picture is neither signed nor ascribed, it is likely the work of Govardhana, an artist not usually associated with animal studies.

In keeping with Govardhana's style about this time, the animal is placed in an almost narrative context rather than in isolation. To the right are gentle slopes, a cluster of buildings, and a line of small-leafed trees. To the left, a cot maker works outside a brick building as a friend or client sits watching him, his back to the viewer. A chipmunk in the left foreground insolently echoes the posture of the white-haired craftsman. A crow sits on the thatch canopy that shelters the men while its mate takes to the air. Another pair of birds flies off to the right. The palette is very restrained. The whole picture is bathed in a warm golden glow, another feature typical of Govardhana. The subdued color, overall tonality, and meticulous brushwork of this picture relate it very closely to an unpublished study of a holy man in the Bharat Kala Bhavan, Varanasi (6974).

This charming animal study is of special interest for its historical significance, exceptional quality, and probable provenance. In 1616, Muqarrab Khān presented the emperor Jahāngīr (r. 1605–27) with "a small elephant from Abyssinia." Jahāngīr was keenly interested in natural history and carefully noted the gift in his memoirs: "In comparison with the elephants of Hindustan it presents some peculiarities. Its ears are larger than the ears of the elephants of this place, and its trunk and tail are longer" (*Tūzuk*, vol. 1, p. 323). There can be little doubt that this painting depicts this gift to the emperor. Muqarrab Khān, who was a child when he entered the service of Prince Salīm, later Jahāngīr, was an excellent hunter and surgeon. He also distinguished himself as an inspired agent of the emperor in gathering curiosities for imperial edification and amusement.

Govardhana was a major artist of the first half of the seventeenth century. His father, Bhavānī Dāsa, was an indifferent painter of the Akbar period, but the young artist absorbed the style of his teacher, the intense, mystically inclined painter Daulat. Govardhana's earliest surviving works are illustrations in the British Library (Or. 12988)/Chester Beatty (Ind. MS. 2) *Akbar-nāma*. The colophon of that manuscript is missing, but the first volume, long lost and now in the British Library, bears a date corresponding to 1604. Govardhana was a critical figure in the evolution of Mughal genre painting. At its richest, his style was well suited to lavish renderings of imperial grandeur. He painted some of the most sumptuous studies of the Mughal court, as well as some of the most intimate evocations of courtly love and superbly unaffected scenes such as this delightful little elephant. Both in style and subject his work exerted a tremendous influence on subsequent Mughal painting. He continued to paint into the reign of Jahāngīr's successor, Shāh Jahān (r. 1628–58), probably until about 1640.

The *nāgarī* inscription in gold letters is significant. It reads *hāthī darīyā rī* ([likeness] of the elephant Darīyā) and is typical of inscriptions on pictures that were once part of the princely collection of Mewar. The Mughals had achieved the submission of Mewar only in 1615, long after the other Rājasthānī states had bowed to imperial hegemony. It is tempting to propose that this picture was among the gifts that passed from the Mughal court to its most recent and most important Rājasthānī vassal, but this suggestion is only speculation. On the reverse (see Appendix, p. 254) are an obscured seal, inventory numbers, and various other notations.

It is interesting to compare this elephant with other, less-individualized studies (see cat. nos. 29, 46, 59, and 65). There is an excellent account of Govardhana in Beach 1978, pp. 118–19. This picture, the study of a holy man cited above, and an ascetic with musicians in the National Museum of India, New Delhi (50.14/11) should be added to Beach's extensive list of ascriptions and attributions to Govardhana. An album leaf border in the Gulistan Palace Library, Tehran, shows Daulat teaching his young pupil Govardhana. See Godard, fig. 14; and Beach 1978, p. 113, fig. 9.

हथीदरीयाई

❀ 23 ❀

Allegorical portrait

Signed(?) by Chitarman

MUGHAL, SHĀH JAHĀN PERIOD, ca. 1630–40

Image 8 × 4¾ in. (204 × 121 mm); sheet 15⅞ × 11½ in. (404 × 292 mm)

Akbar, Jahāngīr, and Shāh Jahān with their ministers and Prince Dārā Shikoh

Against a rocky background and a gold and blue sky, Akbar (r. 1556–1605) and Jahāngīr (r. 1605–27) sit holding falcons and facing Shāh Jahān (r. 1628–58). All three sit on golden thrones, the most elaborate of which is Shāh Jahān's, and are sheltered by parasols of gold, jewels, pearls, and rich fabrics. Shāh Jahān sits with his hands out in a gesture of acceptance as he prepares to receive the falcon held by his grandfather Akbar. The ill-fated Prince Dārā Shikoh (see cat. no. 25) attends his father, Shāh Jahān. Below stand two ministers. The one at the left is ʿAbd al-Rahīm, who served both Akbar and Jahāngīr and was a great patron of painting and literature (see cat. no. 14). Though not identified, he is easily recognizable from other inscribed portraits (see Beach 1981, p. 83, no. 18a, and p. 84, ill.).

In the eighteenth century the picture was in an album owned by John Murray, commissioned to the Bengal army in 1781. He mistakenly assumed it to be a portrait of Akbar, Salīm (later Jahāngīr), and Murād (another of Akbar's sons), but an inserted note in his hand describing the painting reveals a keen appreciation for the Mughal style. He writes:

"This is one of the highest finished Miniature drawings I have ever seen in Hindoostan; and, I may add, anywhere else. I am also satisfied that they are likenesses, from the great number of portraits I have seen, and compared them with, done by different hands and at different times,—of Acbar, Selim, etc. On the side of the Chair of State, on which Murad sits, is, (written in a fine hand) the name of the Painter, which Mr. Francklin has translated for me as follows, 'The picture of the King of the World; done by Chutterman.' I purchased this painting, at Lucknow, selecting it from a Hisser, or collection of others, bound together; which, tho of great merit, none came near it. The book belonged to an old family in distress." Murray bought the picture before 1798, not directly from the distressed family, but from a Lt. J. P. Hoare, who died that year in Barrackpore. The note reveals the discerning eye of a connoisseur, and we envy Murray his opportunities at a time when collections of old families "in distress" were dispersed, just as his has now been.

The "fine hand" of the inscription on the side of Shāh Jahān's throne may be the artist's. Mr. Francklin's translation is correct, but "lord of the world" might be a slightly more literal rendering. Chitarman was a painter who worked during the reign of Shāh Jahān. Few pictures bear his name. Only one other signed "Chitarman" is known to be in an American collection, a portrait of Dārā in the Pierpont Morgan Library that is dated 1639/40 (M.458, fol. 9). For the Morgan portrait and a survey of the artist's work, see Beach 1978, pp. 111–13. In both portraits the prince is nimbated. A later study of Dārā by Chitarman is in the Victoria and Albert Museum, London (I.M.13-1925); see *Indian Heritage*, pp. 44–45, no. 67.

There is another interesting inscription, largely effaced, on the green ground between the standing ministers. It appears to read ——*shn d*——*s*, apparently for Bishn Das (Viṣṇu Dāsa), a great seventeenth-century painter who was unmatched for his skill as a portraitist. The significance of this curious inscription is unknown. It is possible that Chitarman collaborated with the older painter. We do not know when Viṣṇu Dāsa ended his career, but he may have been painting as late as the 1630s. Such a collaborative effort, common in the sixteenth century (see cat. no. 7), would be very unusual during the reign of Shāh Jahān. In his survey of Viṣṇu Dāsa's style, Beach 1978, pp. 107–11, proposes that he painted from about 1590 to about 1645. It is not clear if this inscription was covered by the application of paint or written (and erased) after the picture was completed.

For thematically and compositionally comparable pictures that also serve to underscore the legitimacy of Mughal imperial succession, see *Indian Heritage*, p. 41, no. 52 and p. 42, no. 53; and *Beatty*, vol. 1, p. 33, no. 19, vol. 3, pl. 65.

❀ 24 ❀

Genre scene

Image 9⅝ × 5⅝ in. (245 × 142 mm); sheet 13½ × 9 in. (343 × 229 mm)

A prince meeting a holy man

MUGHAL, SHĀH JAHĀN PERIOD, ca. 1640

Border from the *Farhang-i Jahāngīrī*

MUGHAL, JAHĀNGĪR PERIOD, 1607–8

A young prince with a spear-bearing attendant kneels respectfully before a Muslim divine. The old holy man has a servant behind him with a peacock-feather flywhisk. The scene is set on a terrace outside a simple thatched building overlooking a lake. An old man leaning on a short crutch (see cat. no. 60) and two musicians are in the foreground. A woven mat with a decorated border covers the terrace floor. The prince and the old man are deep in discussion under the shelter of a large tree. In keeping with the development of painting in the reign of Shāh Jahān (r. 1628–58), movement is stilled and the color softened.

Genre pictures of this type first gained popularity in the reign of Jahāngīr (1605–27), probably about 1610 and later. One of the very earliest examples of this theme is in a private collection in northern California (Beach 1978, p. 163, no. 61, and p. 164, ill.). These pictures emerged from earlier literary illustrations. They are commonly assumed to represent portraits of individual princes, and may in some cases, but they are probably most often simply idealized studies of royal piety.

Many Mughal pictures preserve figured borders, either contemporary (see cat. no. 26) or later additions, when the picture was mounted for inclusion in a royal album (see cat. no. 20). In this case, however, the margin was taken from a leaf of the 1607–8 lexicon, the *Farhang-i Jahāngīrī*, by the French dealer Demotte who used it to replace the picture's original border. Demotte was often not satisfied with the appearance of Persian and Indian paintings that passed through his hands. He remounted several leaves of an early-seventeenth-century imperial history in borders from the same lexicon (see Binney 1973, p. 41, no. 20, and p. 43; and Beach 1978, pp. 41–43), trimmed damaged manuscript pages to combine the fragments into disconnected pastiches of text and illustration, and even separated fronts from backs of single folios to have two separate pictures instead of a single item. This leaf seems to have fared rather well, though it has been enlarged slightly on all four sides to fit into its frame. The enlargement at the bottom makes the first step up to the terrace impossibly high.

A thematically related picture of about the same time that retains its original margins is in the Collection of Edwin Binney, 3rd, San Diego (Binney 1973, p. 85, no. 60; and Binney 1979, pp. 52–53, no. 9). For leaves of the *Farhang* that have escaped damage, see *Beatty*, vol. I, p. 50, no. XXXIII; and Binney 1973, pp. 72–73, no. 46.

❀ 25 ❀

Double portrait

Possibly by Hāshim

MUGHAL, SHĀH JAHĀN PERIOD, ca. 1655

Image 8⅜ × 6⅜ in. (213 × 162 mm); sheet 12½ × 8½ in. (318 × 216 mm)

Prince Dārā Shikoh and his son Sulaimān Shikoh

The figures, identified by Persian inscriptions in the upper margin, stand against a cool green ground marked by tufts of grass at their feet. They both wear transparent *jāmās* (full-skirted coats) and golden sashes. Dārā Shikoh, on the left, holds a yak-tail flywhisk in one hand and in the other an emerald-and-pearl turban ornament that he presents to his son.

Dārā Shikoh (1615–1659) was the eldest son and designated heir of his father, Shāh Jahān (r. 1628–58), but he never reached the throne. In 1657 Shāh Jahān fell ill, touching off a war of succession among his sons. The Mughals did not practice primogeniture in selection of an heir. Rather, all legitimate sons of an emperor were eligible for the throne, a Timurid tradition that ensured bloody struggles among princes. Dārā was twice defeated in battle by his younger brother Aurangzīb (1618–1707), who seized the throne, imprisoned his father, and executed his brother. Sulaimān fled to the Hills, but after a brief respite he was betrayed to the emperor and died in prison in Gwalior in 1662, three years after his father. The learned Dārā, a patron of literature and painting, was himself an author. His son was famous for his good looks.

This portrait is unsigned, but the cool detachment of its subjects supports an attribution to the painter Hāshim; see Beach 1978, pp. 127–30. It is very close in style to a signed portrait of Shāh Jahān (Beach 1978, no. 45) from the same album as catalogue number 26. The almost inflated lower bodies of the figures are identical in the two pictures, as are the precise rendering of the yak-tail flywhisks and the cloudlike treatment of the beards. There is a Hāshim portrait of Sulaimān as a child in S. C. Welch 1976, pp. 52–53, no. 20.

Persian captions on the reverse identify the subjects again. There is also an owner's note dated A.H. 1352/A.D. 1933–34.

سلیمان شکوه
دارا شکوه

❀ 26 ❀

Leaf from a royal album prepared for Shāh Jahān

MUGHAL, ca. 1650

Sheet 15¼ × 10½ in. (388 × 267 mm)

Portrait of the Lord Steward ʿAlā al-Mulk Tūnī

Image 7¾ × 4½ in. (197 × 115 mm)

Recto. The Lord Steward, in charge of the stores of the imperial household, stands on a grassy ground. He wears an orange *jāmā* (full-skirted coat) and holds an inventory list in his hand. The background is green with sky at the top. The borders bear portraits of his staff, who count and record the imperial porcelain, jewels, and bolts of rich cloth. Gold flowers surround the figures.

Calligraphic panel in a floral border

Attributed to Mīr ʿAlī

Image 3¾ × 6⅞ in. (96 × 175 mm)

Verso. Though the panel is unsigned, its elegant *nastaʿlīq* script can be attributed to the hand of Mīr ʿAlī, a sixteenth-century Iranian calligrapher whose work appears frequently in Mughal imperial albums (see Beach 1978, nos. 6, 7, 10, 11, 12).

Like his father before him, Shāh Jahān commissioned sumptuous albums of painting and calligraphy from his artists. Portraiture during his reign (1628–58) becomes increasingly formalized and favors flat surfaces and hyper-refinement over the more relaxed and expressive portraits of the early seventeenth century. Robert Skelton (*Indian Heritage*, p. 44, no. 69) has identified the subject of this portrait as ʿAlā al-Mulk Tūnī, an able and accomplished servant of the imperial court who came to India from Iran in 1633–34 and died in 1663 when he was nearly seventy.

This leaf, which was formerly in the Charles LeBargy Collection, comes from an album that passed from India to Iran to France, where it was dispersed in Paris early in the twentieth century. It is published in Laurin et al., no. 188; and Spink & Son 1980, no. 73. Beach 1978, pp. 76–77, publishes a list of the known pages from the same album, to which he gives the title *Late Shāh Jahān Album.* He cites an uninscribed leaf in the Cleveland Museum of Art (45.168), published and identified as ʿAlā al-Mulk Tūnī in Hollis, pp. 180–81, where the subject of that leaf, like that of this page, is identified on the basis of an inscribed portrait in the British Library. See Martin, pl. 187A; and Binyon and Arnold, pl. XXVI. The Cleveland portrait appears to be that of a younger man, and its identity bears re-examination.

❀ 27 ❀

An album page

MUGHAL, ca. LATE 17TH CENTURY

Image 7 × 9½ in. (178 × 241 mm); sheet 9⅛ × 11⅜ in. (232 × 289 mm)

A camel fight

The precise and detailed observation of early-seventeenth-century animal studies (see cat. no. 22) gave way in later periods to an increasing emphasis on abstract shapes curiously reminiscent of the generalized animal studies of the sixteenth century (see cat. no. 8). Though the artist of this thinly painted picture of two camels fighting pays some attention to the textures of their hair, he is much more interested in the interaction of the flowing lines that unite the testy beasts in a single arabesque of humps, legs, and biting heads. The composition is evenly balanced. Only the placement of the camels' heads breaks the symmetry. This is not a "portrait" of two animals, rather it is a study of patterns, shapes, and lines that happen to depict a pair of fighting camels. This approach represents a retreat from the refined naturalism so typical of Mughal painting in the beginning of the century and reveals a style that is reasserting its essentially anti-naturalistic Indian heritage. This tendency becomes even more pronounced in the eighteenth century (see cat. nos. 30–33).

This leaf is published in McInerney, p. 46, no. 16. The study is based on a famous picture of circa 1525 by the celebrated Persian painter Bihzād (d. ca. 1535–36); see Binyon, Wilkinson, and Gray, pl. LXXXVII A. For other Mughal versions, see Krishnadasa, pl. 5; Khandalavala and Chandra 1965, p. 18, no. 19; and Sivaramamurti 1977, p. 422, no. 665.

❀ 28 ❀

Equestrian portrait

MUGHAL, ca. 1660–70

Image 15 × 10¾ in. (382 × 273 mm); sheet 17½ × 12⅝ in. (445 × 321 mm)

Aurangzīb

Aurangzīb is shown on horseback with full imperial regalia. His halo represents both the sun and the moon. Two attendants carry peacock-feather fans, while a third bears the imperial shade adorned with a crowned sun. Ahead of the emperor another retainer carries a bow and a quiver filled with arrows. A cloudy sky of green and blue overlooks a background that is plain save for a small cluster of buildings seen behind the forelegs of the imperial mount. The color is fairly deep, but is applied in washes thinner than the enamel-like pigments that characterize the work of only a short time before (see cat. no. 26). The artist changed the original positions of the peacock-feather fan of the farther fan-bearer and of the lance carried by the emperor. Aurangzīb, who ruled from 1658 to 1707, a reign as long as that of his great-grandfather Akbar (r. 1556–1605), is described conventionally as a bigot with no sympathy for the arts, but he was sincerely religious and deeply troubled by his own shortcomings.

The picture is mounted in a border that suggests it was formerly in the state collection of Kishangarh (see the border of cat. no. 71). Two inscriptions on the back in Persian and Hindi (see Appendix, p. 254) identify the subject as Aurangzīb's son and successor, Bahādur Sh̲āh (r. 1707–12), in his youth, but they must be rejected for two reasons. First, no one but the emperor, not even an imperial prince, would be represented with full imperial trappings and insignias. Second, though Aurangzīb and his son resembled each other strongly, the father is almost invariably portrayed with a blunt-ended beard, as here, while the son's beard is more pointed (see cat. no. 29). For comparable examples of portraits of Aurangzīb, see Binney 1973, p. 94, no. 69; S. C. Welch 1964, nos. 58, 59; Beach 1978, p. 170, ill., and p. 171, no. 67; and *Indian Heritage*, p. 48, no. 80. See catalogue number 29 for references to portraits of Bahādur Sh̲āh.

The inscriptions also attribute the painting to the Mughal artist Honhār, which may be correct. For an earlier work by this artist, see *Indian Heritage*, p. 46, no. 70; it is also published in *Beatty*, vol. 3, pl. 71.

This leaf is published in McInerney, pp. 42–45, no. 15, where the inscriptions are accepted and a list of Honhār's paintings is provided.

❀ 29 ❀

Processional scene

MUGHAL, ca. 1700–1707

Image 14½ × 23⅜ in. (369 × 594 mm), irregular

Bahādur Shāh on a royal progress

Bahādur Shāh rides an elephant. He is attended by a man in pink holding a peacock fan. All around is the controlled confusion of an army on the move. Heavily armed men on foot, horse, and elephant move through a hilly landscape. An orange-covered palanquin heads the procession, carried and guarded by orange-coated attendants and flanked by elephants. Behind are mounted warriors and a phalanx of spear-carriers whose massed weapons form a sharp vertical that divides the composition into distinct sections. After a slight clearing comes Bahādur Shāh, framed by more soldiers. In the foreground three men turn to face the prince and one salutes him. Behind them is a foreshortened horse who seems uncertain of which direction he is to go.

The picture shows Bahādur Shāh (r. 1707–12) without imperial regalia, suggesting that it was painted before his accession to the throne. Late in the reign of his father, Aurangzīb (r. 1658–1707), Prince Muʿazzam was granted the title Bahādur Shāh, under which he was known as emperor. Already sixty-four when he came to the throne, he ruled for only five years. Bahādur Shāh was an able soldier to whom his father entrusted many important missions. This illustration may portray an actual historical incident, though there is no inscription to give an exact identification.

Thinly painted, this princely processional scene is a fine example of Mughal painting at the very beginning of the eighteenth century. The rich enamel-like colors of the mid-seventeenth century, still vestigial in catalogue number 26, have given way completely to a subdued palette applied in broad washes. The style of this picture relates closely to Mughal painting of the late seventeenth and early eighteenth centuries, and a date around 1700 is probably accurate.

The Mughal style that this picture represents was influential in Rajasthan in the eighteenth century. The broad, thin washes of color, linearity, and stylization of facial features directly anticipate later painting in the state of Kishangarh (see especially cat. no. 70), which was tied closely to the Mughal court through bonds of friendship, fealty, and marriage. One of Bahādur Shāh's wives was a Kishangarh princess.

For regnal portraits of Bahādur Shāh, see Binney 1973, p. 98, nos. 71, 72, and p. 101, ill.

❀ 30 ❀

An album page

LATE MUGHAL STYLE AT DELHI, MID-18TH CENTURY

Image 7¾ × 10⅛ in. (197 × 257 mm); sheet 8⅜ × 10⅞ in. (213 × 277 mm)

Bāz Bahādur and Rūpmatī hunting at night

This leaf illustrates a popular subject in Indian painting, the passionate love of Bāz Bahādur, last king of Malwa (r. 1555–61) before its absorption into the Mughal empire in 1561, and his Hindu courtesan Rūpmatī, famous all over India for her skill as a dancer. Here the lovers are shown hunting at night, seemingly more interested in each other than in any quarry. A dark ground gives way to a somber forest and a night sky of deep blue. In the center, the lovers glow as if illuminated by an inner light. A tree directly behind them reflects their effulgence and provides a frame of light-green leaves. The king's robe is a sunny yellow, while Rūpmatī's garment is of opalescent white. She is heavily jeweled. The lightly tinted horses sport rich tack. They rear up, but so gently that the lovers are not disturbed and continue to stare into each other's eyes. A pool is in the lower right. The yellow border is decorated with a conventional pattern of stylized flowers. The lovers' idyllic life together ended in sorrow. When Akbar (r. 1556–1605) and his forces took the city of Mandu, Bāz Bahādur fled without his beloved and she committed suicide rather than submit to a conqueror. Traditional Indian songs still popular today tell the story of the ill-fated lovers.

Delhi was an unhappy city in the middle of the eighteenth century. The Mughal empire was severely weakened from within and subject to attack from without. The looting and massacre of the city and the humiliation of the emperor in the invasion of Delhi in 1739 by King Nādir S͟hāh of Persia left the city acutely aware of its decline. Power was decentralized. Nobles set up rival courts elsewhere, further eroding imperial power even while formally acknowledging the emperor. Lucknow vied with the imperial capital for the position of the main center of North Indian culture (see cat. no. 33). During this period, Mughal painting changed considerably. Though it never entirely lost its refinement of line, the style became flatter, more conventionalized, harder, and more abstract. Materials were less sumptuous as painters and patrons accommodated themselves to the new circumstances of an ever more impoverished empire. Scenes of idealized lovers and rather wistful recreations of past imperial glories became increasingly popular, as if painting could provide relief from grim political reality.

This theme is extremely popular in many styles of Indian painting. Another Mughal version of the subject from about the same time is in the British Museum, London (1920, 9-17-027). An example from Murshidabad is in the India Office Library; see Falk and Archer, p. 199, no. 372, and p. 488, ill. It is later than the picture reproduced here but very similar in composition.

❀ 31 ❀

An album page

LATE MUGHAL STYLE AT DELHI, LATE 18TH CENTURY

Image 15 1/8 × 11 1/4 in. (384 × 285 mm); sheet 15 7/8 × 11 7/8 in. (404 × 302 mm)

Shīrīn mourns the dead Farhād

The story of Khusrau and his beloved Shīrīn is a standard of Persian literature. Their love survived incredible incidents of jealousy, betrayal, and separation. One such story concerns the unfortunate Farhād, King Khusrau's rival for Shīrīn. Thinking that he could set Farhād an impossible task, Khusrau promised him the hand of Shīrīn if he could cut a road through impenetrable mountains. Spurred on by his all-consuming love, Farhād worked night and day. Finally the task was nearly finished, and Khusrau was horrified that Farhād would succeed and win the lovely prize. To avert this event, the king ordered an old woman to tell Farhād that Shīrīn had died. The distraught rival hurled himself to his death, whereupon the grief-stricken Shīrīn rushed to him in mourning.

The Delhi artist who painted this picture set the story near the beautiful seventeenth-century Red Fort, a massive structure built by Shāh Jahān (r. 1628–58) and still standing within the old city, part monument, part tourist attraction, part bazaar, and part military installation. The main scene is at center right. Shīrīn kneels weeping near the dead Farhād as her ladies-in-waiting discuss what has taken place. The old woman, perhaps an unwitting dupe of the clever Khusrau, stands "biting the finger of amazement" (see cat. no. 10) as she surveys the results of her message. The women and the dead hero are within a red, tented enclosure. Outside sit Shīrīn's palanquin and guard. To the left of the center foreground a dark-skinned servant of the king has slain the old woman to keep her from exposing the plot to Shīrīn. At the right the servant tells Khusrau and his ministers of the success of their treachery. Fanciful rocks and a river separate the narrative portion of the picture from the Red Fort. The rocks represent the high mountains where Farhād worked in vain to earn the woman he loved. They are populated by animals rendered with a cheerful disregard of scale. An enormous tiger emerges from the rocks and stalks two tiny antelope by the riverside, while a giant dragon to the left dwarfs a group of women drawing water from a well. The scene at the well is a common motif of Mughal painting in the eighteenth century and is often treated as a separate subject.

On the reverse are a Hindi caption reading *sīrīṃ pharahāta* (Shīrīn Farhād), several numbers, and a few recent notations in English.

The sooty palette and heavily shaded expressionless faces of the figures are typical of painting produced in Delhi during the long reign (1759–1806) of Shah ʿAlam II, who had been very interested in painting but was blinded in 1788 by an upstart chieftain.

For other late Mughal versions of the same subject from Faizabad and Farrukhabad (both in Avadh [Oudh]), see Falk and Archer, p. 138, no. 240, and p. 436, ill. (from Faizabad) and p. 190, no. 362iv, and p. 470, ill. Though the picture reproduced here is more elaborate, its composition is very similar to that of the example from Faizabad. All three pictures include a river that refers to the channel of milk Farhād created for Shīrīn in an earlier feat of engineering.

❀ 32 ❀

Portrait

MUGHAL STYLE AT MURSHIDABAD, ca. 1780–90

Sheet 12 1/8 × 9 3/4 in. (308 × 248 mm)

Muḥammad Riẓā Khān seated smoking a water pipe

Muḥammad Riẓā Khān, the subject of this portrait, was a minister to the ruler of Murshidabad in northeastern India. He was known for his strength and vigor, virtues that did not fail him even in old age. He is shown here seated on a green and gold lacquered seat, facing right, and holding the mouthpiece of a water pipe that stands beside him. His profile is fierce and strong, the hooked nose and hooded eye giving him the appearance of an enormous bird of prey at wary rest. The sway of the beaded tassels that hang from his sash and the agitated drape of his lower garment reinforce the tense anticipation of his angular posture. The floor is covered with a woven grass mat. The background is gray blue. Mughal painting at Murshidabad is characterized by an extremely cold palette, here tempered by the warmer tones of the matting.

On the back *Nawab Mahomed Reza Kaun of Cossimbazaar* is inscribed in an eighteenth-century English hand.

The leaf is published in *Indian Heritage*, p. 51, no. 92. For a general discussion of painting at Murshidabad, see Skelton 1956, pp. 10–22.

❀ 33 ❀

An album page

Ascribed to Faiẓullah

MUGHAL STYLE AT LUCKNOW, ca. 1775

Image 15 1/8 × 10 3/8 in. (384 × 263 mm); sheet 17 1/2 × 12 3/8 in. (445 × 314 mm)

Kṛṣṇa fluting

Kṛṣṇa stands under a tree playing the flute as men, women, children, cows, and peafowl stand entranced. In the foreground several women, overcome with emotion, have fallen insensate as the music pours from the divine musician-lover. Golden bells deck the cows. The animals are adorned with painted floral decorations, their lower bodies painted red in a custom that survives in India to this day. In the background cows and cowherds sheltered by pink rocks strain to hear the distant fluting. Behind them are gardens and a gleaming city of domes and towers under a blue sky streaked with spectacular orange clouds.

Lucknow of the late eighteenth century was an extraordinarily eclectic blend of Islamic, Hindu, and European traditions. As Delhi declined, Lucknow emerged as a major center of Indian cultural and intellectual life, combining in its culture decadence and vigor, imitation and invention. Painting flourished in this atmosphere as artists either interpreted traditional Indian subjects in the city's characteristic late Mughal manner or turned to European models provided by English artists who eagerly sought the patronage of the Indian aristocracy. This work by Faiẓullāh represents a Hindu subject painted in the heavily shaded Mughal style of the late eighteenth century and incorporates a receding vista borrowed from European sources.

The inscription on the city wall (middle left) reads *ʿamal faiẓullāh* (work of Faiẓullāh). Other works by this artist are in private collections and in the British Museum, London (1920, 9-17-0308).

❀ 34 ❀

Colonel Mordaunt's cockfight of 1784

LUCKNOW, ca. 1850

Image 33 × 42½ in. (839 × 1,080 mm)

This curious picture clearly expresses many of the themes and concerns of eighteenth- and nineteenth-century India, a stage for incredible daring and all-consuming greed, enlightened toleration and appalling bigotry. As the East India Company moved relentlessly to consolidate political and economic control of India, the subcontinent's traditional rulers fought to counter British expansionism even while their courts rejected Indian standards of taste and adopted European manners and customs.

The subject of this painting is a cockfight that took place on April 5, 1784, between birds belonging to Nawab Āsaf al-Daula, ruler (1775–97) of Avadh [Oudh], and Colonel John Mordaunt (d. 1790), bastard son of the earl of Peterborough. The original version was painted by John Zoffany (ca. 1733–1810), the finest of the British artists who worked in India in the eighteenth century. Zoffany, a favorite painter of Warren Hastings, Governor-General of British India, first came to Lucknow from Calcutta for a time in 1784, then returned to the city again in 1785–86. He painted at least two versions of the scene, one for the nawab and a more elaborate treatment for Hastings. It is not certain if the Hastings version, now in a private collection in England, is the first version Zoffany painted for him or if it is a second picture made to replace the original, reportedly lost at sea. The nawab's canvas was lost in the events of 1857–58, when a briefly resurgent Lucknow was sacked by vengeful British troops who looted the royal collections and destroyed what they did not steal. Both pictures inspired British and Indian copies. The Hastings picture was published in an engraving in 1792, and the nawab's version was copied in 1817, possibly by the painter Robert Home (see cat. nos. 82–83), as a royal gift to the British Resident of Lucknow.

Either directly or through intermediary copies, the 1792 engraving is probably the ultimate source for the picture reproduced here, which is a reverse of the Hastings composition. The picture contains many portraits of the Indian and European aristocracy who attended the fight, though the representations are considerably generalized. Of special note are Zoffany himself, sitting distractedly under the circular sunscreen to the far left, and the French-Swiss adventurer Colonel Antoine Louis Henri Polier (1741–1795), who stands closer to the center looking over his own shoulder. Polier's large collection of Indian paintings is now divided among the Islamisches Museum and the Museum für indische Kunst, Berlin; the British Library, London; and the Achenbach Foundation of the California Palace of the Legion of Honor, San Francisco.

Both the large size and cloth support of the picture coincidentally recall the achievements of Akbar's workshop in producing the great *Ḥamza* (cat. no. 4), but here reflect the imitation of European models rather than a revival of earlier Mughal practices. The conventionalized shading and essentially flat, decorative conception of form are reminiscent of catalogue number 61, another Europeanized Indian picture.

For a discussion of Zoffany's Indian career, see Webster 1976, especially pp. 77–78, no. 104; and Webster 1973, pp. 588–89. For related material, see M. Archer 1972, pp. 156–57, p. 163, nos. 126, 127, pls. 54–56; M. Archer 1979, pp. 141–55, figs. 91–95; and S. C. Welch 1978, pp. 94–95, no. 39.

❀ 35 ❀

Portrait

DECCAN, GOLCONDA, ca. 1660–70

Image 7¾ × 3⅞ in. (197 × 99 mm); sheet 12½ × 8¼ in. (317 × 210 mm)

ʿAbdullah Quṭb Sh̲āh of Golconda

The king, identified by an elegant gold inscription across the top, stands facing left against a blue ground with a conventionalized landscape indicated lightly in gold. Haloed, he carries a lance and a black shield. He is dressed in a green *jāmā* (full-skirted coat) and wears a transparent gold shawl. The pigment of his face is applied so heavily that it has begun to crack, but there is no paint loss and the picture is in good condition.

ʿAbdullah Quṭb Sh̲āh of Golconda ruled from 1626 to 1672. He was heavily pressured by the Deccani ambitions of Sh̲āh Jahān (r. 1628–58) and in 1635 was forced to become all but a vassal of the empire. Painting in his reign took on a decidedly Mughal manner, the relative naturalism of the Mughal style replacing the heavy stylization of earlier painting in Golconda.

This picture is published in Zebrowski, p. 184, no. 151; for other portraits of the same king, including some that are in a less Mughalized style, see Zebrowski, pp. 179–88, figs. 144, 145, 149, 150, and 152–154. See also Khandalavala and Chandra 1965, p. 22, no. 60; Binney 1973, pp. 160–61, no. 136b; and Czuma, no. 49.

❀ 36 ❀

An album page

DECCAN, GOLCONDA, ca. 1660–70

Sheet 12 × 8 in. (305 × 203 mm)

Portrait of an unidentified man

Image 9 3/8 × 5 3/4 in. (239 × 147 mm)

Verso. A noble figure kneels on a rug. He is flanked by trees and holds a white iris in his right hand. The background is pale green (see cat. no. 26) with an elaborate white palace and conventional trees in the distance.

Calligraphic panel

Recto. The panel is signed by Muḥammad Ḥusain.

The kings of Golconda ruled from a fort near Hyderabad until the final Mughal victory over the Quṭb S̲h̲āhī kings in 1687, but even before that the painting of the state had become heavily Mughalized. The cool color and individualized portraiture of this picture reveal its Mughal debt.

❀ 37 ❀ 38 ❀

Two folios from a manuscript of the *Gulshan-i ʿIshq* (Rose Garden of Love) by Nuṣratī of Bijapur

DECCAN (BIJAPUR?), ca. 1700

37. The poet praises ʿAlī ʿĀdil Shāh II of Bijapur

Image 11¼ × 6 in. (285 × 153 mm); sheet 15¾ × 9¼ in. (400 × 235 mm)

The king (r. 1656–72), shown in a generalized portrait, graciously receives the praises of the poet Nuṣratī, who stands to the right with his hands outstretched, while a courtier stands next to him with his hands folded respectfully. An attendant at the left waves a peacock flywhisk over the king, depicted as a simple and pious monarch deserving of the accompanying verses that emphasize his role as a defender of Islam. An open book is on a stand before him. A double-bladed sword, candelabra, and golden vessels are in the foreground. The palette is predominantly white and gold with few touches of the fervid colors so typical of Deccani painting in the sixteenth and seventeenth centuries. Vertical and horizontal lines dominate the composition. The borders are decorated with a gold lattice pattern.

The fine calligraphy at the top and on the verso is strongly rectilinear. The verses are extravagant in their praises of the king and his children. Unfortunately his heir, Sikandar, had little opportunity to display his virtue. He came to the throne in 1672 at the age of four and lost it to Mughal invaders in 1686 when he was only eighteen.

For royal portraits from the reign of ʿĀdil II, see Zebrowski, pp. 140–42, figs. 107–111.

38. The lovesick Prince Manohara falls unconscious into his father's lap

Image 10⅜ × 5⅝ in. (264 × 144 mm); sheet 15¼ × 9 in. (388 × 229 mm)

This illustration is extraordinary in its combination of disciplined restraint and violent passion. The king and his courtiers are coolly withdrawn, locked into a grid of rectilinear patterning. The insensate prince is delineated in sweeping curves that mirror the form of the red and gold brocade cloth thrown over the ornate gold bed shown above him. At its left is a standing woman, her folded hands red with henna, a practice still prevalent in India, especially at weddings. Beyond lies the royal garden, full of banana trees and coconut palms heavy with fruit. At the top, pairs of birds pick at mangoes that burden a large tree. Mangoes in classical literature symbolize the female breast, and here they increase erotic tension.

The text on the recto describes the king's concern at his son's mysterious illness. He offers rewards to the doctor who can cure the malady, but all who try are unsuccessful. Of course, the only cure for the prince is union with his beloved.

The manuscript from which these miniatures come is dispersed. It is of very fine quality with superb calligraphy, but details of patronage and production are unknown. The text it illustrates was written by a Hindu priest-poet who wrote for ʿAlī ʿĀdil Shāh II of Bijapur under the pen name of Nuṣratī. He completed the work in 1657. It recounts the love story of a prince named Manohara and his beloved Madhumālatī and embodies themes typical of the Indian romance tradition.

Other leaves and related material are published and discussed in Zebrowski, pp. 222–26, figs. 195–198. There is an early-nineteenth-century illustrated version of the same work in Philadelphia; see Simsar 1937, pp. 172–73, no. 98.

❀ 39 ❀

Genre scene

DECCAN, HYDERABAD, FIRST HALF OF 18TH CENTURY

Sheet 8¾ × 6½ in. (222 × 164 mm)

Inebriated ascetics

This delightfully discursive picture shows a group of Hindu holy men in various states of intoxication induced by a marijuana derivative made into a drink. The man in the center middle ground scans a large shallow cup for elusive drops, while his companion above lies back in cheerful oblivion to all around him, including his friend who has been fetching and carrying and now wants to relax. To the left, a young yogi with a peacock-feather fan dances to the tune of the flutist in the lower right. At the top right another of the party brings a load of dried dung cakes for fuel. The holy men have cats on golden leashes and two dogs. In the background small shrines dot the hill to the left; a distant city is to the right; and in the center is a ship in a sea vista that opens to a gold sky.

It is difficult to place this picture precisely, but it is probably from Hyderabad of the early eighteenth century. It is related in style to a group of genre and *Rāgamālā* pictures that are likely to be from Hyderabad and its surrounding region. These pictures are distinguished by discursive compositions, elegantly mannered human and landscape forms, and a pearly palette that uses gold liberally.

For related examples, see Zebrowski, pp. 226–42, figs. 199–203 and 207–217. Deccani painting in this period comes under profound Mughal influence but still preserves its palette and its distinctive distortions of form. See catalogue number 57 for a nineteenth-century treatment of this theme from Rajasthan.

❀ 40 ❀

Folio from a manuscript of the *Gīta Govinda* of Jayadeva

POSSIBLY FROM AURANGABAD IN THE DECCAN, ca. 1650

Image 5 3/8 × 5 7/8 in. (136 × 148 mm); sheet 6 1/2 × 7 5/8 in. (165 × 193 mm)

Kṛṣṇa and Rādhā in the forest at night

Kṛṣṇa, deep blue and richly jeweled, turns to his lover Rādhā. Clad in brilliant garments of yellow, red, and gold and wearing elaborate gold and pearl ornaments, she offers him a necklace as a love token. They walk together in the dark forest along the Jamuna (Jumna) River. Fanciful rocks of deep rose-pink mark the river's banks, which are alive with tiny herons. Somber trees and flowering branches fill the slate-blue sky where storm clouds gather as the lovers' passion mounts. They glow in the darkness, just as the pearls of Kṛṣṇa's ornaments shimmer against his dark skin.

The Sanskrit text on the verso is the second verse of the *Gīta Govinda*, but the picture illustrates the first verse, which faced it in the manuscript:

> "Clouds thicken the sky.
> Tamāla trees darken the forest.
> The night frightens him.
> Rādhā, you take him home!"
> They leave at Nanda's order,
> Passing trees in thickets on the way,
> Until secret passions of Rādhā and Mādhava
> Triumph on the Jumna riverbank.
>
> (Miller, p. 69)

The twelfth-century *Gīta Govinda* explicitly describes the overwhelming power of Kṛṣṇa's divine love. It is still read and sung today in temples in many parts of India. The text was frequently illustrated in virtually every style of Indian painting (see cat. nos. 91, 119, 125, 126).

For another leaf from the same manuscript, see Binney 1973, p. 156, no. 130, where he also lists the locations of additional pages.

The style of this folio, and of catalogue number 41, is difficult to place. It shows close affinities with Mewar painting of the mid-seventeenth century (see cat. no. 48). In a temple library in Udaipur there is an illustrated *Rasamañjarī* manuscript of the same type bound with other texts. One of these bears a colophon from Aurangabad dated 1650; see Doshi, pp. 19–28, pls. 11–13. An illustrated *Gīta Govinda* in the same style is in the Rajasthan Oriental Research Institute in Udaipur (MS. 1586). A text bound in with this manuscript is dated 1723, but so late a date is unlikely for the illustrations; see *Kṛishṇa*, manuscript no. 25.

❀ 41 ❀

Leaf from a *Rāgamālā* series

POSSIBLY FROM AURANGABAD IN THE DECCAN, ca. 1650–75

Sheet 7⅞ × 6⅜ in. (200 × 162 mm)

Probably *Varāḍī Rāgiṇī*

A noble dressed richly in gold brocade sits on a sumptuously upholstered platform and leans on a bolster (the acidic green pigment of which has eaten entirely through the paper). He grasps the right arm of a woman who stands before him and holds a flywhisk in her upraised left hand. He looks directly at her face, but she gazes beyond him. Her bodice is red, draped with a transparent plum-colored veil; her yellow skirt is patterned like the skin of a tiger. A maid stands demurely behind her holding garlands of flowers heaped in a shallow golden bowl. The scene is set in a courtyard walled with shaded pink bricks. A red and white pavilion frames the main figures, its bamboo screen door decorated with tile patterns. A deeply colored floral rug is on the ground. The picture is a striking combination of refined line, flattened forms, and intense color. It is closely related in style to catalogue number 40, but is more finely finished.

If the identification of the subject is correct, the iconography is unusual. Typically, the woman with the whisk is seated with the lord.

Several leaves of this *Rāgamālā* are in public and private collections in India and the United States. For their locations and a list of published examples, see Ebeling, p. 177, no. 27, where the series is identified as from south Rajasthan. See also Zebrowski, pp. 48–50, figs. 32, 33.

❀ 42 ❀

Portrait

Ascribed to the artist Govinda Rāma

PROBABLY THE NORTH DECCAN, ca. EARLY 18TH CENTURY

Image 8½ × 5½ in. (216 × 140 mm); sheet 11 × 7⅜ in. (280 × 188 mm)

Rājā Aniruddha Siṅgha of Ater

Working in a manner that owes much to Mughal realism and refinement, Govinda Rāma achieves a penetrating portrait of a distinguished Rajput noble. Rājā Aniruddha Siṅgha of Ater sits facing right on a terrace. He wears a long white muslin robe and a richly jeweled turban that bears an elaborate feather and pearl aigrette. The unpainted terrace provides a plain ground for the dusty-rose cushions and bolster against which the chieftain rests. His sword and shield lie before him as he contemplates the sprays of flowers in his hands, a conventional pastime for a noble or a prince. The streaky sky is orange and blue. The portrait combines Mughal description with a typical Deccani palette of rose, blue, and orange.

On the reverse is a Hindi inscription that reads *hari anurudhu sigha rājā gopāla siṅgha sutaḥ bhadāvarīyāḥ cahuvānaḥ aṭeraḥ ṭhikānāḥ musavara govinda rāma//1//*, which translates, "O Lord! Rājā Aniruddha Siṅgha, son of Rājā Gopāla Siṅgha, of the Bhāduriā Cauhāna clan [of Rajputs] from the barony of Ater. [By the] painter Govinda Rāma. 1." This is followed by a less detailed Persian inscription giving much of the same information. Ater is located in what is now the district of East Nimar in the modern state of Madhya Pradesh, not far from the town of Bhind-Bhadawar, traditional seat of the Bhāduriā Rajputs. North Deccan was under Mughal power by the very beginning of the seventeenth century and includes the cities of Aurangabad (see cat. nos. 40 and 41) and Burhanpur, from which the Mughals waged their Deccani campaigns. The former principality of Ater is still the site of an important timber market.

This picture is published in Spink & Son 1976, p. 12, no. 34, where it is identified as from the state of Kishangarh; for examples of Kishangarh painting, see below, catalogue numbers 70–75.

❀ 43 ❀

Folio 35 from a manuscript of the *Karṇaparva* of the *Mahābhārata*

SOUTH INDIA, MYSORE, 1670

Image 4½ × 6 in. (114 × 152 mm); sheet 7⅝ × 17⅝ in. (193 × 448 mm), irregular

Verso. The battle between the heroes Kṛtavarman and Śikhaṇḍin

Two warriors, identified by text and inscription as the opponents Kṛtavarman and Śikhaṇḍin, face each other in a fierce fight. Arrows fill the air as men, chariots, and horses clash in one of the seemingly endless string of battles of the *Mahābhārata*, the Indian national epic of dynastic struggles that sweep away the old order. The conventionalized shading of the heavily stylized figures suggests roundness bordering on rotundity. The background is solid red; nothing distracts from the confrontation of the enemies. The horses, who meet in starkly opposing diagonals, are goaded to fury by the charioteers. Gold highlights the animals' trappings. The bold abstraction and rhythmical, circular line of this picture represent continuations of much earlier stylistic elements that were widely distributed throughout south India and the Deccan and contributed to the development of more refined styles.

Though the *Mahābhārata* is very popular, illustrated versions of it are extremely rare. The dark-skinned Śikhaṇḍin, typically represented as blue, is an unlikely hero. The child of King Drupada, he was born a girl, a fact his mother kept secret. The truth remained hidden until after marriage, when Śikhaṇḍin's outraged father-in-law threatened to destroy Drupada's kingdom in revenge. Śikhaṇḍin practiced austerities at the shrine of a nature-spirit who obligingly agreed to trade sexes, thus saving the day for the unfortunate and much-deceived King Drupada. The newly created male was a great warrior, though he fainted during the battle depicted here and was taken from the field. The text on folio 35v is *Mahābhārata* 8.18.60–71. For a translation, see Roy, vol. 7, pp. 63–64.

Other leaves from this manuscript are in the Salar Jang Museum, Hyderabad; the Jagdish and Kamla Mittal Museum of Indian Art, Hyderabad; the National Museum of India, New Delhi; and the Freer Gallery of Art, Washington, D.C. For a discussion of the significance of the manuscript, see Mittal 1969, pp. 26–27, fig. 5. A damaged leaf formerly in the George P. Bickford Collection (now dispersed), published in Czuma, no. 124, is probably from the same manuscript. For related South Indian styles, see Sivaramamurti 1968. Catalogue numbers 13 and 14 above are from Persian translations of the *Mahābhārata* illustrated in the Mughal style.

कृतवर्मा
शिखंडी

❀ 44 ❀

Leaf from a *Rāgamālā* series

DECCAN, WANPARTHY, MID-18TH CENTURY

Image 10½ × 5⅜ in. (266 × 137 mm); sheet 12⅛ × 7 in. (308 × 178 mm)

Naṭa Rāgiṇī

A bearded swordsman rides at full gallop against a foe. Below, another enemy lies dead, headless. The rider has snatched up the severed head as a trophy as he turns his fury toward his next victim, already without shoes and turban in the confusion of the assault. The landscape is a molten orange that glows like flowing lava. Conventionalized plants and trees dot the horizon. The artist has no concern for a ground line. He has placed the fighting figures above the green hillock at the bottom, floating free, so as not to impede their headlong rush. The style is different from that of catalogue number 43, and yet these two battle scenes are close in spirit.

This is a strong statement of traditional Indian painting at a time when most other Indian styles are more closely aligned with the refined line and cool palette of Mughal painting. South India was more culturally isolated than the north and more impervious to change. Conservative painting of great strength and visual power continued to be produced there until well into the nineteenth century.

The text at the top is in Telegu, a South Indian tongue that is one of the world's most spoken languages. It is spoken in the modern state of Andhra Pradesh, the capital of which is Hyderabad, where a very different kind of painting was practiced in the eighteenth century (see cat. no. 39).

This series was formerly in the collection of the raja of Wanparthy. For other examples, see Mittal 1963, pp. 57–64; Binney 1973, pp. 188–89, no. 175; and Spink & Son 1976, p. 30, no. 140.

❀ 45 ❀

Leaf number 9 from a *Bhāgavata Purāṇa* series

MALWA, ca. 1640

Image 5¾ × 6⅞ in. (146 × 174 mm); sheet 6¾ × 8⅛ in. (171 × 206 mm)

The exchange of babes

Kṛṣṇa's parents were imprisoned by his mother's evil brother, Kaṃsa, usurper king of Mathura, who killed their first six children to circumvent a prophecy that a child of theirs would kill him. When Kṛṣṇa was born, his father, Vasudeva, took him secretly to the countryside and exchanged him for the infant daughter of a cowherd couple, really a goddess in the guise of an infant. He took her back to Mathura, where the fearful king dashed her against a rock. But instead of dying she assumed divine form and spoke to Kaṃsa from heaven (see cat. no. 99), telling him his enemy was safe. Frustrated, Kaṃsa fruitlessly sent his demon forces through the land to slay all male infants of the appropriate age, but he could not avert his fate.

In this painting Vasudeva crosses the Jamuna River, here depicted more like a paved road than flowing water. Rain hangs like strings of pearls in the dark sky. Kṛṣṇa's foster mother, Yaśodā, is only dimly aware of him as he begins to nurse. A maid attends her. The border is pink. An inscription in the yellow panel at the top reads *vasudeva krasna hi dai kanyā lai cale* (Leaving Kṛṣṇa and taking the girl, Vasudeva went) followed by the number 9.

Though this picture was painted over a century after catalogue numbers 1 and 2, it preserves the earlier style to an astonishing degree. Costume, ornament, figure type, and the bright red interior of the pavilion are similar. Perhaps slight Mughal influence is discernible in a quieting of movement and a softening of line and color, but the painting takes little notice of the Mughal experience.

The series, formerly in the collection of the Datia State Library, originally contained about one hundred twenty-five miniatures. About fifty leaves of this important set are now in the National Museum of India, New Delhi. Other illustrations are in the Bharat Kala Bhavan, Banaras (Varanasi), and public and private collections in India, Europe, and the United States. See Krishna, pls. 15–16; Archer and Binney, p. 57, no. 41; McNear, pp. 46–47, no. 75; Pal 1976, no. 7; and Pal 1978, pp. 68–69, no. 11.

॥वसुदेव कृस्न हि दै कंन्या लै चले॥ ८

❀ 46 ❀

Leaf from a *Bhāgavata Purāṇa* series

MALWA, ca. 1640–50

Sheet 6¾ × 8⅛ in. (171 × 206 mm)

The slaying of Kuvalayāpīḍa

Kṛṣṇa and his brother, Balarāma, attack Kuvalayāpīḍa, the elephant sent by Kaṃsa to kill them. Kṛṣṇa seizes the animal's tusks as a prelude to ripping them out and using them for clubs. His brother raises a plow, his major attribute. An elephant handler lurches forward from his perch behind the creature's head, little realizing that the simple execution he has planned will turn out rather different from what he had expected. The Sanskrit version of the incident is *Bhāgavata Purāṇa* 10.43.

The flat red ground and curved horizon line are typical of the Malwa style of about 1640 and a little before, but the relatively fine line evident here in the human and animal figures is indicative of a stylistic change that was to become more pronounced as the century progressed. Malwa remains a very conservative style throughout its development, yet a strain of the idiom exhibits a refinement that is difficult to understand without assuming some Mughal influence, however indirect. The history of the style is fairly well understood from its earliest examples dated 1634 to the end of the seventeenth century, but its subsequent development is unclear.

In the panel at the top is a Hindi caption reading *hastīvadha. 36.* (Elephant-killing. [Leaf] 36.). Another hand has altered the number to 33.

Other leaves of this series are in the J. P. Goenka Collection, Bombay; the Colonel R. K. Tandan Collection, Secunderabad; and in various private collections. See Tandan 1982, figs. 21a–c; and Khandalavala and Chandra 1965, p. 24, no. 75.

॥हस्तीवध॥३६॥

❀ 47 ❀

Leaf from a *Rasamañjarī* of Bhānudatta

MEWAR SUB-STYLE, ca. 1625

Image 8½ × 6 in. (216 × 153 mm); sheet 9⅞ × 7⅜ in. (252 × 188 mm)

Madhyākhaṇḍitā Nāyikā

A woman confronts her beloved in a pavilion topped with domed kiosks. They face each other against a deep green ground. She raises her right hand to her face while her left clasps a spouted jug from which water pours unheeded. Another woman sits to the left. The figures are depicted in profile, the preferred manner in traditional Indian painting. The intense color and flat planes preserve the stylistic conventions of pre-Akbar painting (see cat. nos. 1 and 2). There is little trace of Mughal influence. This style is more boldly rendered than standard Mewar painting of about the same time (see cat. no. 48), a difference that may indicate it was produced at a different painting center.

Like the *Rasikapriyā* (see cat. nos. 48 and 67), the *Rasamañjarī* by the poet Bhānudatta classifies types of heroes (*nāyakas*) and heroines (*nāyikās*). The subject here is a woman past early youth but not yet thirty. She is angry because her beloved has returned home in the early morning still bearing on his chest the marks of lovemaking with another woman. Stung by his betrayal, she is speechless, then begins to weep. In order to disguise her tears, she washes her face with the water she carries. The Sanskrit text is verse 45 of Bhānudatta's work. The number 45 is written in faded numerals in the lower right. Another hand has added the number 43 in the center of the lower margin. On the back of the leaf are a Hindi version of the text and a commentary.

This leaf was formerly in the William Theo Brown and Paul Wonner Collection, San Francisco, and is published in Pal 1976, no. 31. Other leaves from this large *Rasamañjarī* are in the Sri Gopi Krishna Kanoria Collection, Patna; the J. P. Goenka Collection, Bombay; the National Museum of India, New Delhi; the Collection of Edwin Binney, 3rd, San Diego; the Paul Walter Collection, New York; and other public and private collections. See Lee, p. 25, no. 14; Archer and Binney, p. 6, ill., and p. 19, no. 3; and Pal 1978, pp. 60–61, no. 7.

॥अन्योपभोगचिह्नितः प्रातरागछति पतिर्यस्याः सा खंडिता॥
॥वक्षोजचिह्नितमुरो दयितस्य वीक्ष्य दीर्घं न निःश्वसिति जल्प
॥ति नैव किंचित्। प्रातर्जलेन वदनं परिमार्जयंती बाला
॥विलोचनजलानि तिरोदधाति॥
मध्याखंडिता
सीया
४३

❀ 48 ❀

Leaf from an illustrated *Rasikapriyā* of Keśavadāsa

Attributed to Sāhibdīn

MEWAR, ca. 1630–40

Image 7¾ × 6⅝ in. (197 × 168 mm); sheet 10¾ × 8¼ in. (273 × 210 mm)

A maid describes the beauty of her mistress to Kṛṣṇa

Kṛṣṇa sits under a mango tree while a maid cajoles him with a vivid description of the physical beauty of her mistress: her lips are deep red, her breasts like the unblemished fruit of the divine tree that grants all wishes. The painter delights the eye with a tree loaded with unripe mangoes, fruits to which the breasts of young girls are often likened in Indian literature, the delightful allusion underlined by the loving pairs of birds that grace the tree's branches. The blue god, here more a chivalrous hero than a divine figure, leans against a yellow bolster as he hears the entreaties of the maid. Two women attend him. All are on a boldly stated rug of red and blue with narrow white borders. Images of fecundity are everywhere. The river at bottom holds a cluster of blooming lotuses. Black bees, images of erotic fulfillment, drift through the flowers on the river bank. Trees and shrubs burst forth in a profusion of fruits and flowers.

The outer border is red, the inner is yellow. In the lower right corner the number 91 is written over another number (4——). A few scattered letters and the number 4 are written in pale ink within the right yellow border.

Keśavadāsa wrote the *Rasikapriyā* in 1591. The work describes the characteristics of heroes (*nāyakas*) and heroines (*nāyikās*) using the lovers Kṛṣṇa and Rādhā as its examples. Keśavadāsa's poetry is still popular today.

Sāhibdīn, a Muslim serving a Hindu monarch, was the dominant painter of the Mewar style from the 1620s to the 1650s. His style expresses continuity with the bright color and abstract values of catalogue numbers 1 and 2, but its increasing refinement and use of shading show that the painter was not unaffected by the Mughal style. Note the three-dimensional form of the trunk of the mango tree and the subtle effects of the nearly transparent veils that drape the upper bodies of the three women. Though this picture is unsigned, its high quality and calm assurance leave no doubt that it is from the master's hand. For a thorough discussion of the artist's style and references to other works by him, see Topsfield 1981b. See also Khandalavala 1951; and Khandalavala, Chandra, and Chandra, pp. 30–34, figs. 29, 30, and plate C.

This leaf is published in Spink & Son 1982, p. 21 and p. 104, no. 97. For the text at the top, see Keśavadāsa, p. 34, chap. 13, verse 5. The verse on this leaf shows several variant readings from the published text; for a translation, see Bahadur, pp. 209–10. Other leaves from this same series are in the Government Museum, Udaipur; the Bikaner collection; the British Museum, London; and private collections.

श्रीक्रष्ण कै विनय ॥

कुंडल के से फूल ले नैन दोऊ स्यौं से दसन अैंन लाल से अधर हास सुधा सौं सुधा स्यौ है।
वैनी पिक वैनी की त्रिवैनी सी वनाई वीर वारी ऊ वास सो करि हा को करि हास्यो है।
कान ऊ च अमल कलप तरकै से फल के सौदा राया तें विधि सुगंध विवास्यो है।
देष्यो नंदपाल सषि मेरी को सरी रूस सुसोनौ सो सचारि मन मैन सो सवास्यो है

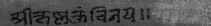

२१

❀ 49 ❀

Folio 32 from the *Uttarārdha* (latter half) of the tenth book of the *Bhāgavata Purāṇa*

MEWAR, FIRST HALF OF 17TH CENTURY

Sheet 9¼ × 16 in. (235 × 416 mm)

Mura, the five-headed demon who sleeps under the waters, rushes to attack Kṛṣṇa

Image 6¼ × 12⅞ in. (159 × 327 mm)

Recto. To the right, against a red ground banded at top and bottom with blue, Kṛṣṇa and his wife arrive on the man-bird Garuḍa. Kṛṣṇa, blue-skinned as usual, is dressed in yellow. Four-armed, he carries a discus, lotuses, and a drawn bow. Mura and his forces attack from the left. The ground is pale yellow. The five-headed demon is dressed in red, carries a sword in his upraised right hand and a shield in his left. Even at the moment of attack there is no doubt of the outcome. Already some of Mura's men have dropped defenseless to the ground. From the upper left corner the demon king Naraka watches anxiously from his citadel. An attendant points to the battle. A moat and rocky fortifications protect the fortress. The outer borders are green, yellow, and red.

Kṛṣṇa slays Naraka

Image 6 × 12⅞ in. (152 × 327 mm)

Verso. Now Kṛṣṇa carries a mace, a drawn bow, and a conch shell as he continues the fight. Celestials, their faces obscured by the borders, rain flowers on the divine hero. Naraka rushes into battle on a lively elephant, surrounded by his followers. He makes a hopeless attempt to shoot arrows at Kṛṣṇa, but already the god's discus reaches its target. Naraka's head lolls back, his face expressionless, the gaping neck-wound gushing blood. A woman within the citadel watches, beating her breast. The battleground is a dull blue, the rocks around the fort mauve, tan, and blue-gray.

The text on the folio is *Bhāgavata Purāṇa* 10. 59.7–16 (recto) and 17–24 (verso); the scribe has confused verse numbers starting with verse 18. Brief commentaries on the verses are on both sides, top and bottom. At the top of the recto a Hindi caption in red reads *pāñcamukha kau bhaumāsura ḍhāla taravāra layaiṃ bhagavāna sauñ juddha karata*, which can be translated freely as, "After Bhaumāsura [an epithet of Naraka] took a sword and shield to the five-headed one, he fought with the lord." The grammatical ambiguity of the caption is reflected in the erroneous labeling of Mura as Bhaumāsura. The caption at the bottom of the verso reads *hāthī pau çaḍha kai narakāsura juddha kaun āyau tā kau bhagavāna naiṃ vāna ghālata main cakra saum māthau kāta ḍārau*, which translates, "Having mounted an elephant, the demon Naraka came to the battle. The lord shot arrows at him and severed his head with a discus." The folio number is written in light blue circles in both right and left margins. For a translation of the Sanskrit text, see Tagare, part 4, pp. 1629–32.

The bold color, flat planes, vigorous yet simple compositions, and square-headed figure types of these pictures compare with those of catalogue numbers 1, 2, 45, and 46. At the same time, the refined line, softly shaded rocks, lessened angularity, and fluttering garments indicate an awareness of Mughal painting. Less complex than paintings done for the Mewar court in the mid-seventeenth century, the illustrations of this *Bhāgavata* were possibly painted in some workshop serving patrons humbler than the rulers of Mewar, perhaps at some outlying center.

The recently discovered manuscript from which this folio comes is probably the earliest illustrated *Bhāgavata* that can be assigned to Mewar with any certainty. It is being dispersed among public and private collections in the West; for other leaves, see Hutchins, pls. 20 and 22.

Though more accomplished in execution, this manuscript is stylistically similar to a *Ḍholā-Māru* manuscript in the National Museum of India, New Delhi (51.52). The *Ḍholā-Māru* is dated, but the obscured date cannot be read with certainty. It was painted in Aghatpur, near Udaipur. See Krishna, pls. 6 and 7; Sharma, p. 12, pl. 29; Andhare, pp. 298–300; and *Image of Man*, p. 166, no. 246.

पांचमुष कौं भौमासुर ढाल तरवार लैंं भगवान सौं जुध्ध करत

हाथी पै चढ कै नरकासुर जुध्ध कौं आयौ ताकौं भगवान नैं बान थाल तैं चक्र सौं माथौ काट डारौ

❀ 50 ❀

Equestrian portrait

MEWAR, ca. 1700–1710

Image 12⅛ × 9½ in. (308 × 242 mm); sheet 16¼ × 12⅛ in. (413 × 308 mm)

Mahārāṇa Amara Siṅgha II

Amara Siṅgha II of Mewar (r. 1698–1710) rides to the right in the company of seven attendants who are on foot. One of his company carries the ruler's water pipe, another a yak-tail flywhisk, and a third shields him with a royal parasol adorned in the center by a golden disk. Amara Siṅgha is nimbated. His halo rivals in splendor the sun in the upper left poking through the unusual frilled cloud forms that rear up in the sky. A rayed sun is the symbol of the Mewar rulers. The harness of the spirited horse is simple but elegant, his mane and forelock carefully brushed and crimped. A misidentification is scrawled above the horse's head in a coarse, uneducated hand.

The heavily shaded and lightly colored style of this picture is extremely interesting. It derives from a kind of lightly tinted Mughal drawing technique very popular in the seventeenth and eighteenth centuries. Like the style of catalogue number 51, it attests to a strong Mughal influence in Mewar painting of the early eighteenth century under the patronage of Amara Siṅgha II, a great lover of painting who died at the age of only thirty-eight. Though never entirely losing the seventeenth-century preference for boldly stated forms, Mewar painting of the opening years of the eighteenth century excels in refined stylization and mannered elegance.

Other examples in this Mughalized manner include works certainly by the unknown artist who painted this portrait. Typical of his style are the swirling and animated edges of the drapery patterns. For his, and closely related, work, see Khandalavala, Chandra, and Chandra, p. 36, nos. 29, 30, figs. 35, 37; Skelton 1961, pp. 33–35, nos. 10, 11; Welch and Beach, pp. 44–47 and p. 120, no. 28; and Topsfield 1980, pp. 60–61, nos. 56, 57. Use of this technique in Mewar painting persisted well into the eighteenth century, but later examples lack the subtle sense of movement so evident in this portrait. For a portrait from about 1761, see Khandalavala, Chandra, and Chandra, pp. 36–37, no. 32, fig. 36.

❀ 51 ❀

Miniature border

MEWAR, EARLY 18TH CENTURY

Sheet 12¼ × 9 in. (311 × 229 mm)

(Illustrated on title page)

A royal hunting party in a fantastic landscape

In each side panel a hunter, one with a gun, the other with a bow and arrow, prowls a rocky landscape in search of a four-winged dragon and a leopard respectively. At the top a dragon and a lion are locked in mortal combat. In the hunters' camp at the bottom a servant prepares food, while seated men in each corner are served by standing attendants. The pair at the left probably represents Amara Siṅgha II (r. 1698–1710) and his son and successor, Saṅgrāma Siṅgha II (r. 1710–34).

This elaborately illustrated border, now lacking the miniature it originally framed, is a fine example of the heavily Mughalized painting produced in the Rājasthānī state of Mewar during the reign of Mahārāṇa Amara Siṅgha II (see cat. no. 50). Such borders are derived from figured Mughal manuscript and album margins produced from late in the reign of Akbar (1556–1605; see cat. nos. 20, 24, 26).

Mewar held out against Mughal control longer than other Rājasthānī states and enjoyed special privileges even after it finally succumbed to Mughal hegemony. Although it was renowned as a center of traditional Hindu culture, the leading Mewar painter of the seventeenth century was a Muslim (see cat. no. 48), and Mughal painting exercised a significant influence on Mewar painting of the eighteenth century. In this work, painted in the opening years of the eighteenth century, the rocks are recognizably derived from the landscape conventions found in painting of the Akbar period (see cat. no. 11).

The style of this border is very close to a portrait of Amara Siṅgha II and his court in the National Gallery of Victoria, Melbourne, and may be by the same hand; see Topsfield 1980, p. 60, no. 55.

❀ 52 ❀

Leaf number 3 from a *Rāgamālā* series

SIROHI, LATE 17TH CENTURY

Image 8¾ × 5¾ in. (223 × 147 mm); sheet 10¾ × 7¾ in. (273 × 197 mm)

Sindhu Rāgiṇī

Sindhu *rāgiṇī* is martial in spirit. At the top, against an Indian-yellow ground, a mounted warrior fights a running swordsman who has discarded his shoes. Below, an elephant with three riders attacks a warrior who has fallen. The movement is emphatic. The animals break through the restraining borders of the pictures, and the men's garments swing out from their bodies in strongly rhythmic patterns. The picture space is conceived as strictly two-dimensional. The only indication of landscape is an occasional, seemingly random, stylized blooming plant. The caption *sindhu rāteṃ rāgiṇī 3* is at the top. This evening melody is relatively rarely illustrated. When it appears, it usually replaces Naṭa, with which it is interchangeable both iconographically and textually (see cat. no. 44).

An offshoot of the Mewar school of painting seems to have flourished in the principality of Sirohi in the late seventeenth century. The style is characterized by saturated colors that glow with molten intensity. Though the background is strongly colored, the pigment is thinly applied, enabling the viewer to see the texture of the paper and several areas of underdrawing. The artist has made several small alterations in the placement of figures and animals. Most interesting is the complete elimination of the sword-bearing arm of the hapless soldier at the bottom. Completely outnumbered and overpowered, he is thus denied even the barest chance of resistance.

Leaves from the same and similar series are scattered throughout the world; see Ebeling, pp. 92–94 and 182 for a brief survey of this material. See also Pal 1978, pp. 82–83, no. 18, pp. 86–89, nos. 20, 21; Pal 1976, no. 24; and Binney 1979, pp. 80–81, no. 23. A leaf in the Rietberg Museum, Zurich (RVI 866) is very close in style to this leaf and is probably from the same series. A closely related leaf is in the Worcester Art Museum (Massachusetts; 1953.42); see Findly, pp. 52–55. The Worcester leaf is from another series, and it is interesting to note that it has been in this country since the early 1930s, a time when most Rājasthānī paintings were still in traditional collections in India.

❀ 53 ❀

Hunting scene

Attributed to Bagatā

DEVGARH, ca. 1775

Sheet 9⅞ × 19⅞ in. (251 × 505 mm)

Anupa Siṅgha and a companion shoot a boar who mauls a man

Anupa Siṅgha of Devgarh mounted on a dapple-gray horse shoots arrow after arrow into a wild boar who gores one of the noble's retainers. A companion rides behind Anupa Siṅgha, but there is no doubt whose arrow will kill the beast. The chief and his companion are lightly colored, but the paint does not obscure the active and vibrant line. The drawing is composed in two broad arcs. One encompasses the riders and their weapons, directing the eye to the middle right where the helpless victim of the boar is hurled head-over-heels by the angry beast. The other arc starts with the hunting dog who runs beside his master and whose form merges with the furious wild pig. The two opposing curves intersect where arrows pierce the boar. A smaller arc created by the mauled man accents and reinforces the line that leads the viewer's eye to the animal's wounds, suggesting that perhaps the man will be saved by his chief's intercession.

The picture is not inscribed, but an attribution to Bagatā is confirmed by another Anupa Siṅgha hunting scene ascribed to him and dated 1769; see Andhare and Singh, pl. 2. In the scene reproduced here the noble is older, with a heavier beard, suggesting a slightly later date for this study. Bagatā was the father of the famous Cokhā, who served the Mewar court at Udaipur during the first quarter of the nineteenth century. Before he came to Devgarh, Bagatā, too, painted in Udaipur, where he was active about 1760–65; see Topsfield 1980, pp. 24, 103, and 118–19, nos. 130 and 167, pls. 9 and 13. Devgarh was a barony of Mewar, so it is not surprising that artists traveled to and from Udaipur and worked in closely related idioms. Though it exhibits significant local differences, Devgarh painting is essentially a sub-style of the late-eighteenth-century Mewar style as practiced in Udaipur.

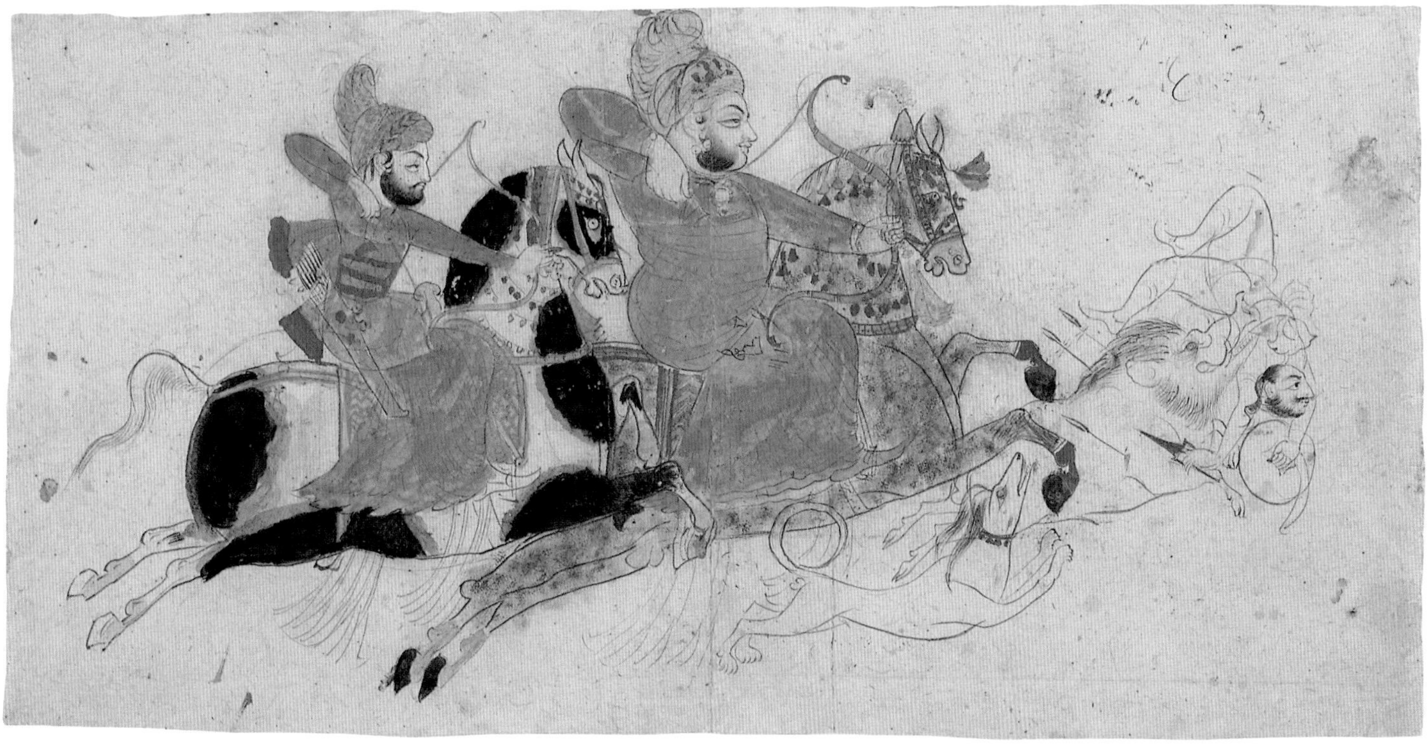

❀ 54 ❀

Idealized portrait

Possibly by Bagatā

DEVGARH, ca. 1810

Image 8¾ × 6¼ in. (222 × 159 mm); sheet 12 × 9 in. (305 × 229 mm)

Pṛthvī Rāja, last Hindu king of Delhi

The twelfth-century Hindu king of Delhi, Pṛthvī Rāja, is still celebrated in Indian bardic tradition for his valor in resisting the Muslim invasions. Idealized portraits of him were popular in Rajasthan and elsewhere in north India. Here he is depicted preparing to draw a bow as he kneels on a terrace at night. He wears a dark green upper garment, a tightly wrapped sash, and fawn-colored leggings that tuck into leather boots. Conventional clouds are at the top.

A caption on the top margin identifying the subject reads *cavāṇa prathī rājanī*. More Persian and Hindi captions are on the reverse, below which is a two-line Hindi note that appears to have been added later.

Though this picture is neither signed nor ascribed, it may be the work of Bagatā toward the end of his career at Devgarh. It bears close affinities with his dated works of the early nineteenth century. Typical of his style are the extreme exaggeration of the bulging of the eye; the markedly hooked nose; and the heavy, finely shaded face atop a body that is flat and monumental. For comparable examples, see Beach 1970–71, pp. 23–35, especially figs. 11–13; and Andhare and Singh, pl. 1. Bagatā's style at this time is very close to that of his son Cokhā, but is less heavily shaded, more colorful, and more linear.

रावलप्रथीराजजी

❀ 55 ❀

Animal studies

Ascribed to Svarūpa Rāma

MEWAR SUB-STYLE, ca. 1800

Sheet 10⅝ × 13⅛ in. (270 × 333 mm)

A hunting hound with its keeper

Image 7⅝ × 9¾ in. (193 × 248 mm)

Recto. A gray-brown hunting dog stands facing right and straining forward. The artist lovingly renders the silky texture of the dog's coat. The animal's ears are covered with long hair, a tuft of hair marks his nose. His intelligent face is fixed not on prey but on a flowering shrub. Svarūpa Rāma's close attention to detail is evident in the subtle shading of the dog's ribs, the scar on his back, and the burr caught on his left foreleg. The magnificent animal wears three collars, one functional, of red and gold, and two light, jeweled bands. One of these is decorated with a ruby and two pearls set in gold, while the other bears silver and enamel amulets. These rich adornments show the high value placed on such dogs, the ancestors of modern Afghan and saluki hounds. The attendant in green, dwarfed by his charge, holds a rope attached to the red collar and a bamboo frond to brush away flies. A spray of flowers decorates his turban. The background is yellow. A butterfly flutters through the vegetation at the right, and a tiny bird nestles in the spiky leaves of a white-flowered plant near the border. Villages and shrines are in the distance. Faint underdrawing reveals that the artist altered his original conception slightly at the collar and tail.

Fighting elephants

Image 6⅞ × 8¾ in. (175 × 223 mm)

Verso. The struggle of the animals in this tinted drawing raises clouds of dust, obscuring the surrounding trees and the attendants who seek to control the beasts with fireworks on long poles, a common practice. A very interesting inscription is on a panel at the top. Decorative scribbles obscure the original first line, but below, a verse begins which reads, *māsa do yatnoṅ kīnoṅ kāma/likhyoṅ citrakavi svarūpa rāma/śrīr astu kalyāṇam asthu* (Having worked for two months, the poet Svarūpa Rāma painted this picture. May there be prosperity! May there be good fortune!).

If the sensitive and complex dog study on the recto indeed took two months to paint, Svarūpa Rāma must have been a very exacting artist. Perhaps this is the colophon of a series of portraits of a noble's favorite animals. The more spontaneous elephants may have been added as an afterthought. Their immediacy makes them every bit as appealing as the elegant and polished canine. The style resembles the Mewar sub-style practiced at Devgarh (see cat. nos. 53 and 54), but the exact provenance is unrecorded.

The recto is published in Tooth and Sons, no. 14. An interesting sculpture of a similar dog is in the Collection of Mr. and Mrs. James W. Alsdorf, Chicago; see *Indian Heritage*, p. 28, no. 14. Another dog sculpture of this type is in the Doris Wiener Collection, New York. A drawing by the same artist, showing three ascetics and four more dogs, is in the Los Angeles County Museum of Art (M.81.180).

Catalogue number 56 can be attributed to Svarūpa Rāma on the basis of this picture.

॥मासदोयलों कीनों कांम॥॥॥
॥लिषौ चित्र कौ वे स्वरूप राम॥॥॥
॥श्रीरस्तु॥कल्याणमस्तु॥॥॥

❀ 56 ❀

Hunting scene

Attributed to Svarūpa Rāma

MEWAR SUB-STYLE, ca. 1800

Sheet 6¾ × 13¾ in. (171 × 349 mm)

A hunter kills a lion

As a lion kills the bait left near a water hole, a mounted hunter spears him and another shoots a gun at him from atop a rocky hill. A faintly sketched figure with a sword rushes forward from the left. The landscape is quickly drawn, the trees and sky indicated with broad washes of color. The mounted man and the lion are lightly colored, the other, more spontaneously rendered figures are not.

The artist's name is not given, but the use of washes for shading, the figure types, attention to textures, and the swirling horizon line suggest an attribution to Svarūpa Rāma, the painter of catalogue number 55. The more thinly painted verso of that leaf is perhaps more closely comparable than the fully finished dog study on the recto.

There is an inscription on the reverse (see Appendix, p. 254), but it seems to be a fairly conventional tribute to the noble hunter. Perhaps it will yield more information when fully deciphered.

❀ 57 ❀

Genre scene

Attributed to Prema-jī

MEWAR SUB-STYLE, PROBABLY AT BADNORE, BEFORE 1820

Image 9 3/8 × 6 3/8 in. (239 × 162 mm); sheet 11 1/8 × 8 1/4 in. (282 × 210 mm)

Intoxicated ascetics

Caricatures of ascetics are popular subjects in Indian painting. This late example is perhaps even more delightful and pointed than the earlier Deccani version of catalogue number 39. A group of ascetics sit in rows before a thatched hut in which sits a yogi devoted to Śiva, apparently their leader. They are completely intoxicated from smoking and ingesting marijuana. Their turbans loose, they wander heavy-eyed, or sleep, or keep smoking more and more of the inebriating weed. In the lower right a crow pecks at a man's head, but he is oblivious. In the opposite corner a rat scampers over another of the ascetics who has collapsed in a tangle of arms, legs, and turban. Above this amusing scene another of the party watches without comprehension as a dog eats from his food plate. Above them another dog barks to keep at bay a monkey who is out to see what he can get while the men are too far gone to care. To the dog's right a man with a round face, bulbous nose, and spiky hair scratches his back and his hip at the same time. Two men in the middle look at a caged bird. The trees behind the hut include two mangoes putting forth new leaves, a ubiquitous motif. The background is green, the sky streaked with red, yellow, and blue.

A Hindi inscription on the back has been partly covered with paper tape. Below is another that reads *pānoḥ amalya koḥ* (the sin of intoxication). In the upper right, in a nineteenth-century English hand, is "1820" and below, "Chittor," presumably the date and place it was acquired. Above, in a modern hand, is "Pemji of Chitor 1820." "33/-" is in the lower left, and an owner's stamp has been obliterated in the lower right.

The postures of many of the figures have parallels in catalogue number 60 which are in turn derived from Mughal models, another example of the continuity of motif over time, style, and place in Indian painting. This leaf is from a group of stylistically related pictures said to have been painted in the barony of Badnore in Mewar by the artist Prema-jī in the early nineteenth century. Other examples are in the Jagdish and Kamla Mittal Museum of Indian Art, Hyderabad, and an American private collection. See *Image of Man*, p. 77, ill., and p. 155, no. 213; and S. C. Welch 1973, p. 37, no. 14. In these pictures one can see Prema-jī's distinctive style, which is characterized by angular movement, a wiry line, and a strong preference for yellow and green.

❀ 58 ❀

Leaf from a *Rāgamālā* series

BUNDI SCHOOL, ca. 1670

Image 7⅞ × 4⅜ in. (200 × 111 mm); sheet 11⅞ × 9⅜ in. (302 × 244 mm)

Dhanāśrī Rāgiṇī

This superbly and richly worked picture shows a painting within a painting. An intent dark-skinned woman paints a portrait of her lover on a tablet while her maid kneels before her. The two are on a terrace before a pavilion. The surrounding courtyard has a red and white wall. Behind are trees and a blue sky full of swirling coils of cloud. Gold has been lavished on the painting. The brushwork is vigorous and assured. The painter shades the women with ruddy tones and has constructed a pavilion that is convincing if not completely consistent. The dash of his brush makes the composition pulsate with life. The line, in constant motion even when describing inanimate objects, is strong and quick. The margins are silver and deep red.

The dispersed *Rāgamālā* series to which this leaf belongs is modeled after the earliest of the known Bundi sets, the *Rāgamālā* painted at the fort of Chunar, near Banaras (Varanasi), in 1591 by artists trained in the Mughal workshop. In spite of three-quarters of a century of independent Bundi development, the artist of this picture has not forgotten the Mughal concern with three-dimensionality, though here it is reinterpreted in a way that does not detract from the typical Rājasthānī use of broad planes of flat color.

In the yellow text panel at the top an untidy hand has written *dhanāsarī rāgana*, under which are the numbers 15 and 3.

Other leaves from this splendid series are in the Jagdish and Kamla Mittal Museum of Indian Art, Hyderabad; the Colonel R. K. Tandan Collection, Secunderabad; the J. P. Goenka Collection, Bombay; the Israel Museum, Jerusalem; and the Collection of Edwin Binney, 3rd, San Diego. See Beach 1974, pp. 30–31, fig. 62; and Tandan 1982, pl. XV. For a thorough and far-reaching discussion of the 1591 set, see Skelton 1981. The colophon of this early series is in the Freer Gallery of Art, Washington, D.C.

❀ 59 ❀

Animal studies

BUNDI SCHOOL, PROBABLY AT KOTA, EARLY 18TH CENTURY

Sheet 11¾ × 16⅜ in. (299 × 416 mm)

A bull elephant surrounded by the young of the herd

The Bundi school excelled in elephant studies that rank among the most engaging of all Rājasthānī paintings and drawings. Here a bull elephant stands patiently, ignoring his chains, while the young of his herd scamper around him. Two seem to play hide and seek around his ponderous legs while two others caress his trunk and tusks. The anonymous artist has captured all the awkward charm of young elephants as well as the quiet grace of the bull.

From the earliest times Indian artists have exhibited a special sensitivity in their animal studies, and the elephant has always occupied a prominent place in the painting and sculpture of the subcontinent. The elephant is a beast of burden, a royal attribute, and a symbol of the Waters that are the source of all life. The subjects of this drawing make an interesting comparison with the early-seventeenth-century elephant portrait probably by Govardhana (cat. no. 22). The Bundi school animals are more generalized and abstract, but in their very stylization they portray the essence of the elephant no less effectively than the highly individualized portrait by the Mughal master. He describes a single elephant; the artist of the Bundi school describes all elephants in a single picture.

This drawing is very close in style to a famous hunt scene that shows a bull elephant in furious activity rather than in calm repose. See Lee, p. 44, no. 36, and p. 45, ill.; and Beach 1974, p. 34, fig. 71. The hunt scene has been assigned to Kota on the basis of the identification of the elephant's rider with Rāma Siṅgha I of Kota (r. 1695–1707).

❀ 60 ❀

Genre scene

BUNDI SCHOOL, POSSIBLY AT KOTA, MID-18TH CENTURY

Sheet 10 3/8 × 14 1/4 in. (263 × 362 mm)

A group of men at ease

This group of men smoking and resting as they wait for food is not unlike scenes that may still be seen along the Indian roadsides of today. Our attention is drawn immediately to the barber who grooms the elegant posturing man in white seated under a tree. Though simply dressed, the barber's customer is obviously a bit of a fop. The artist takes special delight in portraying the perfect drape of his garments. Among the man's possessions is a short crutch with a curved handle used for support during long periods of sitting (see cat. no. 24, and *Indian Heritage*, pp. 118–19, no. 359). Some of his companions are hunters with falcons. One lets his bird roost on his head, a cap protecting his scalp from the fierce talons of the creature. Other men sit meditatively, chew *pāna* (a mildly narcotic digestive), loll on a pallet, or absentmindedly play with a caged bird. A few are more active. One strips bamboo, another prepares a bowl of food, and a third tends a cooking fire. In the lower right a poor snake charmer plies his trade, to the complete indifference of those around him. The atmosphere of the picture is one of careless ease. The lurid sky is typical of the Bundi school. The gently rolling green ground is modeled with finely streaked shading, another characteristic of the style in the eighteenth century.

Genre pictures such as this are ultimately derived from Mughal examples, though it is not always clear how directly. The Bundi school derives stylistically from painting of the late Akbar period, but by the time this picture was painted it had enjoyed a century and a half of independent development. Still, it is probable that the painter of this picture was familiar with Mughal genre scenes of the early eighteenth century.

An example of about 1700–1720 in the Cleveland Museum of Art (71.90) is not only compositionally similar, but also provides specific prototypes for the angular postures of several of the seated figures; see Leach, p. 153, fig. 163. There is a similar later Bundi/Kota composition in the Collection of Edwin Binney, 3rd, San Diego; see Binney 1979, pp. 76–77, no. 21.

❀ 61 ❀

Genre scene

BUNDI, ca. THIRD QUARTER OF 18TH CENTURY

Image 10¾ × 7⅞ in. (273 × 200 mm); sheet 13½ × 10⅜ in. (343 × 263 mm)

A Dutch family

Though Mughal adaptations of European pictures are not uncommon, Rājasthānī versions are more unusual. This delightful picture shows a Dutch family gathered together in a courtyard. An old woman spins, assisted by a girl. A dog is curled up at the feet of the spinner. Her bearded husband sits to the left, a staff resting between his legs, and fondles another dog. A young man in red and green leans on the old man's chair. A stylized tree curves up the left, and a gabled, two-story house fills the right background.

The cross-hatching so evident in the fabric and the architecture indicates the painting is based on a print. The specific source is unknown, but the subject suggests Dutch genre pictures of the seventeenth and early eighteenth centuries, or possibly an illustration from an emblem book depicting household tasks. The Indian artist has flattened the Dutch picture, relying for effect on pattern rather than description. The spokes of the squared-off spinning wheel resemble a feather fan, and the patterning of the crosshatched walls suggests they are made from Indian rattan rather than Dutch brick. The house is a fantastic structure of colors, patterns, and shapes that outstrip in invention any Dutch building.

The sooty shading and chalky whites, blues, and grays of the palette make unlikely a date before the middle of the eighteenth century. Such a picture does not indicate Western stylistic influence on Bundi painting of this time, but is simply a curiosity. Its unusual subject and imitation of European printmaking techniques make it difficult to cite exact stylistic parallels, but the treatment of figures and drapery is closely related to that in an unpublished festival picture in a private collection in Calcutta.

The margins are red with a narrow, yellow inner border and black and white rules. The leaf is published in Christie's 1978, lot 146.

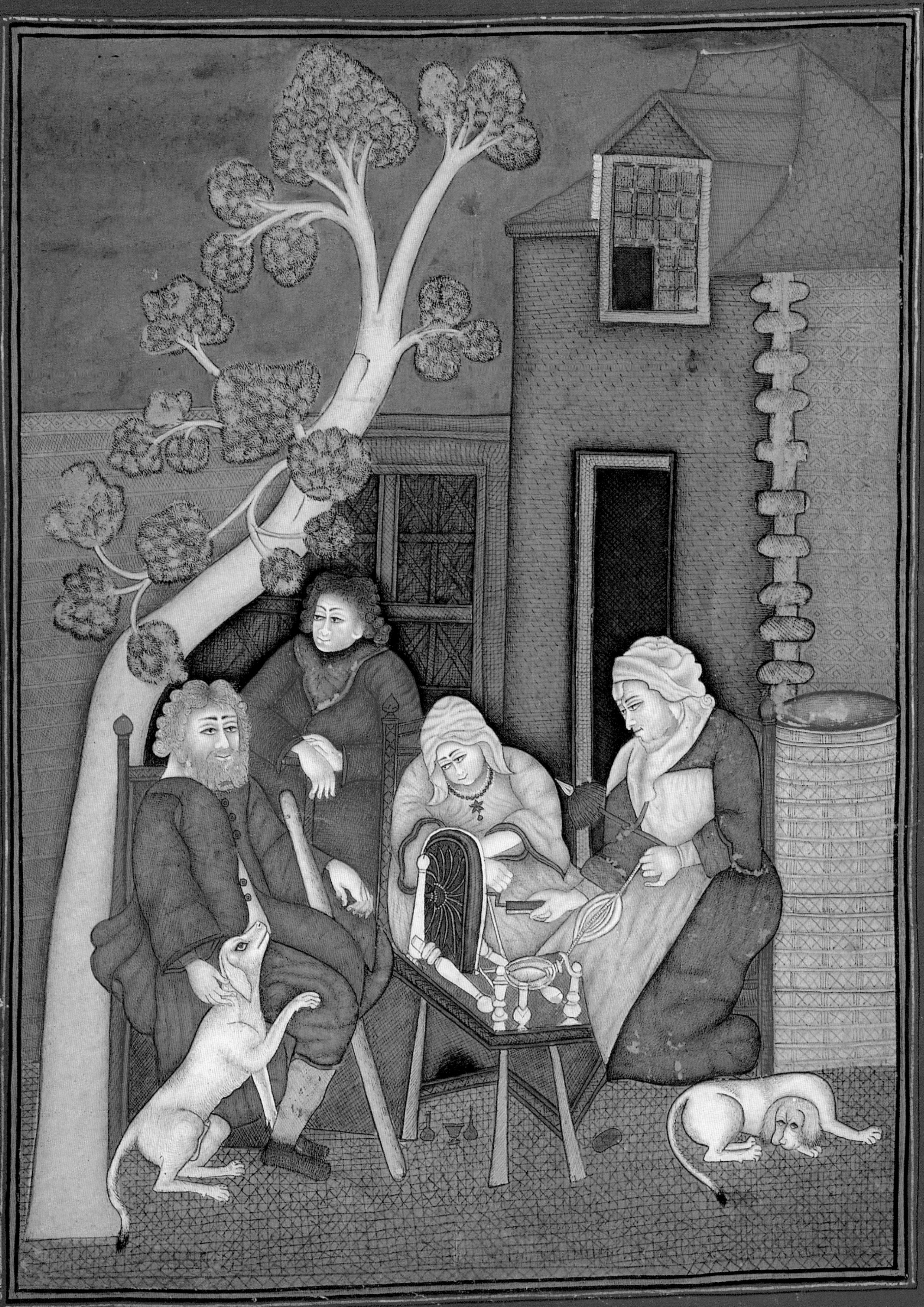

❀ 62 ❀

The goddess Durgā slaying demons

BUNDI SCHOOL, PERHAPS AT KOTA, MID-18TH CENTURY

Image 8 × 7¾ in. (204 × 197 mm); sheet 8¾ × 8⅞ in. (222 × 226 mm)

Durgā, a four-armed windmill of destruction, kills five demons at once as a dark-skinned dwarf attendant raises a dagger to help her. Blood explodes from the demons' wounds. Durgā's doglike lion sinks its fangs into one of the enemy. The goddess is impassive as she fulfills her destiny of demon-killing, the reason for her manifestation in this form. Above her hangs a tasseled hat that once belonged to the buffalo demon, another of her victims. At the bottom is a swirling river bordered with pink rocks and tufts of intensely green grass. A stand of bamboo is to the left. The background is a brilliant orange.

For other representations of the Goddess, who can be fierce in aspect or benign, see catalogue numbers 87, 88, and 123. Examples closely related to this one are published in Lee, p. 38, no. 30, and p. 39, ill.; Czuma, no. 81 (now Dr. Kenneth X. Robbins Collection, Maryland); Kramrisch, pp. 214–15, no. P-46; and S. C. Welch 1973, pp. 46–47, no. 21.

❀ 63 ❀

Leaf from a *Rāgamālā* series

BUNDI SCHOOL, ca. 1750–75

Image 7⅜ × 4⅞ in. (187 × 124 mm); sheet 13⅜ × 9⅜ in. (340 × 239 mm)

Baṅgāla, Rāgaputra of Hiṇḍola

Baṅgāla, an ascetic, is worshiping at a shrine in front of a hut (see cat. no. 16); a tame leopard rests nearby, and a tree is in the background. It is night. The heavily shaded opalescent palette is typical of Bundi painting in the third quarter of the eighteenth century, another example of Bundi's absorption of Mughal influence. The style is extremely smooth and shows little trace of the bold brushwork we usually associate with the idiom. A more conventionally colored and more vigorously painted version of the Bundi style continued to be produced at the same time, but the so-called white style that this picture represents was dominant. The margins of the leaf are plain paper that has been block-printed with a floral device. Across the top is the caption *hīṇḍola kau putra baṅgālo pāchalai pahara gāvaije* (Baṅgāla, the son of Hiṇḍola, to be sung in the last watch [of the night]).

This large and attractive series is iconographically distinct from most other *Rāgamālās* of Rajasthan. It follows a system that differs from the typical thirty-six-leaf classification of Rājasthānī sets and includes sons (*rāgaputras*) and daughters-in-law (*rāgaputrīs*) as well as wives (*rāginīs*) of the various *rāgas* (males). When complete the set should have consisted of over one hundred fifty paintings, or twenty-five in each of the six "families," plus a frontispiece (now in the Rietberg Museum, Zurich). Published reports to the contrary, no colophon is known. The date is unlikely to be earlier than mid-century and is probably closer to circa 1760–70. The paintings are said to have been in the collection of the chieftain of Dilwara, near Ajmer.

For the other surviving leaves, see Ebeling, pp. 192–93. Several of the leaves cited by Ebeling, including this one, have since changed hands. They are now in the Paul Walter Collection, New York; the William Theo Brown and Paul Wonner Collection, San Francisco; the Polsky Collections, New York; and other private collections. See Pal 1976, no. 27; and Pal 1978, pp. 126–27, no. 40. Thirteen leaves are in the Museum of Fine Arts, Boston. See Pal 1967b, nos. 11, 13, 34, 47, 51, 58, 60, 62, 68, 70, 71, 73, 87; and Beach 1974, pp. 38–39, fig. 100. Unpublished leaves are in the Collection of Edwin Binney, 3rd, San Diego, and other collections.

भैरोंकोपुत्रबंगालीपाछलेपहरगावेजे

❀ 64 ❀

Group portrait

KOTA, DATED V.S. 1910/A.D. 1853

Image 17¾ × 12 in. (451 × 305 mm); sheet 20⅜ × 14⅝ in. (517 × 372 mm)

Rāma Siṅgha II of Kota rewards his elephant handler

Rāma Siṅgha II of Kota (r. 1827–65) rides an elephant from the upper level of the ramparts of a fort to a terrace atop a domed pavilion. The king is attended by two flywhisk bearers. The occasion is explained by an inscription on the back. Rāma Siṅgha grants his elephant handler Vākānī a robe of honor and a gift of money. Vākānī is the paunchy man in pink who stands before the elephant, identified in the inscription as Subudha. Musicians and a female dancer stand with the king's sunshade bearer on the ramparts to the left, alerting us to a dance performance to follow the formal presentation of the honors. Below at the left is a richly dressed horse, Rāṇā by name, and the nobles of the court stand to the right of the domed pavilion. The colors are deep and rich, the movement lively yet controlled. Every figure glitters with jewels and trappings. Activity is everywhere, except in the quiet landscape beyond, to which the eye is led through open arches. The dark sky is full of elegant arabesque clouds and golden lightning that has startled cranes into flight.

The inscription on the reverse (see Appendix, p. 254) is very difficult to decipher, and I am grateful to B. N. Goswamy for extracting the information summarized above. Also on the reverse is a stamp indicating that this picture was formerly in the collection of the maharaja of Bikaner, now dispersed (see cat. nos. 17, 18, 66–69).

Rāma Siṅgha II of Kota reigned during a late efflorescence of the Bundi school that flourished in the state of Kota in the nineteenth century. At this time changing patronage patterns and tastes had relegated much traditional Indian painting to mechanical and static recapitulations of the achievements of the past, but a few styles held out against encroaching European influences (see also cat. nos. 78 and 79).

There are many fine portraits that chronicle the official life of Rāma Siṅgha. For examples, see W. G. Archer 1959, fig. 48; Chandra 1971, pp. 75–76, no. 123; Beach 1974, fig. 101; and Topsfield 1980, pp. 22, 46–48, nos. 35, 36, pl. 7. There are also a few more intimate paintings of Rāma Siṅgha in less formal situations. There is an extraordinary hunting scene in the Sri Gopi Krishna Kanoria Collection, Patna (Beach 1974, fig. 103), and an unpublished picture in a private collection in London shows the king in a sexual encounter with five women.

❀ 65 ❀

Leaf number 16 from a *Gajendra-mokṣa* series

POSSIBLY FROM AJMER, ca. 1640

Image 7¾ × 11½ in. (197 × 292 mm); sheet 8¼ × 12 in. (210 × 305 mm)

The King of Elephants and his retinue enter the Ganges River

Seeking relief from scorching heat, the elephant monarch, his queens, and their young enter the Ganges. The King of Elephants and his court are ponderous yet graceful as they play in the water's welcome coolness. A few of the pachyderms are nearly submerged, and in the center a bold baby has turned tail up to search for a tasty plant on the river bottom. To the left a school of aquatic beasts swims hastily away. Among their number is a fierce, crocodilian creature that will seize the lumbering monarch and try to pull him into the depths. They will fight for a millennium until Viṣṇu intervenes to save his elephant devotee, a reincarnated human king cursed to elephanthood by an angry sage who mistook his meditative silence for thickheaded rudeness. Śiva sits above in his half-male/half-female form. The god rests on a tiger skin as the Ganges flows through his matted hair, an indication that the incident takes place near the Himalayan source of the river. His bull is with him.

The descriptive text in the upper left is numbered 16. The standard version of the liberation of the elephant is recounted in the eighth book of the *Bhāgavata Purāṇa*, chaps. 2–4.

The flattened perspective and basket-weave water of this picture derive from much earlier Indian styles, but the refined line and subdued, coordinated palette show that the artist was influenced by Mughal innovations.

Other leaves from this series are in the National Museum of India, New Delhi; a private collection in Cambridge, Massachusetts; the Sri Gopi Krishna Kanoria Collection, Patna; and the J. P. Goenka Collection, Bombay. See Khandalavala, Chandra, and Chandra, pp. 57–58, nos. 140a–140d, fig. 99; Welch and Beach, p. 63, ill., and p. 118, no. 13; *Image of Man*, p. 158, no. 220; and S. C. Welch 1985, no. 229.

१६

❀ 66 ❀

Lakṣmī-Nārāyaṇa attended by women

Attributed to Lūphā

BIKANER, LATE 17TH CENTURY

Sheet 7⅝ × 5½ in. (195 × 142 mm)

Nārāyaṇa (a name of Viṣṇu) sits on a throne with his consort Lakṣmī on his lap. He is four-armed, carries a discus, conch, club, and lotus, and wears elaborate ornaments of gold and pearls. Deep blue in color, he wears an orange lower garment and leans against a pink bolster. Behind the pair rises the back of a yellow throne decorated with a tulip pattern. Women in multicolored clothes attend the divine couple, some playing musical instruments. A canopy shelters the figures. Its poles are arranged to form a pleasing pattern and emphasize the strong vertical lines of the composition rather than to convey to the viewer any sense of their spatial reality. A low carved marble screen separates the heavenly court from the dark trees and blooming vines in the background. A fountain and flower beds are in the foreground.

The miniature has lost any inscription it may have had, but it can be attributed to the artist Lūphā, a skilled Bikaner painter of the late seventeenth century of whom we know almost nothing but his name. His style is close to that of his better-known contemporary Rukn al-Dīn (see cat. no. 67), but his colors are clearer, his rhythms bolder. His figures are intimately involved with one another, unlike the coolly isolated and detached figures painted by Rukn al-Dīn. Lūphā's women are unmistakable. High-breasted and with cascading side curls, they have long, slender arms bent at sharp angles. For a closely comparable picture, see Khandalavala, Chandra, and Chandra, pp. 51–52, no. 96, fig. 75.

This leaf pictures a simpler version of the famous dream vision of the king of Bikaner painted about 1650 by ʿAlī Riẓā, a master from Delhi. (For another interpretation of this latter artist's background, see *Indian Heritage*, p. 42, no. 55.) ʿAlī Riẓā's portrait of Lakṣmī-Nārāyaṇa (Khandalavala, Chandra, and Chandra, pp. 48–49, no. 83, pl. E) is stylistically identical to painting from the imperial workshop under Shāh Jahān (r. 1628–58) except for its hotter palette, a characteristic Lūphā inherits. The theme became standard in Bikaner painting. An example by the artist Rashīd dated 1699 is published in Goetz 1950, fig. 79.

See catalogue number 111 for an aniconic representation of Lakṣmī-Nārāyaṇa.

❀ 67 ❀

Leaf from a *Rasikapriyā* series

Attributed to Rukn al-Dīn

BIKANER, LATE 17TH CENTURY

Image 8¾ × 5½ in. (222 × 140 mm); sheet 10⅞ × 7¾ in. (277 × 197 mm)

A maid encourages Rādhā to join Kṛṣṇa as he waits alone

Rādhā sits on a cool white terrace as her maid tells her of the virtues of her lover, Kṛṣṇa, who stands in the lower left. A stairway leads up to the terrace, but Kṛṣṇa waits for a sign of approval. A bed awaits their union. A dark forest is in the background under a cloudy sky of brooding gray. The beautiful black border is decorated with tiny stylized gold clouds.

This miniature has been remounted, obscuring the inscription it probably carries on its back. It is clearly the work of Rukn al-Dīn who, after ʿAlī Riẓā, was the most influential Bikaner painter of the late seventeenth century. The subdued, even smoky palette is typical of his style, as are the meticulous, refined line and the pronouncedly pointed noses of the figures. Also characteristic of Rukn al-Dīn is the distinctive manner in which the maid's transparent lower overgarment catches on the fabric it covers and ripples from her waist to her feet. Rukn al-Dīn was active from about the 1660s to the 1690s. A Muslim, he painted Hindu themes for a Hindu patron in a style derived from the Mughal idiom, a testament to the pluralistic character of Indian culture. Catalogue number 48 is another *Rasikapriyā* illustration by another Muslim painter who served a Hindu patron.

For other examples of this artist's work, several of them dated, see Khandalavala, Chandra, and Chandra, pp. 48, 50–51, nos. 85, 86, 89, 92; Goetz 1950, figs. 78, 83; Welch and Beach, p. 70, ill., and pp. 119–20, no. 23; and S. C. Welch 1973, p. 64, no. 32.

❀ 68 ❀

Leaf number 13 from a *Bhāgavata Purāṇa* series

BIKANER, ca. 1700–1710

Image 8 3/8 × 12 in. (213 × 305 mm); sheet 11 7/8 × 14 7/8 in. (302 × 379 mm)

The naming ceremonies of Kṛṣṇa and Balarāma

Garga, the family priest of Kṛṣṇa's clan, comes from Mathura to perform secretly the naming ceremonies of Kṛṣṇa and his brother, Balarāma. He approaches Vraja from the right, converses with Nanda, Kṛṣṇa's foster father (left), while the boys stand nearby, and then performs the rites (above) while the boys' mothers converse in a pavilion (upper left). All the events are presented continuously in a cool green landscape. High-towered Mathura is on the far right, separated from the rest of the composition by the silvery Jamuna River flowing through the picture in a steep diagonal from right to left. Another settlement is in the upper right behind a rocky hill and a line of trees, perhaps intended to represent Vṛndāvana and Govardhana (see cat. nos. 73 and 93). The rocks and the landscape in the lower right look like extrusions that have hardened on contact with the air. Beautifully patterned conventionalized trees fill the landscape, their trunks swelling and twisting gently. Still evident here is the sense of refinement derived from the Mughal style, but the composition has become conceptual rather than descriptive.

It is curious that Kṛṣṇa, shown twice, is represented as fair rather than his typical blue. This is not the case in other leaves from this series I have seen.

The leaf is numbered 13 both front and back. On the verso is a Hindi summary of the events of *Bhāgavata Purāṇa* 10.8.1–20. There is also the number 53 and the Bikaner collection stamp.

This series is dispersed, but it seems to have been large. It may have been painted over several years. Some illustrations appear to be late seventeenth century in date while others, like this one, are early eighteenth. Other examples are in the J. P. Goenka Collection, Bombay; the Collection of Edwin Binney, 3rd, San Diego; the Paul Walter Collection, New York (by the same artist as the leaf reproduced here); the John Kenneth Galbraith Collection, Cambridge, Massachusetts (also by the same hand); and several public and private collections. See Binney 1979, pp. 82–83, no. 24; Pal 1978, pp. 96–97, no. 25; and Welch and Beach, p. 75, ill., and p. 120, no. 29.

13

❀ 69 ❀

Group portrait

BIKANER, ca. 1715

Image 8³/₈ × 5⁷/₈ in. (213 × 149 mm); sheet 13¹/₂ × 9¹/₈ in. (343 × 232 mm)

Rājā Sujāna Siṅgha and Prince Zorāvara Siṅgha of Bikaner meeting with Devakīnandan, a Vaiṣṇava holy man

The holy man, identified by the inscription above, sits cross-legged on a floral-patterned carpet. He wears the sacred thread, rich jewels, and a lower garment and shawl of mustard yellow. His hair is pulled back and gathered neatly in a bun. His right hand is upraised in a gesture of benediction, his left holds a manuscript. A small water vessel, two manuscripts resting on their cloth wrapper, and a box of *pāna* (a mildly narcotic digestive) are before him. To the right, kneeling on a large light carpet, are Rājā Sujāna Siṅgha of Bikaner (b. 1690; r. 1700–1735) and his son Prince Zorāvara Siṅgha (b. 1703; r. 1736–46). Both are richly dressed and heavily jeweled. Sujāna Siṅgha wears a deep green robe covered with gold flowers and a matching turban. His thick sash is white with a gold border. He rests his folded hands on a shield. Zorāvara Siṅgha is dressed like his father, except that his robe is solid orange and his jewels are more elaborate. The trio is sheltered by an intricately decorated, domed marble pavilion supported by four lotus pillars. Trees flank the scene. Flowering shrubs are in the background. The sky is green with patches of blue near the top. Birds fly in the distance.

The top recto bears a Hindi inscription reading *gosvāmi śrī chote raghunāthajī ke putra śrī devakīnandanajī mahārāja kī chabi āge bīkānera ke rājā sujāna siṃhajī kuvara zorāvara siṃhajī*, which translates, "Portrait of Śrī Devakīnandana-jī Mahārāja, son of Gosvāmi Śrī Chote Raghunātha-jī, faced by Rājā Sujāna Siṅgha-jī and Prince Zorāvara Siṅgha-jī of Bikaner." Though apparently accurate, the inscription follows neither the form nor the placement typical of contemporary Bikaner inscriptions and was probably added later. On the reverse a short caption identifies Sujāna Siṅgha, and another hand has added an inspection date of the fourteenth day of the light half of the month Śrāvaṇa [July-August] Vikrama saṃvat 1805 [A.D. 1748].

Sujāna Siṅgha left immediately for imperial Mughal service in the Deccan following his accession to the throne of Bikaner in 1700 at the age of ten. He stayed away for a full decade, returning to an unsettled and difficult political situation threatened by both internal and external forces. His own son Zorāvara Siṅgha rebelled and had Sujāna Siṅgha's favorite advisor murdered, though father and son eventually reconciled. Sujāna Siṅgha died in 1735 while on a mission to restore peace between two feuding nobles. He was succeeded by his son, who continued the struggles of their house against Jodhpur, Bikaner's traditional enemy. He, too, faced serious internal threats, dying, perhaps of poison, in 1746 while returning from an expedition to secure a border area of the state.

This picture is the earliest-known portrait of Zorāvara Siṅgha. Stylistically it indicates the direction Bikaner painting was to take in the eighteenth century. Though it never lost its Mughal sense of refinement (see cat. nos. 66 and 67), Bikaner painting became more flat and abstract, taking on a more Rājasthānī character as the century progressed.

This portrait is stylistically similar to a slightly earlier *Rāgamālā* series, two leaves of which are in the Earnest C. and Jane Werner Watson Collection, now in the Elvehjem Art Center, Madison, Wisconsin; see Chandra 1971, p. 108, nos. 176, 177. For other portraits of Sujāna Siṅgha, see Goetz 1950, fig. 84; and Gangoly, pl. XXIIA. For later portraits of Zorāvara Siṅgha, see Goetz 1950, fig. 88; W. G. Archer 1960, pl. 54; and Topsfield 1980, p. 39, no. 20.

॥ गोस्वामिश्री छोटे रघुनाथजी के पुत्र श्री देवकीनंदन जी महाराज की ॥
॥ छबि म्हाराजश्री कानेरके राजा सुजानसिंहजी कुवर जोरावरसिंहजी ॥

❀ 70 ❀

Illustration of an unidentified story

KISHANGARH, ca. 1740

Image 12 × 9 in. (305 × 229 mm); sheet 14 × 11 in. (356 × 280 mm)

An Afghan servant shames his masters in front of a king

A king and his four sons sit behind a screen watching a curious scene in the courtyard below. A huge Afghan with a bristling mustache points belligerently at two men identified by Hindi and Persian inscriptions on the base of the wall above their heads as Kapūra and Lāū. Attendants flank the group, and another in the right middle ground makes a gesture of supplication toward the king. They, too, are named, in inscriptions above or near their heads.

Inscriptions on the reverse (see Appendix, p. 254) are of some help in explaining the story, but certain details are still obscure. A short Hindi caption is followed by a Persian text in clear *nastaʿlīq* script. The caption reads *syāha jahām bādasyāha*, thus identifying the king as "the emperor Shāh Jahān [r. 1628–58]." As the story below goes, two men named Kapūra and Lāū had an Afghan servant who frightened them. The king commanded them to come to court; he spread rich gifts before them, ordered a tray of food containing the cooked head of a lamb (an Afghani delicacy), and summoned the Afghan servant to fan away the flies while his masters ate. Instead, the greedy Afghan snatched away the gifts—a bag of a thousand rupees, a string of pearls, and a golden sash, which he wrapped around his head—then pulled the food over to himself and began to eat, ignoring the protestations of the unhappy Kapūra and Lāū. Thus the greedy Afghan revealed his character before the king and his sons, but to what end the story does not report.

As this picture suggests both thematically and stylistically, the Kishangarh style of the eighteenth century emerges directly from the Mughal idiom. The thinly applied paint, fine line, and subdued, coordinated palette of this leaf are very close to early-eighteenth-century Mughal painting (see cat. no. 29), and the stylized features of the attendants anticipate the exaggerations and distortions of human form that characterize later painting in Kishangarh.

For stylistically comparable works that show the close relationship of Kishangarh and Mughal painting, see Dickinson and Khandalavala, pls. II and VII, both of which share a similarly chalky palette. See also Chandra 1971, pp. 96–97, no. 158. For other Kishangarh examples of curious subject matter from about the same time, see S. C. Welch 1973, pp. 57–58, no. 28; and S. C. Welch 1976, p. 118, no. 66.

❀ 71 ❀

Portrait

KISHANGARH, MID-18TH CENTURY

Image 6½ × 10⅛ in. (166 × 258 mm); sheet 9½ × 13 in. (242 × 331 mm)

Ānanda Siṅgha and Joṣī Śyāma

This double portrait depicts a confrontation between two men who face each other on a terrace. Ānanda Siṅgha, right, a fat man in white holding nothing but prayer beads, seems to be challenging his companion, Jośī Śyāma, who is heavily armed. The heads of two men carrying spears are at the far left. A camel runs free on the horizon.

The details of this incident are obscure, but we can still enjoy the vivid depiction of the two men. Jośī Śyāma bristles with weapons, each one elaborately patterned with gold and rich color. He draws back from Ānanda Siṅgha, his heavy mustache quivering with indignation. Ānanda Siṅgha has set down his black shield and sword, but he exudes an air of confidence and authority. Whatever the situation, he is clearly the master. The running camel and the supercilious spear carriers add a note of quiet humor to the picture.

The back bears identifying inscriptions. One reads, *bhāṭī rāvalota aṇada sigha jīḥ/betau bhāṭī hara nātha jī rau. 1.* (Bhāṭī Rāvalota Ānanda Siṅgha-jī, the son of Bhāṭī Hara Nātha-jī. 1.); the other, *josī syāma jī mana malukaḥ/tana pracaṇda mahābhuja daṇḍa balabaḍaḥ.* This second inscription is difficult to translate exactly, but roughly describes Jośī Śyāma as a man of powerful body and great, strong arms.

The palette and the handling of the faces and the running camel relate this picture to a slightly larger scene of women in a landscape in the Earnest C. and Jane Werner Watson Collection, now in the Elvehjem Art Center, Madison, Wisconsin; see Chandra 1971, pp. 97–98, no. 160. Another picture very close in style which shows the court at worship includes a portly figure in white standing at the far right in the foreground, who is certainly Ānanda Siṅgha; see Dickinson and Khandalavala, p. 18, fig. 4. The two pictures may be by the same artist, along with the tinted drawing reproduced in the same publication as pl. XVI.

❀ 72 ❀

Idealized study

KISHANGARH, ca. MID-18TH CENTURY

Image 11⅞ × 9 in. (302 × 229 mm)

Head of a woman

This large profile study of a woman is broadly rendered and shaded with washes. It is very lightly tinted, the color restricted to the woman's lips, her jewels, and the flowers in her hair. The stylized "Kishangarh" eye is very apparent. Actually, this elongated eye-type is common in many styles of Indian painting, though it is especially exaggerated in the Kishangarh idiom from the mid-eighteenth century on (see cat. nos. 73–75). The rather strong profile of this woman is softened by the subtle shading and the flowing hair that cascades from under an elaborate bun. The relaxed line gives a feeling of naturalism rare in the painting of Kishangarh.

This drawing is based ultimately on Mughal prototypes. Such idealized portrait heads of women were common in eighteenth-century Mughal painting. Kishangarh painting, strongly dependent on the Mughal style, also borrowed Mughal themes and motifs.

This picture is published in McInerney, p. 65, no. 27. It is by the same artist as a similar but less freely drawn portrait in a private collection. A famous later portrait of a woman, which is much more heavily stylized than this example, is published in Dickinson and Khandalavala, pl. IV. For a Mughal treatment of a similar subject, see Mehta, p. 88, pl. 36, who publishes it as the work of the seventeenth-century Mughal artist Govardhana (see cat. no. 22), but it is by an eighteenth-century painter of the same name. The Kishangarh picture avoids the heaviness of the Mughal version.

❀ 73 ❀

Kṛṣṇa raises Mount Govardhana as Indra acknowledges his power

KISHANGARH, ca. MID-18TH CENTURY

Sheet 11 5/8 × 7 5/8 in. (295 × 193 mm)

The ruling family of Kishangarh were ardent worshipers of Kṛṣṇa, and his life was by far the favorite theme for painters in the state. Here is a subject that has been painted countless times in India, the raising of Mount Govardhana to protect the inhabitants of Vraja from torrential rains unleashed by a jealous Indra. The King of the Gods is angry because Kṛṣṇa has persuaded his companions to worship the mountain instead of making their traditional offerings to Indra (see cat. no. 93). But, of course, no one can defeat the blue god, and he elegantly and effortlessly raises the mountain into the stormy sky. Cowherd men and women crowd around to pay him homage as an astonished Indra kneels humbly at his feet, his royal regalia and weapons before him. In the upper right is Indra's vehicle, a great white elephant. Kṛṣṇa and Rādhā are nimbated. As is usually the case, they are rendered in a far more stylized manner than the other figures.

Deep rich colors and gold glow against the dark landscape. The broadly washed ground and hills recall the modeling technique used in catalogue number 72.

There is a version of the same subject (but lacking Indra) in the Bharat Kala Bhavan, Banaras (Varanasi), by the Kishangarh master painter Nihāla Canda.

❀ 74 ❀

Kṛṣṇa, Rādhā, and maids on a terrace

KISHANGARH, ca. 1775

Image 12⅝ × 9½ in. (320 × 241 mm); sheet 15½ × 11⅜ in. (394 × 289 mm)

Kṛṣṇa, nimbated, pale blue, and wearing a long white garment, stands holding a flower while Rādhā shyly approaches him. She pulls her veil forward as if to shelter her face from her lover's gaze, but still she moves toward him. Two maids whisper behind her. They lack the extreme stylization and attenuation of the lovers. The four are framed by two masses of foliage. Kṛṣṇa's horse stands half-hidden in the bushes to the left. A lotus lake is in the foreground. The modeled green background is dotted with shrines, a lake, a lavish palace, and a walled city. The somber sky is filled with huge dark clouds. The intense greens of this picture are typical of the Kishangarh palette (see cat. nos. 71, 73, 75).

Here Kṛṣṇa is as much elegant prince as divine hero. Earlier in the century, a Kishangarh prince named Sāvanta Siṅgha lived in the land of Kṛṣṇa's youth and became a famous devotional poet under the name of Nāgarī Dāsa. He was less successful as a ruler; when his father died in 1748, a brother seized part of the state, and Sāvanta Siṅgha ruled haphazardly at best until 1764, spending most of his time away from the state. Himself trained as a painter, he infused the painting of his reign with a profound spirit of devotion and exalted spirituality (see cat. no. 73). If the religious fervor of earlier times has lessened in this picture, it still charms with its very human treatment of the theme of divine love. It is published in Colnaghi, p. 64, no. 73, and p. 102, ill.

❀ 75 ❀

An album page

KISHANGARH, ca. 1780

Image 7¾ × 6 in. (198 × 153 mm); sheet 10½ × 8½ in. (267 × 217 mm)

A nimbated ascetic worships at a Śiva shrine

Kishangarh painting is overwhelmingly concerned with Viṣṇu, and scenes associated with Śiva are unusual. Here an ash-smeared ascetic sits cross-legged on a tiger skin worshiping the phallic emblem of the god Śiva. The shrine consists of a low platform under a tree. The trident, Śiva's symbol, and the flag that traditionally marks a holy place are among the tree's branches. A small pool is in the foreground. Three followers attend the ascetic, whose eyes are fixed unwaveringly on the object of his veneration. His devotion is so intense that his halo sends out rays of gold. A simple hut of bamboo and thatch is on the right. Dense foliage in the middle ground parts to reveal distant hills, a river, and a city. Behind the city gate the cloudy sky glows with gold and orange. The pink margins have triple leaf patterns.

For a related scene of a Vaiṣṇava holy man, see Pal 1976, no. 43.

❀ 76 ❀

Hunting scene

Signed(?) by Gopāla

JAIPUR, ca. 1790

Image 18⅞ × 27¾ in. (480 × 705 mm); sheet 21 × 28 in. (533 × 711 mm)

A maharaja on a tiger hunt

A king and his courtiers hunt tiger in a softly rolling landscape of green hills. The style is broad and flat, relying for its effect on strong outline and superb patterning. The tiger has been shot, but the violence of its injuries is lost in the elegant statement of appliquéd stripes and pinwheel wounds. The horses' manes are patterned in a formal design, the locks of hair arranged like curving dagger blades. Two horses in the foreground are dappled with densely placed polka dots. The elephant is splendidly arrayed in fabric and gold trappings. So richly worked are its gold ornaments that they give the illusion of being in high relief though they are raised only barely above the painted surface. Note especially the bell that swings in an arc that follows the curves of the back cinch of the harness and the tail. The quiet landscape behind the hunt is delightful. Minuscule animals, mostly antelope and black buck, who welcome the death of a tiger, pack the distant hills. At the far right an impossibly large camel steps out of a city gate.

There are two inscriptions in gold, one identifying the prince and the other the artist. Unfortunately, the one at the top begins *mahārājā* and then is too abraded to tell us who he is, though it is clear enough a few words later to reveal that he hunts from the elephant named Maṅgalagaja. The inscription identifying the artist has fared better. Placed humbly under the right rear foot of the king's elephant, suggesting that it may be an actual signature, it reads *sabī likhī gopāla catera* (a portrait painted by Gopāla the artist).

❀ 77 ❀

Erotic study

JAIPUR, ca. 1800

Image 14⅞ × 21 in. (378 × 534 mm); sheet 17¾ × 24 in. (452 × 610 mm)

Two lovers

Two lovers sit facing each other on a terrace, the man on the right, the woman on the left. The man touches the breasts of his companion. He wears white garments and a red cap. Her clothing is white, bright blue, and red with gold trim. Her blouse is nearly transparent. Its bottom hem is slightly raised, exposing the join of lower breast and body. The lovers rest against a large bolster. Conventionally arranged flowers are visible beyond the terrace railing. The background is pale blue.

As is typical in Indian erotic paintings, the figures are distant and withdrawn. They intersect physically, but do not interact emotionally. This is a symbolic statement of sexual activity, not a literal description.

The picture is a highly formalized expression of late-eighteenth-century Jaipur painting. Its cool color and preference for broadly stated forms relate it to the famous Jaipur drawings formerly in the Collection of Ananda K. Coomaraswamy (now in the Metropolitan Museum of Art, New York) and to a splendid, slightly earlier "Europeanized" painting of Śiva and Pārvatī in the Collection of Edwin Binney, 3rd, San Diego. See Coomaraswamy 1916, vol. 2, pls. IX and X; Lee, p. 52, no. 49, and p. 53, ill.; and Archer and Binney, p. 49, no. 38. The women's profiles in Coomaraswamy, pl. X, the Binney picture, and this painting are closely comparable.

❀ 78 ❀

Portrait

JAIPUR, ca. 1830–35

Image 18¼ × 21⅝ in. (464 × 549 mm); sheet 20⅛ × 23¼ in. (511 × 591 mm)

Mahārājā Jaya Siṅgha of Jaipur receives Mahārāṇā Javāna Siṅgha of Mewar

The raja of Jaipur and the rana of Mewar sit talking within a tented enclosure hung with panels of red velvet painted with gold designs. The rulers are nimbated and are attended by kneeling retainers arranged symmetrically on a white ground cloth. The beautiful borders of flowers and insects at the sides are ingeniously incorporated into the structure of the tent by continuing the pattern in the tent top. Ropes in the upper corners secure the structure.

The slight boy-king and his ponderous guest are surrounded by the trappings of royal might, but in fact both their states had submitted to British power in 1818. Jaya Siṅgha III was his dissolute father's posthumous heir, becoming the ruler of Jaipur on his birth in 1819. His mother ruled as regent until her death in 1833. The unfortunate Jaya Siṅgha was only sixteen when he died two years later, probably of poison. Javāṇa Siṅgha of Mewar (r. 1828–38), after an upright and promising youth, did not distinguish himself during his reign. He turned to debauchery in the face of corruption, confusion, and the erosion of princely power by the British.

Nineteenth-century Jaipur painting is very common but is usually flat and uninteresting, seldom approaching the excellent quality of this double portrait. For typical Jaipur work of the period, see Ebeling, pp. 226–28. Paintings of this type were produced in large numbers and sold in many parts of north India. Though court painting in Jaipur seems to have resisted a general decline in quality, the same was not true in Mewar at this time. Works produced in the reign of Javāṇa Siṅgha are uniformly dreary, their colors dead and their subjects dull and repetitious; see Topsfield 1980, pp. 149–59, nos. 233–263.

Closely similar gold and velvet tent panels from the princely textile collection of Jaipur are now in the Victoria and Albert Museum, London; the Calico Museum, Ahmedabad; the Metropolitan Museum of Art, New York; and private collections in New York. These panels are virtually identical to the ones pictured here; see *Indian Heritage*, p. 83, no. 208, and p. 146, ill.

❀ 79 ❀

Processional scene

Attributed to Govinda

ALWAR, LATE 18TH–EARLY 19TH CENTURY

Image 19¾ × 27¾ in. (502 × 706 mm); sheet 21 × 29 in. (534 × 738 mm)

Bakhtāwar Siṅgha of Alwar

The formal composition is densely textured. The prince rides an elaborately outfitted elephant. Around them are nobles and retainers, most of whom are on horseback. Two in the upper left ride camels depicted with heads pulled back and long necks thrust forward, a typical convention of the period. Above, bearers carry an empty palanquin, while behind them is a European-style carriage with greenish wheels and a red plush interior. The picture is an interesting blend of observation and abstraction, of description and convention.

This large and impressive processional is related to catalogue number 76 in both style and scale, revealing the powerful influence of Jaipur painting in north India in the late eighteenth and nineteenth centuries. Indeed, it is possible that such pictures were produced by itinerant artists trained in Jaipur but serving patrons elsewhere. It is also possible that the picture could have been painted in Jaipur, where Bakhtāwar Siṅgha spent time, part guest and part prisoner.

Bakhtāwar Siṅgha (r. 1791–1815) came to the throne at the age of twelve. Previously he had chosen a sword and shield from toys spread out before the noble youth of the state, thus indicating that he was worthy to succeed the current ruler, who had no sons of his own. Bakhtāwar Siṅgha allied himself with the British to counter the threats of his Indian foes. He became unhinged near the end of his reign, expressing his madness in extreme acts of cruelty toward Muslims. When he died his chief wife burned herself on his pyre. The site is marked by a cenotaph near Alwar Palace. His successor distinguished himself as a patron of literature and painting, though the heavily decorated style he preferred is distant from the cool restraint and elegance of this picture.

The picture is not inscribed, but similar large studies in other private collections, including one in the Collection of Edwin Binney, 3rd, San Diego, bear identifying captions and ascriptions to Govinda. A posthumous portrait of Bakhtāwar Siṅgha is in the British Library (Add. 27254, fol. 92). It is an illustration in a history of North Indian princely families completed in 1830 by Colonel James Skinner. The portraits may have been added later; see Losty 1982, p. 149, ill., and pp. 152–53, no. 136.

❀ 80 ❀ 81 ❀

Two processional scenes

Ascribed to Pyāra Canda of Mandasor

SITAMAU, DATED V.S. 1904/A.D. 1847

80. Mahārājā Rāja Siṅgha in procession

Image 11¾ × 16⅝ in. (299 × 422 mm); sheet 13¾ × 18½ in. (349 × 470 mm)

The hilly landscape is green. In the upper left a tiger kills a black buck. The ruler, Rāja Siṅgha, rides an elephant, surrounded by the trappings of state. Prince Bhavānī Siṅgha, identified by inscription as age eleven, rides ahead on horseback. Other inscriptions identify the court retainers and the elephant Bakhtāwar Gaja.

In the top margin is written *saṃvat 1904 mītī āsojī dasarāve najara hucha* (This was a gift on the date of Daśaharā [It is the custom to present gifts on the occasion of Daśaharā.] in the month of Āsoja [September-October] of the [Vikrama] year 1904 [A.D. 1847]). This is followed by an inscription reading *mahārāja dharāja mahārāja śrī rāja siṅgha jī umara barasa 59* (Mahārājā Dhīrāja Mahārājā Śrī Rāja Siṅgha-jī at the age of 59 years). In the lower left is written *musavara pyāra canda mandasora bāsī* ([By] the painter Pyāra Canda, a resident of Mandasor). On the verso are four verses in praise of the king. An abraded inscription dated [V.S.] 19—— is almost invisible below.

81. Prince Ratana Siṅgha in procession

Image 11½ × 16 in. (292 × 406 mm); sheet 12⅞ × 17¾ in. (328 × 451 mm)

The composition is similar to that of catalogue number 80 except that the subject is Prince Ratana Siṅgha. Though also signed by Pyāra Canda and dated 1847, this picture is more freely rendered than the previous one. Instead of the conventional landscape at the horizon, it has darkly coiled clouds with serpentine bolts of lightning.

The inscriptions are similar. This picture, too, was a Daśaharā gift in V.S. 1904. Prince Ratana Siṅgha is thirty-nine. He apparently predeceased his father, who died in 1885 at the extraordinary age of ninety-seven.

On the verso, in a heavier hand than on the back of catalogue number 80, are four Hindi verses written by one Uddhava Dāsa in V.S. 1909/A.D. 1852 in praise of the prince (see Appendix, p. 254). They are followed by another verse in a third hand. This is identified as by Svarūpa Dāsa.

These pictures belong to a series that chronicles the court life of the small state of Sitamau in what is now Madhya Pradesh. Though the pictures are very late, they are of good quality. The painter Pyāra Canda of Mandasor avoided European influence to produce pictures that continue to embody the brilliant color and abstract statement of traditional Indian styles. His small group of pictures from Sitamau, dated examples of which range from 1831 to 1847, compare stylistically with other nineteenth-century paintings (see cat. no. 64) that held out against the English watercolor style that was ultimately to supplant Indian styles under colonial political and social pressures.

A painting in a private collection with the same date as these two pictures shows the painter Pyāra Canda sketching the ruler of Sitamau. The inscriptions on these pictures identify the artist as from the ancient and archaeologically significant city of Mandasor, only a little way from the state of Sitamau where he worked. Most Indian painters are anonymous, and it is unusual to have both a name and a city of origin. The identification of these pictures with Sitamau was made by Robert Skelton; see Topsfield 1981a, pp. 170–71, fig. 183. For other pictures from this group, see Spink & Son 1976, pp. 25–27, nos. 108–112.

❀ 82 ❀ 83 ❀

Two folios from an album of architectural studies prepared for Robert Home by Shaikh Laṭīf of Agra

COMPANY STYLE AT AGRA, ca. 1820–34

82. Inlaid panels from the frame of the cenotaph screen in the Taj Mahal

Sheet 13⅞ × 5⅛ in. (353 × 130 mm);
14 × 5 in. (356 × 127 mm);
14⅛ × 5¼ in. (359 × 133 mm)

Laṭīf's rendering of these three flowering-plant inlays captures precisely the luminous beauty of marble and colored stones. The panels, included on a list of drawings executed for Robert Home, are cited as part of a group of "Flowers on the Framework of the Screen—outside" and are numbered 10–12 from the left.

83. A portion of the ornamentalized crenellated band around the top of the cenotaph screen in the Taj Mahal

Image 10¼ × 18⅜ in. (260 × 468 mm);
sheet 19⅝ × 25⅞ in. (498 × 658 mm)

The cool blue ground and elegantly shaded arabesque forms of this decorative study must have appealed strongly to a patron like Robert Home whose tastes were formed in the atmosphere of late-eighteenth-century Britain. The inlaid flowers are especially well rendered. Laṭīf communicates something of the extraordinary skill of the craftsmen who built and adorned the Taj for Shāh Jahān in the seventeenth century. This study is numbered 18 and described on the list as "Carved ornament around the top of the Screen with the Flowers on the outside."

The album from which these leaves have been removed includes a sheet headed "List of Drawings for Mr. Home executed by Shekh Latif of Agra." A note attached to the leather and marbled-paper binding indicates that the album was once the property of the nineteenth-century surgeon and scholar T. H. Hendley.

Though the British came to India primarily for commercial reasons, they marveled at the exotic sights of this ancient land. Foreign residents and travelers bought great quantities of literary and mythological illustrations, portraits, architectural and landscape views, and ethnological, zoological, and botanical studies. At first these generally were rendered in late Mughal idioms, but as British control and influence increased, Indian painters changed their styles to conform with prevailing European standards. A leading Agra painter of the first half of the nineteenth century, Shaikh Laṭīf seems to have mastered English watercolor techniques of the day without abandoning entirely the penetrating clarity and refined draftsmanship of late Mughal painting. His work is thus of greater interest than that of his less gifted contemporaries. He prepared the album from which these two studies come for Robert Home (1752–1834), an English artist who came to India in 1791 and stayed until his death. During his long Indian career Home chronicled the Mysore campaigns against Tipu Sultan, painted portraits of wealthy Calcuttans, and served as painter to the court of Lucknow.

Most Indian painters, even those of the nineteenth century, are anonymous, but we are fortunate in knowing some interesting details of Shaikh Laṭīf's life. In about 1820–22 he prepared an architectural album for John Bax (1793–1863) of the Bombay Civil Service which Bax presented to the India Office on September 9, 1824. In 1835 the celebrated traveler Fanny Parks visited Laṭīf and bought from him "a large collection" of pictures at prices ranging from "three to forty rupees each." Parks used engravings of two of these studies as illustrations for her famous travel book; see Parks, vol. 1, pp. 349, 375, 418, and pls. following pp. 348 and 374. It is to her keen interest in detail that we owe the knowledge that Laṭīf was the architect of the tomb of Colonel Hessing at Agra, a work she describes as being "in excellent taste," and that he was also an inlayer of "marble with precious stones, after the style of the work in the Taj." It is perhaps for the latter reason that his studies of inlay work, of which these leaves are excellent examples, are rendered so beautifully.

For the Bax album in the India Office Library, see M. Archer 1972, pp. 181–85, no. 142, pls. 65–67. There is a chapter on Home in M. Archer 1979, pp. 299–332. See also Archer and Lightbown, nos. 14, 40, 41, 68.

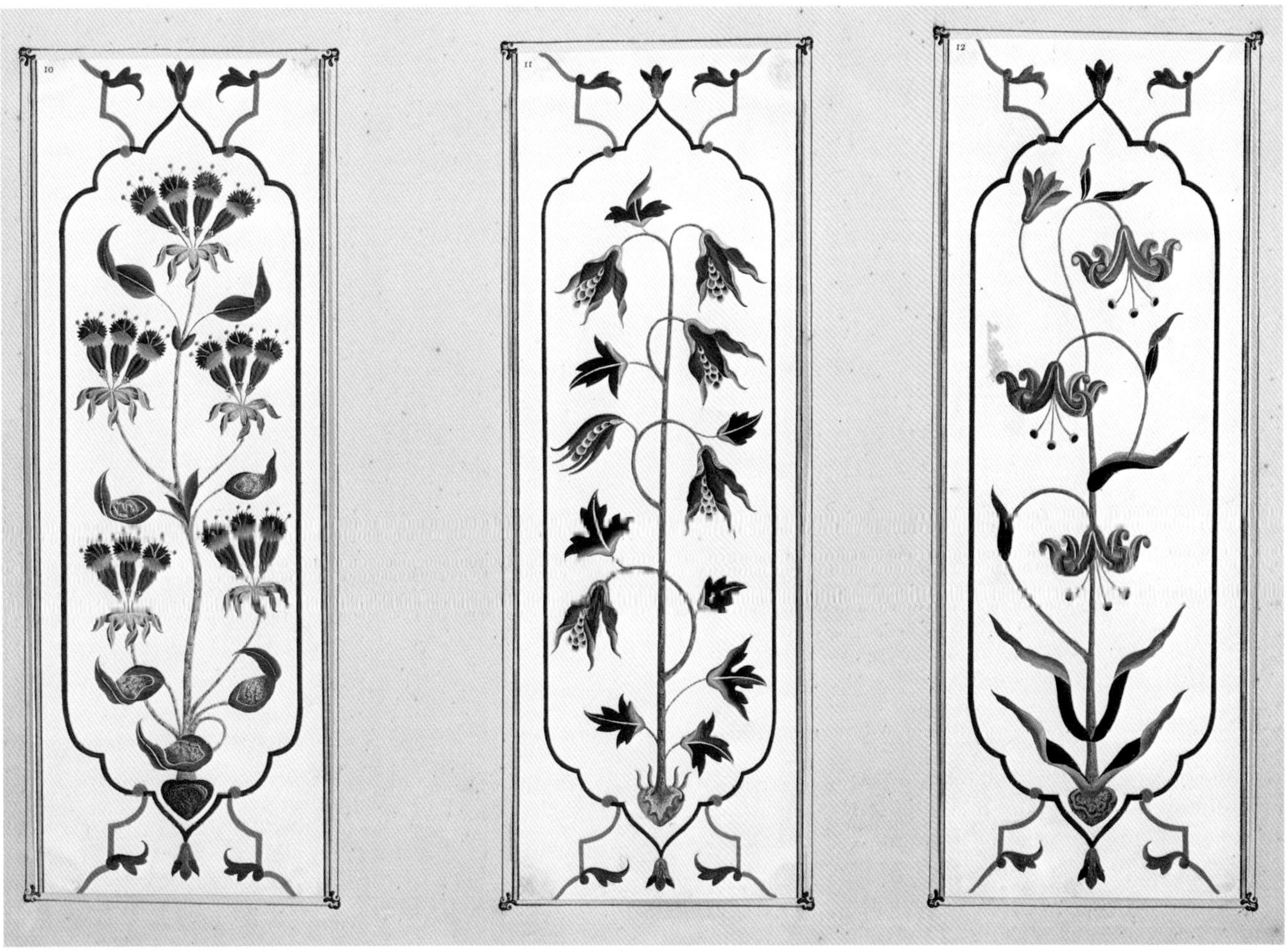
10
11
12

❀ 84 ❀

Genre scene

NORTH INDIA (PROBABLY PUNJAB PLAINS), COMPANY STYLE, 19TH CENTURY

Image 7¾ × 11 in. (197 × 279 mm); sheet 9 × 12⅜ in. (229 × 314 mm)

Pottery makers in a village courtyard

This delightful genre scene shows potters at work in a crowded courtyard. A man in the middle left prepares clay while farther back a woman near the kiln holds a pot. Her child stands behind her, his arms around her. At the right a man approaches with a leather bag of water to fill the large vessel in front of him. Finished pots tower behind the busy workers. The bustle of village life is everywhere. A child crawls through the courtyard and fat dogs wander at will. A mare suckles her colt in the upper right. In the center foreground a weary traveler squats on the ground with a water pipe, while a more fortunate smoker sits comfortably on a nearby cot. More travelers arrive at the lower right. Above these an old man lies sick in bed but is still able to take a long drag from his pipe. At the foot of his cot a bearded man eats intently, completely oblivious to the action around him. A ram is tethered at the left. Nearby a hen watches over her chicks and a goat rears up to eat tender tree leaves. A water tank and a village are in the distance under a blue sky filled with billowing clouds. The yellow border is decorated with flowers.

Though genre painting was popular in India as early as the beginning of the seventeenth century, the advent of the British created a new market for scenes of Indian workers pursuing their trades. Few of these pictures are as amusing and interesting as this example, being for the most part dull and repetitious. The style and costumes of this painting suggest that it was painted in the Punjab Plains, possibly in Lahore, by an artist whose work derives from the nineteenth-century Kangra idiom of the Hill schools (see cat. nos. 124–126). The Sikh kingdom centered in Lahore and Amritsar absorbed many Hill states in the early nineteenth century before itself falling under British control in 1849.

For stylistically and thematically similar works, see Chandra 1971, pp. 50–51, nos. 79, 80; Czuma, no. 100; and Falk and Archer, p. 137, no. 238, and p. 435, ill.

❀ 85 ❀

Leaf number 33 from a *Bhāgavata Purāṇa* series

NEPAL, ca. 1775

Image 12¾ × 19¼ in. (324 × 489 mm); sheet 14⅜ × 20¾ in. (365 × 527 mm)

The story of Pradyumna's birth

Pradyumna was a son of Kṛṣṇa and an incarnation of the god of love. When he was six days old a demon kidnapped him and threw him into the sea, where he was swallowed by a big fish. Fishermen netted the creature and took him to the demon as a gift. When the fish was cut open cooks found the baby and entrusted it to Māyāvatī, the rice and legume chef in the demon's kitchen and the incarnation of the goddess of love. When he grew up she explained his birth and kidnapping to him, whereupon he killed the demon, married Māyāvatī, and returned home.

This illustration shows Pradyumna, blue like his father, being carried from the kitchen (right) and presented to Māyāvatī (center), and Māyāvatī in the court of the demon (left). The leaf bears the number 33 at the top and a brief summary of the story. For the standard version of the tale, see *Bhāgavata Purāṇa* 10.55.1–40.

The demonic palace is elaborate and multistoried. The upturned eaves and arched gateway are typically Nepali, but the bright colors, flat planes, and conventionalized trees may be derived from Indian painting. There is some evidence that Malwa painting (see cat. nos. 45 and 46) influenced eighteenth-century painting in Nepal, but the exact relationship between the two styles is unclear. It is true, however, that the compositions of this *Bhāgavata* are demonstrably connected to those of the famous 1686/88 *Bhāgavata* in the Malwa style, of which the first volume is dispersed and the second volume is in the Sri Gopi Krishna Kanoria Collection, Patna. It is also true that certain Nepali illustrations of the Viṣṇu story of about 1600 (University Library, Cambridge [Add. 864]) relate compositionally to the dispersed *Bhāgavata* of circa 1520–30 from the Delhi-Agra region (cat. nos. 1 and 2), so such compositional parallels could be the result of independent developments from common sources.

Other leaves from this series are in the Collection of Edwin Binney, 3rd, San Diego (see Archer and Binney, p. 10, ill., and pp. 64–65, no. 49, where the locations of many additional illustrations are given); the Paul Walter Collection, New York (Pal 1978, pp. 196–97, no. 73); and the Dr. Kenneth X. Robbins Collection, Maryland. For the other Nepali and Malwa material cited above, see Pal 1967a, p. 25, figs. 1 and 2; Krishna, p. 36; and W. G. Archer 1958, pp. 12–13, pl. 5.

❀ 86 ❀

Portrait

BASOHLI, LATE 17TH CENTURY

Image 7¼ × 6¾ in. (184 × 171 mm); sheet 8 × 7½ in. (204 × 191 mm)

Kṛpāla Pāla

Strong-featured Kṛpāla Pāla sits on a floral rug and smokes. His attending maid is tiny, an example of hierarchical perspective in which important pictorial elements are large and less important elements are small. The king wears a white robe. A four-lobed jeweled pendant hangs around his neck. He leans against a yellow bolster on a rug of pink and blue. The background is green, the margins burnt orange.

Very little is known about Kṛpāla Pāla of Basohli (r. ca. 1678–93) except that he was a patron of painting and a kindly and scholarly devotee of both Śiva and Viṣṇu. This picture bears no inscription, but Kṛpāla Pāla is easily identified from other portraits (although portraits of this ruler are rare); see W. G. Archer 1973, vol. 1, pp. 42, 374–75, vol. 2, pp. 27, 286–87.

W. G. Archer 1973, vol. 1, p. 42, vol. 2, p. 27, no. 11 (ii), also publishes a posthumous portrait of Saṅgrāma Pāla (r. 1635–ca. 1673), Kṛpāla Pāla's paternal uncle, which is very close in style and format to this portrait and may be by the same hand.

❀ 87 ❀

Leaf number 36 from a *Devī* series

BASOHLI, ca. 1660–70

Image 7⅛ × 6¾ in. (182 × 171 mm); sheet 8¾ × 8½ in. (222 × 216 mm)

Brahmā, Śiva, and Viṣṇu worship the goddess Indrākṣī

The goddess takes many forms. Here she is Indrākṣī (literally, the Indra-eyed woman). Indra, a Vedic god downgraded in later Hinduism, was lascivious. After seducing a sage's wife, he was cursed with a thousand vaginas on his body. These were eventually transformed into eyes, hence the many eyes on the goddess here, whose eyes are like Indra's. Indrākṣī is six-armed. She carries cymbals, a conch, a lutelike instrument, a double-headed drum, a lotus, and a trident. Beetle-wing cases glitter from her crown and jewels, a characteristic of Basohli painting but very rare in other Indian styles. She sits on a lotus that rises from a pool. The leaf pattern on her lower garment is suggestive of the eyes that cover her limbs. Incense rises from a small, footed burner below her left leg as Śiva pours flowers from his cupped hands. Viṣṇu stands with his hands full of flowers. Brahmā, as usual, has four heads and is also four-armed. Two hands hold flowers for offering, another carries a manuscript, and the fourth carries the water pot of a pilgrim. A beetle-wing diadem is set in Śiva's hair. The other two gods wear crowns with beetle-wing jewels. The intense colors of the figures stand out against a background of chocolate brown. Red margins surround the picture.

The number 36 is in the upper left margin, *indrākhī devī* in *ṭākarī* script in the upper right. The Sanskrit verse on the back (see Appendix, p. 254), also numbered 36, describes the gods' worship of the goddess and her attributes.

This is a leaf from an important series of goddess pictures that stand at the very beginning of the development of Basohli painting. They are flat, brilliantly colored, and truly monumental in conception. In a sense they preserve the concerns of catalogue numbers 1 and 2, but their elegant sophistication sets them apart from the direct simplicity of the earlier style. Extraordinary in their skill of execution, they suggest a significant period of prior development for the Basohli style, yet they are among the earliest pictures known in the idiom.

The series may have been very large. Examples are in Lahore; Chandigarh; New Delhi; the Los Angeles County Museum of Art; the Boston Museum of Fine Arts; the Dr. Alvin O. Bellak Collection, Philadelphia; the Polsky Collections, New York; the Kronos Collections, New York; and various other private collections. For published examples, see W. G. Archer 1973, vol. 1, pp. 33–34, vol. 2, p. 16; Aijazuddin, pp. 3–4, pls. 6, 7; Kramrisch, pp. 216–17, no. P-47; McInerney, pp. 70–71, no. 30; and *Polsky Collections*, cover and pp. 28–29, no. 18.

❀ 88 ❀

Leaf from a *Devī* series

BASOHLI, LATE 17TH CENTURY

Image 7 1/8 × 6 1/2 in. (182 × 165 mm); sheet 8 7/8 × 8 1/4 in. (226 × 210 mm)

The Goddess standing on the corpse of a man

The Goddess stands on a corpse, symbolic of the male power of the universe that is inert without the activating force of the female. Four-armed, she holds a string of prayer beads, a lutelike instrument, a conch, and a severed human head. She has three eyes, golden skin, and a radiating golden halo. Her white garments are decorated with silver. Sharp teeth protrude from the corners of her mouth and her dark hair is gathered in a topknot like that of her consort, Śiva. Both she and the corpse are marked with auspicious symbols of devotion to the lord. In a sense, the corpse is Śiva himself, and the picture recalls the Goddess animating the cosmos by stepping on her husband's body as it lies on the burning ground. The background is yellow, the margins red.

This picture is similar in style to catalogue number 87, but is a bit quieter in color and rhythm, suggesting that it is a little later in date. That it is from another series is confirmed by its slightly different size and proportions, its more elaborate marginal rulings, and the distinctive inscriptions written in a careless hand on the recto.

Similar subjects from the earlier series are cited in the preceding catalogue entry.

❀ 89 ❀

Leaf from a *Rāgamālā* series

BASOHLI, ca. 1690–95

Image 6¾ × 6⅞ in. (172 × 176 mm); sheet 8 × 8⅛ in. (204 × 207 mm)

Maṅgala, First Son of Hiṇḍola Rāga

Maṅgala, a richly jeweled prince pictured here with two attendants, is dressed in a mustard-yellow garment with a white sash and sports a gold turban. Kneeling on a blue and green floral carpet, he rests against a deep-rose bolster with black tassels. His companions kneel before him. One is clad in white and wears a red turban, the other is dressed in rose with a white turban. The background is a rich chocolate brown, a favorite color of the Basohli style. A streaked blue and white sky is at the top. The margins are deep orange.

The inscription in *ṭākarī* script at the top reads *maṅgala rāga hindole da putra* (Maṅgala, the son of Hiṇḍola *rāga*) and is followed by the number 1. The schools of the Punjab Hills followed a different iconographic and classification system for *Rāgamālās* from those of Rajasthan and the plains of north India.

The figures are boldly rendered. There is an acknowledgment of the Mughal style in the flower-spray fabric patterns and the slight muting of the colors. Like other conservative Indian painting styles, the emotionally charged and brilliantly expressive Basohli idiom is characterized by abstract and stylized forms and a lack of concern for the third dimension. Paintings of this type dominated the Hills in the late seventeenth and early eighteenth centuries. The style was practiced with local variations in many centers outside of Basohli proper.

The leaf is published in Spink & Son 1982, p. 23, no. 107, and p. 109, ill. Other leaves from the same set are in W. G. Archer 1973, vol. 1, p. 43, vol. 2, p. 28. For another Pahāṛī example of the same subject, see Ebeling, p. 273, no. 303.

❀ 90 ❀

Leaf from a *Rāgamālā* series

BASOHLI, ca. 1700

Image 6¾ × 6¼ in. (172 × 159 mm); sheet 8½ × 8 in. (216 × 204 mm)

Naṭanārāyaṇa Rāgaputra

A figure, half male and half female, stands facing the viewer. The male half, which is blue, wears a yellow lower garment and a lotus crown and carries a lotus. The female half wears an orange blouse and a red lower garment and carries a trident. She is fair skinned and wears a ring on her thumb. The figure wears necklaces of pearls. A tree grows on either side of the bisexual divinity. The background is green.

At the top are two inscriptions in *nāgarī* and *ṭākarī* scripts identifying the subject as Naṭanārāyaṇa, the son of Megha *rāga*.

This picture, which represents a combination of Viṣṇu and the Goddess, is of special iconographic interest. More typical treatments of this *rāgaputra* consist of a combination of the male forms of Viṣṇu and Śiva, or a combination of Śiva and Pārvatī. And usually Viṣṇu occupies the true left, or female, half of the figure. In his final incarnation at the destruction of the universe Viṣṇu is associated with the Goddess. For a discussion of the typical iconography of this image, see Ebeling, p. 274, where he gives references to more usual examples. For representations of Śiva in half-man/half-woman form and in combination with Viṣṇu, see Kramrisch, pp. 162–68, nos. P-3–P-8.

Most of this series is in the Colonel R. K. Tandan Collection, Secunderabad. Like this leaf, the others have suffered water damage. Luckily, here the damage is restricted largely to the red margins and only minimally affects the picture area. For other examples, see Tandan 1982, pp. 82–84, frontis, figs. 49a–s, pls. XXI–XXX; Tandan 1980; and Spink & Son 1976, pp. 32–33, nos. 149, 150.

❀ 91 ❀

Leaf number 79 from a *Gīta Govinda* series

By the painter Māṇaku

BASOHLI, DATED 1730

Sheet 6⅛ × 10¼ in. (156 × 260 mm)

Kṛṣṇa awaits Rādhā

Kṛṣṇa sits expectantly on a bed of yellow flower petals as a maid advises Rādhā to go to her waiting lover. A tree divides the blue-skinned god from his beloved and her maid. Kṛṣṇa's lower garment is orange and he wears a garland of white flowers. Rādhā wears a blouse of the same color as the petal bed, a red skirt, and a blue veil. Her clothes are patterned and edged with gold. All three figures are richly jeweled. Iridescent beetle wings flash from their ornaments. The background is green. A river is in the foreground, a band of sky at the top. The leaf has been repaired. There are a few spots of minor in-painting.

The leaf is numbered 79 on the back and bears the Sanskrit verse *Gīta Govinda* 5.12:

> Your garlands fall on Krishna's chest like
> white cranes on a dark cloud.
> Shining lightning over him, Rādhā, you
> rule in the climax of love.
> In woods on the wind-swept Jumna
> bank,
> Krishna waits in wildflower garlands.
>
> (Miller, p. 92)

The painter Māṇaku was one of a large family of Hill painters who served in many different states. His younger brother was the artist Naiṇasukha (see cat. no. 111), but their styles are very different. Māṇaku preferred a more traditional, bolder style than his brother.

The colophon of this series is obscure in meaning and has been much debated. For a general discussion of the set and references to its scattered pages, see W. G. Archer 1973, vol. 1, pp. 46–48, vol. 2, pp. 32–34. A lesser painter contributed pictures to the set, but stylistic comparison leaves no doubt that this leaf is by the superior hand of the painter Māṇaku, the only artist named in the colophon. Through careful analysis of the records of family priests at a pilgrimage site, Goswamy 1968, pp. 17–62, has been able to reconstruct the family of Māṇaku and Nainasukha, which came from the state of Guler.

❀ 92 ❀

Dancing women

BASOHLI, ca. 1720–30

Image $9\frac{1}{2} \times 6\frac{7}{8}$ in. (241 × 175 mm); sheet $11\frac{7}{8} \times 8\frac{1}{8}$ in. (302 × 207 mm)

Two women with hennaed hands dance under a tree outside a two-story building. A woman emerges from the building carrying a tray with a covered dish. In the upper right another woman watches from a second-floor balcony. A peacock rests in the tree and two pairs of white birds fly from the upper left corner. A vine twines around the feathery-foliaged tree. The background is yellow. Tufts of vegetation mark the ground. Wavy clouds of white, blue, and gold are in the sky.

The women compare with those of the preceding entry, but the rendering of the tree is more detailed and less free. The exact subject is difficult to place, but the motif of two women with their hands joined over their heads in dance is common in Mughal painting. For a seventeenth-century example, see Khandalavala and Chandra 1965, pp. 35 and 42, color plate 1.

❀ 93 ❀

Cowherds seek Kṛṣṇa's protection from the rain

KULU, ca. 1700

Image 9⅝ × 5¾ in. (245 × 146 mm); sheet 11½ × 7⅞ in. (292 × 200 mm)

This is a devotional picture of great beauty and deep meaning. The composition is simple. Kṛṣṇa sits on a rock while cows and cowherds gather around him seeking shelter from the torrential rains that fill the dark sky. The cowherds carry umbrellas made of woven leaves and wrap their cloaks around themselves. A kneeling boy raises his hands in supplication, but the cows have no fear. They sleep, graze, and raise their heads to their protector as Kṛṣṇa, oblivious to the rain, casually bestows his grace with his right hand, extended as if to scratch the neck of the nearest cow. A lotus pool is in the foreground. Coiled clouds that flash golden lightning are at the top. A dark forest is at the left. The margins are yellow. There is a minor repair in the upper left margin.

This incident takes place just before Kṛṣṇa raises Mount Govardhana, indicated here by the rock on which he sits, to protect the inhabitants of Vraja from rains sent by the King of the Gods. Two cowherd boys have already found shelter under the boulder, curled up like embryos, secure in the knowledge that Kṛṣṇa is their salvation. This is a visual reference to Kṛṣṇa's statement that he is Mount Govardhana made manifest, whereupon he eats the offerings made to the mountain in place of those usually made to Indra, thus incurring the god's wrath and bringing the devastating rains (*Bhāgavata Purāṇa* 10.24.35–36). The two boys have merged with Kṛṣṇa, the goal of all his devotees, who seek to break down the barriers between adorer and adored. This message is underscored by the inscription in *ṭākarī* script at the top which reads *ramaṃya sadakaha* (literally, the bestowal of [divine] sporting). For his followers Kṛṣṇa's earthly actions are part of divine play. By entering into the spirit of this play, made manifest in the world by Kṛṣṇa's grace, worshipers can lose their own identities through participation and eventual union with the divine.

The style of this picture is very similar to Style I of the Shangri *Rāmāyaṇa*. See catalogue numbers 95–97; and W. G. Archer 1973, vol. 2, pp. 244–45. It is closely related to a painting of Rādhā and Kṛṣṇa in the Lahore Museum; see W. G. Archer 1973, vol. 1, p. 331, no. 12, vol. 2, p. 244. The Lahore picture and this leaf, which was formerly in the collection of Dr. Alma Latifi, Bombay, may be by the same hand. They are certainly from the same workshop. This strain of painting—the movement stilled, the palette subdued, yet retaining the same figure types and sense of exalted lyricism—continued in Kulu until at least circa 1720–30. See W. G. Archer 1973, vol. 2, pp. 25–52; and Coomaraswamy 1916, vol. 2, plates XXX–XXXII A and B.

❀ 94 ❀

Leaf from a *Rāgamālā* series

KULU, ca. 1700–1710

Image 6¼ × 6⅛ in. (159 × 156 mm); sheet 8⅛ × 8⅛ in. (207 × 207 mm)

Saṃverī Rāgiṇī, Wife of Śrī Rāga

A woman sits on a platform between two trees, facing right. A falcon perches on the embroidered leather gauntlet that covers her left hand. In her right hand glowing with henna she holds the severed leg of a large bird. Her clothing is boldly patterned. The rhythms of the picture are strong and angular, even jagged. Woman and bird face each other as equals, her stark profile a match for his jutting beak. Her spiky eyelashes and escaping tendrils of straggly hair are typical of the style. The leaves of the flanking trees surge upward. Molten orange in color, the tree on the right is especially striking. A green background gives way to a cloudy sky at the top. The borders are red with white and black rules.

There are two inscriptions in *ṭākarī* script across the top of the leaf, one in white letters, the other in very faint black. Both read *saṃverī raganī srī rage dī bharaja* (Saṃverī *rāgiṇī,* wife of Śrī *rāga*). The fainter of the two inscriptions was written first, then covered over with the red pigment of the border.

Of the original eighty-four leaves of this set, thirty-two are in the Victoria and Albert Museum, London, and six are in the Boston Museum of Fine Arts. The members of the same "family" all have matching border and background colors. See W. G. Archer 1973, vol. 1, pp. 331–34, vol. 2, pp. 247–49; and Coomaraswamy 1926, nos. 67–72, pls. 32, 33. A stylistically identical leaf is in the Rietberg Museum, Zurich; however, its border color indicates that it may belong to a different series. See Skelton 1961, pp. 54–55, no. 35. Saṃverī is an unusual *rāginī* without a consistent iconography. For other examples, see Ebeling, p. 145, no. C60; p. 280, no. 325; and p. 282, no. 333, which is almost identical compositionally to this picture, but reversed.

❀ 95 ❀ 96 ❀ 97 ❀

Three leaves from the Shangri *Rāmāyaṇa*

KULU, ca. 1690–1710

95. Rāma in procession with his father and brothers, from the *Bālakāṇḍa* (Book 1) of the *Rāmāyaṇa*

STYLE II, ca. 1690–1700

Image 7¾ × 11¼ in. (197 × 285 mm); sheet 8⅞ × 12½ in. (226 × 317 mm)

Against a sweeping Indian-yellow ground, Rāma and his brothers lead a procession including King Daśaratha and their family priests. The party has halted before a standing prince carrying a bow and a bowstring. Daśaratha leans forward to see what is happening; Rāma turns to look back at him and reassures him with a raised hand. The artist delights in brilliant colors boldly juxtaposed. The composition is choppy as men, horses, and chariots vie for attention, but any sense of disunity is suppressed by the embracing curve of the vivid background. A lone tree with pinwheel foliage rises to the right.

It is difficult to identify the exact scene depicted, for the series has no text. It does not agree with the accepted account of Rāma proving his prowess by stringing a bow, but the *Rāmāyaṇa* exists in many variant versions. The procession may be connected with the marriages of Rāma and his brothers. On the verso an effaced number and the word *bāla* are written in *nāgarī* script in the upper left. Below is the number 50 in Arabic numerals.

96. Rāma and Sītā visit the hermitage of Atri and Anasūyā, from the *Araṇyakāṇḍa* (Book 3) of the *Rāmāyaṇa*

STYLE IV, ca. 1700–1710

Image 6⅞ × 11⅛ in. (174 × 282 mm); sheet 8¼ × 12⅝ in. (210 × 320 mm)

Rāma and Sītā kneel before the illustrious sage and his virtuous wife. Lakṣmaṇa stands at the right holding his and his brother's bows and arrows. A pot of sacred basil plants stands before the hermit's hut. The yellow background is filled with tufts of vegetation and tall trees. A river runs diagonally across the lower right.

Though the incident depicted is usually considered part of the *Ayodhyākāṇḍa* (Book 2), this version of the *Rāmāyaṇa* is among those that place it near the beginning of the *Āraṇyakāṇḍa* (Book 3), the section of the text that narrates the story of the forest exile of the brothers and Sītā. Here Atri suggests that Rāma send his spouse to Anasūyā so that the venerable female ascetic can instruct her in the proper duties of a wife (*Rāmāyaṇa* 2.109.7–13). A caption in *ṭākarī* script identifies the incident. The leaf is numbered 2 in the upper left.

Style IV, which is drier and more restrained than other work in the series, shows a close connection with painting generally associated with Bilaspur in the early eighteenth century.

97. Sugrīva gives clothing to *brāhmaṇas*, from the *Kiṣkindhākāṇḍa* (Book 4) of the *Rāmāyaṇa*

STYLE III, ca. 1700–1710

Image 7⅛ × 12 in. (182 × 305 mm); sheet 8½ × 13½ in. (216 × 343 mm)

Set simply in a large pavilion, this scene of ascetics and monkeys is arranged in a gently sloping pyramid. The monkeys, headed by the crowned Sugrīva and clad in shorts of various colors, advance bearing garments for the priests. The gift-giving is part of the ceremonies marking Sugrīva's accession to the throne after Rāma slew his older brother at the request of the monkey prince (*Rāmāyaṇa* 4.25.26). The new king wears a chain of gold, an amulet given to him by his noble sibling as he lay dying. (See catalogue number 102 for an illustration of the death of Sugrīva's predecessor, painted at Mankot.) *Kiṣkindhā* is written on the reverse.

This *Rāmāyaṇa* series is named after the small state of Shangri, where it was part of the ancestral collection of the ruling family. Its size, stylistic range, and high quality place it among the major documents of early Pahāṛī painting. Now dispersed, on its discovery in 1956 it contained some two hundred seventy leaves. Most of these are now in the National Museum of India, New Delhi. Other examples are in various public and private collections, including the Mr. Michael Archer and Mrs. Margaret Lecomber Collection, London; the Collection of Edwin Binney, 3rd, San Diego; the Paul Walter Collection, New York; the Rietberg Museum, Zurich; the Bharat Kala Bhavan, Banaras (Varanasi); the Sri Gopi Krishna Kanoria Collection, Patna; the Colonel R. K. Tandan Collection, Secunderabad; the Jagdish and Kamla Mittal Museum of Indian Art, Hyderabad; and anonymous private collections in San Francisco, London, and New York.

The series is in four related but distinct stylistic groups; leaves in Style I are very scarce. For a detailed discussion of the set and a complete bibliography of its scholarly consideration, see W. G. Archer 1973, vol. 1, pp. 322–29, vol. 2, pp. 238–43. See also W. G. Archer 1976, pp. 86–95, nos. 47–51; Pal 1978, pp. 162–63, no. 56; and Tandan 1982, pp. 98–99, fig. 81, pl. 61.

❀ 98 ❀

Portrait

MANKOT, ca. 1700

Image 9¼ × 4¾ in. (235 × 121 mm); sheet 10⅝ × 6 in. (270 × 152 mm)

Kṛpāla Deva of Jammu

A man in a white robe stands against a yellow ground. He holds a flower in his left hand and a banded staff in his right. His turban is red with a large black plume. The ground curves up slightly and is speckled with black to indicate vegetation. The margins are red with black and white rules.

The inscription in *ṭākarī* script at the top reads *raje jomala kṛpala dea*, identifying the subject as Kṛpāla Deva, the raja of Jammu, who ruled from circa 1660 to circa 1690. Little is known about this ruler except that he joined with some of his Hill allies to expel a marauding Mughal governor of the Punjab Plains about 1670–80. W. G. Archer 1973 publishes two portraits of him, one from Kulu (vol. 1, pp. 177, 329–30, vol. 2, p. 246, no. 7) and another from Mankot (vol. 1, pp. 177, 373, vol. 2, p. 284, no. 4). The Mankot portrait, like this study, was formerly in the collection of Dr. Alma Latifi, Bombay, and has a similar inscription.

❀ 99 ❀ 100 ❀ 101 ❀

Three leaves from a *Bhāgavata Purāṇa* series

MANKOT, ca. 1730

99. The evil Kaṃsa slays Yogamāyā

Image 9 × 6¾ in. (229 × 172 mm); sheet 11 × 8½ in. (279 × 216 mm)

When Kṛṣṇa's father, Vasudeva, took the newborn god to the safety of the countryside (see cat. no. 45), he brought back a female child as a replacement. When Kaṃsa, the evil king of Mathura, heard that Devakī, his sister and Vasudeva's wife, had delivered her eighth child, he rushed from his bed to seize the infant, not even stopping to dress, for it had been prophesied that Devakī's eighth child would slay him. Ignoring Devakī's pleas, he dashed the baby against a rock, but the child, an incarnation of the goddess Yogamāyā, rose in glory to the sky and mocked the wretched king.

Kaṃsa stands stupefied outside an elaborate pavilion with a chocolate-brown interior in which a single lamp burns, indicating that it is night. Two women are in the pavilion, probably Devakī and a maid. Kaṃsa is clad only in a pink cloth wrapped around his middle with one end over his right shoulder, and he gestures helplessly toward a loaf-shaped gray rock as the goddess in all her glory foretells his doom. She is dressed in red with a transparent golden overgarment and holds her attributes in her eight arms. Clouds like tongues of fire emanate from her and fill the dark sky. The background is solid green.

The incident is narrated in *Bhāgavata Purāṇa* 10.4.1–13. Having realized his mistake, Kaṃsa next orders his demon allies to scour the kingdom, killing all male children of a certain age. Again Kṛṣṇa will escape his uncle.

100. Celebrations of Kṛṣṇa's birth

Image 9 × 6 in. (229 × 152 mm); sheet 11¾ × 8⅜ in. (299 × 213 mm)

As musicians play, a priest offers Nanda, Kṛṣṇa's foster father, tufts of grass, auspicious gifts to mark the occasion of Kṛṣṇa's birth. He sits on a footed platform, leaning against a fat red bolster and holding out his right hand to accept the offering from the priest who stands before him. Earlier offerings of grass are in his left hand, at his knees, and tucked into his turban. An attendant in brilliant red salutes his chieftain. The preceding picture and the next one are certainly by the same hand, but this painting with its livelier line and slightly different facial types may be by another artist. The musicians are especially well rendered. The background is solid yellow. The story is from *Bhāgavata Purāṇa* 10.5.1–18. This leaf is numbered 5 in the lower left corner.

101. Kṛṣṇa slays the bull demon

Image 9 × 6 in. (229 × 152 mm); sheet 11¼ × 8¼ in. (285 × 200 mm)

In a composition unusually complex for the series, Kṛṣṇa slays the bull demon Ariṣṭa as his foster parents, his brother, Balarāma, and another cowherd marvel at his exploits. The main scene is at the bottom along a river bank. Kṛṣṇa grabs the bull by its horns and twists them until the blood flows. Ariṣṭa bellows in pain, defecating and urinating in terror as he realizes that death is near. But he need have no fear, for death at the hands of Kṛṣṇa frees even a demon's soul from the cycle of birth and rebirth. The arrangement of god and demon locked in combat, the hero striding forward from the left to grab the demon on the right, is very ancient. The same composition can be traced back through Indian painting and sculpture to as early as the first and second centuries A.D.

Kṛṣṇa's foster parents sit on a terrace within an enclosure of lashed bamboo. Their house is simple but their garments are brilliantly colored and elaborately patterned, like the complex decoration of the pavilion of catalogue number 99. The broad, lightly shaded faces are also identical. A decorated cart sits within the enclosure. White-skinned Balarāma and the cowherd stand outside. Cows and flowering trees fill the landscape. For the story, see *Bhāgavata Purāṇa* 10.36.1–15. The leaf is numbered in the lower left. A caption in white *ṭākarī* script across the top of the picture identifies the subject. The margins are red with white rules.

The large, and unfortunately dispersed, series to which these pictures belong is prized for its simply stated, starkly powerful vertical compositions. Their bold color and form well suit the economy of expression. They are closely related compositionally to an earlier, horizontal series formerly in the state collection of Mankot and now in the Government Museum and Art Gallery, Chandigarh. The vertical series was formerly in the collection of the ruler of Lambagraon in Kangra, the same collection that once contained catalogue numbers 125 and 126. For examples of these two sets and other related material, see W. G. Archer 1973, vol. 1, pp. 376–77, 379, vol. 2, pp. 289–92, 296.

३

❀ 102 ❀ 103 ❀

Two folios from a manuscript of the *Kiṣkindhākāṇḍa* (Book 4) of the *Rāmayāṇa*

MANKOT, ca. 1700–1710

102. Folio 18. The monkey prince Añgada clasps the feet of his dead father, Vālī, at the request of his mother, Tārā

Image $6^{5}/_{8} \times 10^{1}/_{2}$ *in. (169 × 267 mm); sheet* $8^{1}/_{4} \times 12^{1}/_{8}$ *in. (210 × 308 mm)*

Against a predominantly green background the distraught wife of Vālī, the monkey king, laments her noble husband's death at Rāma's hand. Sugrīva, though instigator of his brother's death, mourns him nonetheless as Prince Añgada grasps his father's feet in grief. Rāma and Lakṣmaṇa, dressed like forest dwellers in leaf garments, watch the pathetic scene with Hanumān, their chief monkey ally. The dead Vālī is white. Absolutely still, his bloody corpse contrasts sharply with the alert and active figures around him. Tārā and her maids have already loosened their hair in grief. A tree bends as if to shelter the sorrowful women, its branches echoing the curvilinear forms of the rocks and tufts of vegetation to the right and in the foreground.

The text on the back (see Appendix, p. 254) is *Rāmayāṇa* 4.23.21–30 and the chapter ending.

103. Folio 46. Having told the monkeys that the abducted Sītā is in Laṅkā, the vulture Sampāti regains his wings

Image $6^{1}/_{2} \times 10^{1}/_{2}$ *in. (165 × 266 mm); sheet* $8 \times 12^{1}/_{8}$ *in. (204 × 308 mm)*

Añgada, the bear king Jāmbavān, Hanumān, and other monkeys sent by Sugrīva confer with Sampāti in the mountains. Sampāti's wings were burned off when he shielded his brother Jaṭāyu as they flew too close to the sun. Later, mortally wounded in battle with Rāvaṇa, Jaṭāyu lived just long enough to tell his brother that the demon king had abducted the virtuous Sīta. As a sage had predicted, Sampāti regains his wings when he tells the searching monkeys the news. The monkeys are delighted to learn Sītā's whereabouts, for now they will avoid the wrath of their king who has warned them severely against failing in their mission.

The picture is composed in curves. Ranges of mountains arch protectively over the animals seated in an opposing half-circle in the middle. Long monkey tails frame the loaf-shaped mountains. Trees dot the landscape, their twisting trunks emphasizing the curvilinearity of the style.

The text on the back (see Appendix, p. 254) is a version of the conclusion of *Rāmayāṇa* 4.62 with interpolations and variant readings. It includes the chapter ending.

A simpler version of the brightly colored styles associated with Basohli and Kulu was practiced in Mankot. Around the beginning of the eighteenth century artists in this state produced several devotional series, including this *Rāmāyaṇa* and at least two *Bhāgavata Purāṇas*. Their style is less concerned with minute detail than those of Basohli and Kulu, deriving its dramatic force from curving rhythms and starkly placed figures.

Catalogue number 103 is published in Spink & Son 1976, pp. 38–39, no. 163. Several other leaves from this manuscript have been published. See W. G. Archer 1976, pp. 122–25, nos. 65, 66; Pal 1976, no. 4; Pal 1978, p. 160, no. 55; and Tandan 1982, pp. 96–97, fig. 77, pl. 38. For the related *Bhāgavata* series, see W. G. Archer 1973, vol. 1, pp. 376–77, vol. 2, pp. 289–92. There is an illustration of the court of Rāma in the Chandigarh Museum that appears to be from another Mankot *Rāmāyaṇa* series of about the same time; see W. G. Archer 1973, vol. 1, p. 376, vol. 2, p. 289.

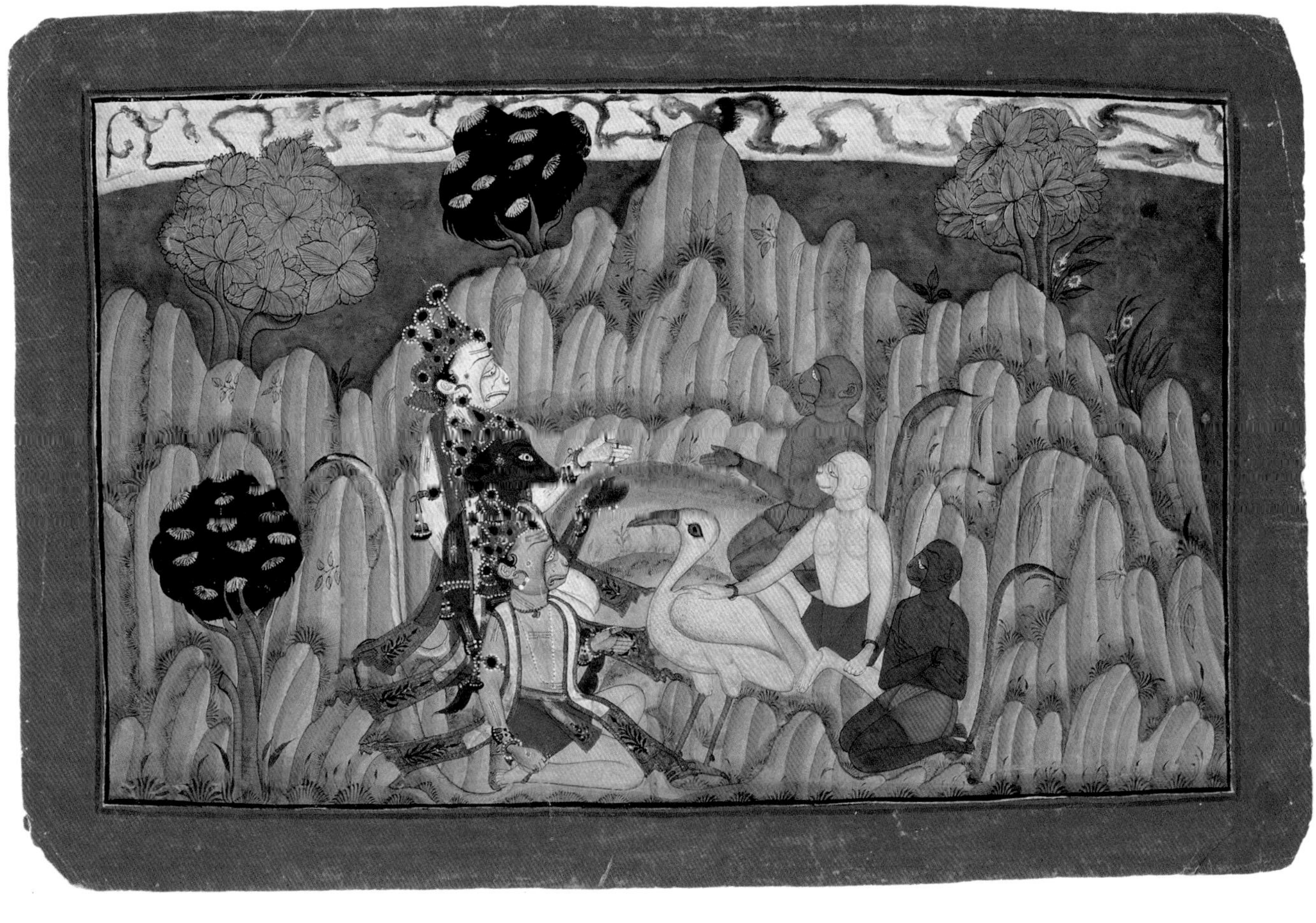

❀ 104 ❀

Leaf from a *Daśāvatāra* series

Attributed to Maheśa

CHAMBA, ca. 1740–50

Image 6½ × 9½ in. (163 × 241 mm); sheet 8 × 11 in. (204 × 279 mm)

Viṣṇu in the boar incarnation

Viṣṇu, four-armed with an attribute in each hand (discus, conch, club, and lotus), lifts Earth from the Chaos of the Eternal Waters. The god has taken the form of a boar, one of the many incarnations he assumes when he intervenes in earthly affairs. The Waters are represented as a swirling lotus pond. Viṣṇu emerges raising Earth on his tusks as he strikes down a demon with one of his right arms. Earth is represented as a cloudlike hill on which are a cow (a common form of the Earth Goddess), a peacock (a bird closely associated with Viṣṇu), and a temple. The sky is cloudy. A strip of land with tufts of vegetation marks the horizon. The borders are red with white rules. In the upper left corner are the numbers 53 and 3, followed by a caption in *ṭākarī* script.

The concept of Earth emerging from the Cosmic Waters is central to Indian religious thought. Viṣṇu in the boar incarnation is both rescuer and creator.

V. C. Ohri has attributed illustrations from this series to the artist Maheśa, who contributed embossed panels of silver and gold to the adornment of a temple gate in Chamba in 1747; see Ohri 1967, p. 50.

This leaf is published in Spink & Son 1976, pp. 40–41, no. 173; and Colnaghi, p. 75, no. 86, and p. 106, ill. Other leaves are in the Jagdish and Kamla Mittal Museum of Indian Art, Hyderabad; the Birla Collection, Calcutta; the Bhuri Singh Museum, Chamba; and the Collection of Edwin Binney, 3rd, San Diego. See W. G. Archer 1973, vol. 1, p. 86, no. 16; and Archer and Binney, p. 15, ill., and p. 106, no. 82.

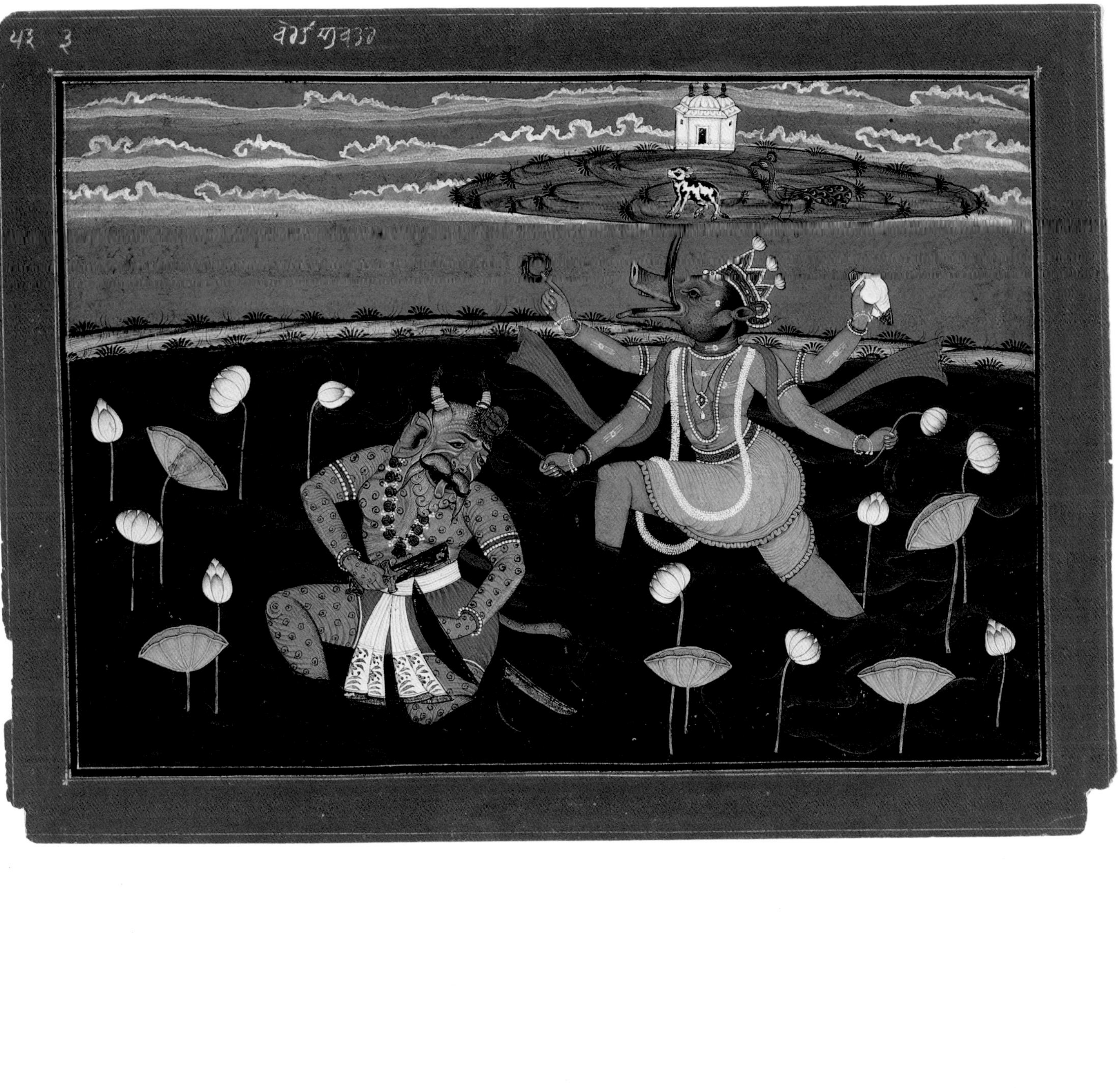
५२ ३

❀ 105 ❀

Leaf from a *Rāgamālā* series

BILASPUR, ca. 1680–90

Image 8 × 5¾ in. (204 × 146 mm); sheet 10¼ × 7⅜ in. (260 × 187 mm)

Vivaca, Rāgaputra of Hiṇḍola

In this brilliantly colored composition, a kneeling prince attended by a flywhisk bearer listens to a drummer and a horn player. The calm repose of the audience is in sharp contrast to the ecstatic fervor of the musicians, just as the cool mauve rug under the listeners stands out against the boldly striped carpet under the players. The figures are composed in a series of complementary and opposed curving forms. This is obvious in the representation of the drummer. His upraised arms are countered by the downward curve of the drumsticks and the downward thrust of his head. The upward curve of the drums echoes the arc of the drummer's arms as it opposes the downturn of his lower torso and legs. This tension of form is emphasized by the solid red background, relieved only by bands of white and blue at the top suggesting clouds and sky. Every element in the picture directs the observer's eye to the utterly absorbed drumming figure.

Vivaca is the *putra* (son) of Hiṇḍola *rāga* and is generally found only in *Rāgamālā* series painted in the Punjab Hill states.

This leaf was formerly in the William Theo Brown and Paul Wonner Collection, San Francisco, and is published in Pal 1976, no. 29. Other leaves from this vivid and lively series are in the Los Angeles County Museum of Art and in the Collection of Edwin Binney, 3rd, San Diego. See Archer and Binney, pp. 92–93, no. 70; and W. G. Archer 1973, vol. 1, p. 231, vol. 2, p. 172. A mid-eighteenth-century version of this composition is among the many leaves of a Bilaspur *Rāgamālā* now in the Museum für indische Kunst, Berlin. See W. G. Archer 1973, vol. 1, p. 237, no. 32(ii), vol. 2, p. 180, ill.; and Waldschmidt and Waldschmidt 1967, color plate B. For examples from other schools, see W. G. Archer 1973, vol. 2, p. 247; and Ebeling, p. 294, no. 377.

❀ 106 ❀

Leaf from a *Bhāgavata Purāṇa* series

BILASPUR, ca. EARLY 18TH CENTURY

Image 8¼ × 11 in. (210 × 280 mm)

Brahmā hides the cows and cowherds

After Brahmā abducted Kṛṣṇa's companions and their cows (see cat. no. 17) he secreted them in a remote mountain cave. This extraordinary illustration evokes a mood of poetic isolation. The exquisitely rendered forms and soft, luminous colors of gray, blue, green, and violet combine with an organically flowing line that is at once elegant and active. The anxious cowherds look to the right where a rocky hillock cuts off escape. In the upper left, four-headed Brahmā can keep watch in all directions at once, even as he rides his goose out of the picture. The boys are unaware of his observation, which heightens the sense of entrapment.

The Sanskrit text on the back is *Bhāgavata Purāṇa* 10.13.15. A number appears to have been whited over and replaced with the number 49.

The subdued palette is clearly the result of Mughal impact on the styles of the Punjab Hills. The rocks, too, recall the landscape conventions of the Akbar period over a century before (see cat. no. 11), a testament to the continuity of tradition in Indian art. Innovation has become convention, nevertheless freshly and vitally interpreted. The stark juxtapositions typical of more traditional Hill painting are not apparent here, but close examination of the seemingly unified compositions reveals disquieting disjunctions. The convulsive roll of the landscape in the lower left corner is particularly disturbing.

This leaf was formerly in the collection of James Ivory; it is published in S. C. Welch 1973, pp. 76–77, no. 43. Another leaf from the same series is in the collection of Mr. and Mrs. Peter Bienstock, Boston.

❀ 107 ❀

Leaf from a *Bhāgavata Purāṇa* series

BILASPUR, ca. 1770–80

Image 10½ × 13⅛ in. (266 × 333 mm); 12¼ × 15¼ in. (311 × 388 mm)

Cowherds beat a demon with sticks as Kṛṣṇa watches

A demon in the lower right vomits blood as cowherd boys beat its body with sticks. Kṛṣṇa, wearing a garland of flowers, watches from the upper left as he leans against a large bolsterlike cow. Other cows and calves—one with a hide like the skin of a leopard, some colored as though they were made of stone—stand placidly by or run away in fear. A river with a zigzag bank cuts across the right foreground. Large trees shelter the scene. Puffs of clouds streaked with gold roll through the blue sky. There is some minor inpainting.

It is difficult to identify precisely what incident from Kṛṣṇa's life this represents, but the setting and the vomiting of blood suggest that it may be associated with the death of Pralamba, who was killed by a powerful blow from Balarāma as the cowherds played in the forest (*Bhāgavata Purāṇa* 10.18).

Certain motifs and stylistic elements of this series have led to the suggestion that it may be related to contemporary painting in Mewar. These include the angular river bank, the stiff, explosive movement of the figures, the subdued palette, and the landscape conventions. Similarities are certainly present, but it is difficult to assess their meaning. They may reflect common sources but independent courses of development, or simply be coincidental affinities. Certain conventions appear and reappear in many different styles in different periods of Indian painting, and they do not necessarily indicate direct contact between separate idioms.

The series to which this picture belongs was once owned by a Bilaspur noble family; most of it is now in the Svetoslav Roerich Collection in India. For a discussion of this set, see W. G. Archer 1973, vol. 1, pp. 241–42; two other examples from the set are published in vol. 2, pp. 188–89. See also Khandalavala, figs. 43, 44, and color plate F. The published examples are from the Roerich Collection.

❀ 108 ❀

Śiva and Pārvatī with worshipers

MANDI, ca. 1730–40

Image 8 × 12 in. (204 × 305 mm); sheet 9¼ × 13¼ in. (235 × 335 mm)

Śiva stands on the terrace of a temple holding the hand of his consort, Pārvatī. The god's hair is gathered in a large bun. His third eye and a crescent moon are on his forehead and he wears a necklace of human heads. A snake coiled around his waist arches protectively over the shy Pārvatī. The divine couple is attended by three women, one of whom carries a peacock-feather fan, while another holds Śiva's trident and his double-headed drum. Śiva's bull, Nandi, and three devotees approach the terrace. Śiva's grace literally flows from his right hand raised in blessing. The god wears wooden sandals; the others are barefoot. Śiva, the women, and the worshipers all have ashes on their foreheads. All carry bags that contain their prayer beads. A banner flies from a trident over the dome of the shrine and a gilded parasol fringed with pearls shelters the temple's lotus finial. The background is light green with tufts of grass to indicate the ground plane.

Śiva is the great ascetic, yet he cannot exist without his female companion. They are shown here as gentle and demure, but this is not always so. Pārvatī can be angry with her husband, as when after intercourse of a celestial millennium Śiva withdrew without ejaculating and let his seed fall into Fire.

This picture is more delicately painted than is typical of the Mandi idiom. For closely related examples, see W. G. Archer 1973, vol. 2, p. 266, nos. 13, 14.

❀ 109 ❀

Equestrian portrait

MANDI, ca. 1765–80

Sheet 9⅞ × 7¼ in. (251 × 184 mm), irregular

Śamaśera Sena of Mandi

In strong contrast to most other Hill painting of the period (see cat. nos. 114–119), the style of Mandi remained bold and flat. This expressive and forceful portrait of the ruler of the state shows him riding a tassel-bedecked horse while smoking a water pipe carried by an attendant in white who stands behind him. The ruler is dressed simply in red and wears a curious turban which is perhaps intended to imitate the piled-up hair of the god Śiva, whose passionate worshiper he was. In fact, the state of Mandi was dedicated to the god, and the rulers considered themselves to be acting as his ministers. The monarch's forehead and neck are marked with ashes, another mark of his devotion.

Śamaśera Sena came to the throne in 1727 when he was only five years old. His reign was long and difficult. He died in 1781.

By the nineteenth century, painting produced in Mandi was more in line with the standard Kangra idiom that began to dominate Hill painting about the time this portrait was painted (see cat. no. 123). For other portraits of this ruler (in some of which he takes the guise of Śiva), see W. G. Archer 1973, vol. 1, pp. 358–60, vol. 2, pp. 270–72; Skelton 1961, pp. 70–71, no. 53 and pl. 53; Archer and Binney, p. 89, no. 67; and Chandra 1971, pp. 136–37, no. 231.

❀ 110 ❀

Leaf of an unidentified series

PROBABLY JAMMU, MID-18TH CENTURY

Image 13¼ × 9¼ in. (335 × 235 mm); sheet 13¾ × 10¼ in. (349 × 260 mm)

Courtiers and their mounts rest under a tree

In the foreground a group of courtiers rest under a tree, their horses clustering around them. Two men are in earnest discussion, but the others seem to have little interest in their conversation. In the middle ground a bowman and an armed man carrying an ax walk through a hilly landscape. In the background at the right a woman on a terrace looks longingly across a valley, her way barred by serpents. Opposite her the door-keeper of a palace gives a cloth to a messenger, while inside, a woman smoking a pipe listens to female musicians.

The subject of this picture is unclear, but it is probably from some romantic narrative. The style is very close to that of the painter Naiṇasukha from Guler, the artist of catalogue number 111. It is tempting to relate this illustration to Naiṇasukha's work of the middle of the eighteenth century (see W. G. Archer 1973, vol. 2, pp. 141–48), but in the absence of more precise compositional parallels than those now available, any attribution is only speculation.

A reading of the text on the reverse (see Appendix, p. 254) might clarify the unknown subject. Underneath the text is an almost invisible Persian inscription. Under this, in English, are printed "Kangra painting" and "Guler collection," both in capitals. In the upper left corner in an old-fashioned English hand is "No. (1)." Underneath this, in *nāgarī* script, is the number "74——."

❀ III ❀

Balavanta Siṅgha's personal shrine

Attributed to Naiṇasukha

JAMMU, ca. 1750

Image 5⅞ × 7½ in. (150 × 191 mm); sheet 7½ × 9¼ in. (191 × 235 mm)

Attendants wearing crisp white garments wave peacock-feather fans over an altar set up inside a tent enclosure of cool gray. The cult figure is veiled in white and adorned with jeweled attributes, a peacock feather crest, and a garland of marigold petals. Tufts of grass dot the green ground. Treetops and a cloudy sky are visible over the tent wall. The inscription in *ṭākarī* script across the top identifies the image as Viṣṇu in Lakṣmī-Nārāyaṇa form.

Though this picture of a shrine to Viṣṇu has neither signature nor attribution it is certainly from the hand of Naiṇasukha (ca. 1725–1778). The detached refinement of the attendants and the simplicity of the setting are typical of this artist's style. (For comparable material, see W. G. Archer 1973, vol. 1, pp. 194–208, vol. 2, pp. 139–53.)

The mid-eighteenth-century court of Balavanta Siṅgha of Jammu (1724–1763) was the scene of a remarkable collaboration between the monarch, a discerning patron of painting, and Naiṇasukha, one of the greatest of all Pahāṛī artists and the younger brother of the artist Māṇaku of Guler (see cat. no. 91). The brothers' styles could hardly have been more different. The elder represents the culmination in the Hills of traditional Indian stylistic values, while the younger anticipates and formulates the highly refined expression that was to dominate Pahāṛī painting in the late eighteenth and nineteenth centuries.

For a meticulous reconstruction of Naiṇasukha's biography, see Goswamy 1968, pp. 17–62.

The picture was formerly in the collection of James Ivory; it is published in S. C. Welch 1973, pp. 80–81, no. 46.

❀ 112 ❀

Leaf from a *Bhāgavata Purāṇa* series

BASOHLI, ca. 1769

Image 9 1/8 × 13 1/8 in. (232 × 334 mm); sheet 12 × 16 in. (305 × 407 mm)

Kṛṣṇa and his companions rest along the river

Kṛṣṇa and his brother, Balarāma, each shown twice, relax by a river as their companions run and play. The scene is set in a softly shaded green landscape. Massive trees shelter the boys as their cows graze contentedly at the right. Puffy clouds of pink, blue, white, and orange and a golden sun fill the sky. At the bottom a cowherd boy sticks his feet in a plain gray river as he tries to coax a wary fish. The line is more refined and the color more muted than in earlier Basohli painting.

Sanskrit verses from *Bhāgavata Purāṇa* 10.15 are on the verso.

It is an interesting fact that the *Bhāgavata Purāṇa* series of catalogue numbers 1 and 2 provides exact compositional prototypes for this series painted in the Hills over two centuries later. A leaf of the same subject from the earlier *Bhāgavata* now in private hands in London has almost exactly the same arrangement of figures, trees, cows, and river as this painting. Even the compositional registers of the early illustration are preserved, though obscurely, in this Basohli leaf. Notice how the artist of this picture composes the scene in three bands. The first is the river; the second begins with the tree at the left and includes the supine Balarāma, his kneeling brother, the sporting cowherds, and four cows; and the third runs across the top, including the reclining Kṛṣṇa and his attendants, the second tree, and a lone cow. Compare this with the more emphatic use of compositional registers evident in catalogue number 1.

Though this series of paintings was painted in Basohli and is obviously related to the earlier work of Maṇaku (see cat. no. 91), it clearly shows the impact of the more refined idiom gaining favor in the Hills at this time. The work of his brother Naiṇasukha is probably responsible for this change (see cat. no. 111) and indeed, evidence suggests that he spent time in Basohli after the death in 1763 of his primary patron, Balavanta Siṅgha of Jammu.

This large and important series of paintings is dispersed. For examples in the Mr. Michael Archer and Mrs. Margaret Lecomber Collection, London, the Royal Scottish Museum, Edinburgh, and the Victoria and Albert Museum, London, see W. G. Archer 1973, vol. 1, pp. 49–51, vol. 2, pp. 36–39; and W. G. Archer 1976, pp. 14–19, nos. 8–10. A colophon is lacking, but a leaf in the Collection of Edwin Binney, 3rd, San Diego, bears an Indian date equivalent to 1769; see Binney 1979, pp. 94–95, no. 30. For other leaves in the Binney collection, see Archer and Binney, p. 75, no. 55.

❀ 113 ❀

Leaf from a *Bhāgavata Purāṇa* series

GARHWAL, ca. 1780–90

Image 10 × 13⅞ in. (255 × 353 mm); sheet 11⅞ × 15¾ in. (302 × 400 mm)

The abduction of Rukmiṇī from the temple of the goddess

Rukmiṇī, unwilling to marry the man most people expect her to, has gone to pray at the shrine of the goddess. Kṛṣṇa comes to abduct her, sending the kings who oppose him into fury. The gray shrine rests on a white platform. The enemy kings come from the left, where Rukmiṇī's elephant waits. To the right Rukmiṇī willingly enters Kṛṣṇa's chariot, for she has secretly sent a message asking for his help. She is shown twice, once to the immediate left of the shrine and once joining her new husband. Kṛṣṇa's forces await his return in the upper right. The background is a deep yellow, the sky a flat blue. Trees are behind the shrine and in the upper left. The borders are red with double white rules.

The text on the back is an incomplete version of *Bhāgavata Purāṇa* 10.53.44–55. It lacks verses 46–49, 51, 54, and portions of 50 and 52. Above the *nāgarī* text are three lines in *ṭākarī* script, a summary of the Sanskrit verses. There are various numbers at the top. The original leaf number appears to be that in the upper left, identifying the illustration as number 202. Another hand has changed the second 2 to an 0. Under this number the *Bhāgavata* chapter is identified as 53. If all ninety chapters of the text were illustrated, this series must once have numbered about three hundred sixty leaves, the same number as that originally planned for the set to which catalogue numbers 1 and 2 belong.

For stylistically and thematically related examples, see W. G. Archer 1973, vol. 1, pp. 115, 117, vol. 2, p. 83, no. 12, and p. 85, nos. 20(i), 20(ii).

❀ 114 ❀

Double portrait

KANGRA, ca. 1765

Image 8¾ × 7⅞ in. (222 × 200 mm); sheet 9¼ × 8⅜ in. (235 × 213 mm)

Ghamaṇḍa Canda of Kangra with Devī Canda of Bilaspur

The two kings sit smoking on a terrace. Each has two attendants. Those in the foreground are probably their chief ministers. Ghamaṇḍa Canda (r. 1761–74), the austere king of Kangra, is at the left dressed simply in white with a grayish-green shawl wrapped around him. His guest is more elaborately dressed in clothing of muted colors. The terrace is covered with rugs decorated with very finely rendered floral tracery. The horizon is high, edged at the top with orange and gold. The sky is cloudy. An identifying caption is on the reverse.

Ghamaṇḍa Canda of Kangra was a powerful and able ruler. Son of the previous monarch's younger brother, he took advantage of his cousins' unpopularity when their father died and seized the throne in 1761. Here he sits with his ally, Devī Canda of Bilaspur, who married his sister. Painting of this type in Kangra, related in style to the refined idiom then gaining popularity through the influence of Naiṇasukha and his followers (see cat. no. 111), seems to be fully formed at the moment of its inception. This suggests that the vigorous new court of Ghamaṇḍa Canda attracted artists seeking his patronage, but so far only some portraits from this period are known. This is the earliest.

This portrait was once in the collection of Raja Anand Chand of Bilaspur. It is published in W. G. Archer 1973, vol. 1, pp. 280–81, vol. 2, p. 194, no. 1; for other portraits of these rulers, see vol. 2, p. 182, no. 38, and p. 194, no. 2. See also Ohri 1974, p. 43 and pl. XVI, fig. 2, for a portrait of Ghamaṇḍa Canda now in the Bhuri Singh Museum, Chamba.

❀ 115 ❀

Court scene

KANGRA, ca. 1788

Image 10¼ × 7⅝ in. (260 × 195 mm); sheet 10⅝ × 8¼ in. (270 × 210 mm)

Saṃsāra Canda of Kangra at court

Saṃsāra Canda sits at court smoking, a hunting hawk perched regally on his gloved right hand. Lightly bearded and wearing a flowing pink garment, he leans against a pale yellow bolster on a matching floral-patterned carpet. A canopy of similar pattern is above. A portly noble and his companion petition the king. Behind Saṃsāra Canda is his court. There are no inscriptions, but comparison with other portraits suggests a few identifications. The man in deep blue directly behind the young king is probably his vizier, Lābha, and the young man in yellow at his left seems to be Saṃsāra Canda's younger brother, Māna Canda (born ca. 1770). The bearded attendant who holds a peacock fan and the bearded man in puce in the lower right both appear in several portraits, but their names are never given; see W. G. Archer 1973, vol. 1, pp. 284–86, vol. 2, pp. 198–200.

The numbers 1 and 2 are on the verso along with a smudged Persian word.

Saṃsāra Canda (r. 1775–1823), the grandson of Ghamaṇḍa Canda (see cat. no. 114), came to the throne at the age of ten after the brief reign of his father. His reign was at first brilliant. The young king grew in wisdom and power, achieving supremacy in the Hills. In the last decades of the eighteenth century he was a perceptive and deeply involved patron of the Kangra idiom, the dominant style in the region until well into the nineteenth century (see cat. nos. 116–122). In 1806, however, his fortunes reversed, and he ended his reign in much-diminished circumstances, his power greatly eroded by invaders and a humiliating "protection" treaty with the Sikh ruler of Lahore.

A picture of Saṃsāra Canda and his court examining paintings, now in the Government Museum and Art Gallery in Chandigarh, is identical in style and very close in composition to this one. The canopy is duplicated exactly and so is the flowing line of the king's sash and the hem of his robe. The two pictures are certainly by the same artist. See W. G. Archer 1973, vol. 1, pp. 285–86, vol. 2, p. 200, no. 16.

❀ 116 ❀ 117 ❀ 118 ❀

Three leaves from the *Āraṇyakāṇḍa* (Book 3) of a *Rāmāyaṇa* series

KANGRA, ca. 1775–80

116. Lakṣmaṇa cuts the nose off the demoness Sūrpaṇakhā

Image 8¼ × 12¼ in. (210 × 311 mm); sheet 9⅞ × 14⅛ in. (251 × 359 mm)

The idyllic forest landscape of Rāma's retreat is the setting for an act that sets in motion the central event of the epic. Sūrpaṇakhā, a hideous demoness, has fallen in love with Rāma, who suggests that she marry his brother Lakṣmaṇa instead. White-skinned Lakṣmaṇa, however, teases her by telling her that Rāma finds her attractive, so Sūrpaṇakhā decides to eat her rival, Sītā, who raises her hand to her mouth in horror. In anger, Rāma orders his brother to mutilate the amorous ogress. Dutiful Lakṣmaṇa cuts off her nose (*Rāmāyaṇa* 3.18). In the upper left Rāma, his wife, and Lakṣmaṇa meet Jaṭāyu, the giant bird destined to die in defense of Sītā. (The meeting actually takes place before the encounter with Sūrpaṇakhā, in *Rāmāyaṇa* 3.13). This series frequently uses the ancient technique of continuous narration to present in a single composition events that take place at different times. Note how the artist places Lakṣmaṇa and his victim on a wedge of land jutting out into the river to isolate and emphasize the main scene.

117. Sūrpaṇakhā instigates her brother Rāvaṇa to abduct Sītā

Image 8¼ × 12¼ in. (210 × 311 mm); sheet 9⅞ × 14⅛ in. (251 × 359 mm)

Seeking revenge, Sūrpaṇakhā has sent many demons to their deaths in assaults on Rāma and his brother. In desperation she finally turns to her brother Rāvaṇa, the ten-headed demon king of Laṅkā. She reviles him in front of his demon ministers, then convinces him to abduct Sītā (*Rāmāyaṇa* 3.32). The scene is set in a brilliantly gleaming golden palace of flat planes and sharp corners that contrast with the softly undulating forest retreat of Rāma. Rāvaṇa's court is around him, comically demonic figures who little realize that death awaits them in their monarch's next adventure. The artist shows Rāvaṇa twice and his horned, yellow charioteer thrice, again utilizing continuous narration. The actions of the king and his attendant underscore the strong diagonal of the outer palace wall. Movement is directed to the upper right, then back down to the bottom middle as Rāvaṇa goes forth in his mule-drawn chariot (*Rāmāyaṇa* 3.33.1–7).

118. Rāvaṇa abducts Sītā after sending Mārīca in the guise of a golden deer to lure Rāma and Lakṣmaṇa away

Image 8⅛ × 12¼ in. (206 × 311 mm); sheet 9⅞ × 14⅛ in. (251 × 359 mm)

Having arrived at the retreat, Rāvaṇa tries to woo Sītā, first in the guise of a mendicant. Rāma has gone to kill Mārīca (upper left). The demon assumes its true form as it dies and calls out in Rāma's voice to Sītā and Lakṣmaṇa. Against his better judgment Lakṣmaṇa goes to his brother's aid after Sītā shames him. Left alone, she falls easy prey to the deceitful Rāvaṇa, who assumes his real form and carries her off. The pivotal act of the epic is accomplished.

In a tour de force of continuous narration, the artist includes six chapters of the *Āraṇyakāṇḍa* (*Rāmāyaṇa* 3.42–47) within a single illustration. The narrative sequence of the incidents, from the slaying of the golden deer to the abduction, is emphasized by the subtle diagonals of the sloping hill at the left and of the river at the bottom. The earliest painted representations of these incidents come from Gujarat in the middle of the fifteenth century; see Chandra and Ehnbom, p. 22, no. 3, pl. 2A for an example from the Collection of Edwin Binney, 3rd, San Diego.

Lyrical and gentle, the Kangra style at its best presents a world of refinement and delicacy. Rolling hills, cool green forest bowers, and labyrinthine palaces are the settings for scenes of amorous dalliance of strangely detached violence. The *Rāmāyaṇa* series to which these three leaves belong has come to be known only in the last decade. It is close in style to a similarly large *Bhāgavata Purāṇa* series of about the same time, also dispersed, but fortunately well documented (to which cat. no. 121 is related). Such paintings seem at first to have little in common with the bolder and generally earlier idioms of the Hills (see cat. nos. 86–105), but research continues to reveal both stylistic and iconographic continuity.

Other published leaves from this *Rāmāyaṇa* series are in the Mr. Michael Archer and Mrs. Margaret Lecomber Collection, London, and the Paul Walter Collection, New York. See W. G. Archer 1976, pp. 72–77, nos. 40–42; and Pal 1978, pp. 184–85, no. 67; Pal publishes leaves of a later Kangra *Rāmāyaṇa* series on pp. 186–87, no. 68.

❀ 119 ❀

Leaf from a *Gīta Govinda* series

KANGRA, ca. 1780

Image 6 × 10 in. (153 × 255 mm); sheet 6⅞ × 10¾ in. (175 × 273 mm)

Rādhā pines in her bower as her maid speaks to Kṛṣṇa

In a lyrical and gentle riverside setting Rādhā suffers in her retreat while her maid implores Kṛṣṇa to go to her, the opposite situation of that depicted in the earlier *Gīta Govinda* illustration of catalogue number 91. The sorrowing Rādhā is the main focus of the picture. All other details recede from her huddled figure. She is cut off from the idyllic landscape by dark trees. The stump of a tree juts out between her and Kṛṣṇa, but its stark branches burst forth in delicate foliage as if to assure the viewer that the lovers will eventually reunite. The ground is shaded with fine horizontal streaks, a convention of Kangra painting. In the foreground is a silvery gray river, its bank dotted with boulders and plants. The page illustrates *Gīta Govinda* 6.9:

May poet Jayadeva's song
Bring joy to sensitive men!
  Lord Hari,
  Rādhā suffers in her retreat.

(Miller, p. 96)

The rather untidy text on the back is *Gīta Govinda* 6.10 with a translation into the Punjabi of the Kangra region, but this relates to the picture that originally followed this leaf in the series.

A detail of the leaf is published in Randhawa 1963, p. 62, fig. 22. Plate IX in Randhawa 1963 (*Gīta Govinda* 6.4–9 on the verso) apparently preceded this leaf in the series' original order. Its composition is very similar, but the scene is set at night. Instead of crouching in her bower, Rādhā desperately searches the night for her lover.

The series from which this miniature comes was formerly in the ancestral collection of the maharaja of Tehri-Garhwal, now dispersed. It has a curious colophon that duplicates that of the series to which catalogue number 91 belongs. Such peculiar problems plague the study of Pahāṛī painting. For a general discussion of the set and references to its frequent publication since it first appeared in 1926, see W. G. Archer 1973, vol. 1, pp. 291–93, vol. 2, pp. 205–8. See also Pal 1978, p. 182, no. 66.

Catalogue numbers 125 and 126 come from a Kangra *Gīta Govinda* series of about half a century later.

❀ 120 ❀

Leaf from a *Satasaī* of Bihārī

KANGRA, ca. 1785

Image 7¾ × 5½ in. (213 × 133 mm); sheet 8¼ × 6 in. (210 × 153 mm)

A barber's wife paints the heroine's feet with henna

A young beauty sits on a terrace in the morning with two whispering maids while a barber's wife applies henna to her feet. The scene overlooks a mountain lake. In the distance are low rolling hills dotted with stands of trees and two clusters of buildings. The cloudy sky is streaked with gold and orange. Grays and whites predominate. Our eyes are drawn to the heroine by the brilliant red of her lower garment.

The text on the reverse tells us that a barber's wife who has come to dye the heroine's feet mistakes the reddened heel for a lump of pigment and rubs it to extract color. (For the text with a commentary and a translation into modern Hindi, see *Bihārī Satasaī*, p. 331, verse 403.)

Indian women traditionally dye their palms and the bottoms of their feet red as marks of beauty (see cat. no. 38). Barbers' wives had great freedom of movement and often acted as go-betweens for separated lovers. The erotic tension of this picture is achieved through the moment's intimacy and the illicit contact implied by the presence of the barber's wife.

The poet Bihārī lived in the seventeenth century and wrote in Vrajabhāṣā, the Hindi of the Mathura region that is widely used as a literary language. Like the *Rasamañjarī* of Bhānudatta (see cat. no. 47) and the *Rasikapriyā* of Keśavadāsa (cat. nos. 48 and 67), the *Satasaī* (Seven Hundred Verses) of Bihārī describes the attributes of lovers. As is typical in Hindi poetry of this kind, the supreme lover is Kṛṣṇa.

The series to which this picture belongs was once in the ancestral collection of the maharaja of Tehri-Garhwal, now dispersed. About forty leaves are known. This one is published in Randhawa 1966, pp. 76–77, pl. 16. See also W. G. Archer 1973, vol. 1, pp. 296–97, vol. 2, p. 214. There is an illustrated manuscript of the *Satasaī* painted in a rougher version of the Kangra style and dated V.S. 1836/A.D. 1779 in the National Museum of India, New Delhi (63.1171); see *Kṛishṇa*, manuscript no. 39.

❀ 121 ❀

Drawing from a *Bhāgavata Purāṇa* series

KANGRA, ca. 1790

Image 8¼ × 12¼ in. (210 × 311 mm); sheet 10⅜ × 14¼ in. (264 × 362 mm)

Kṛṣṇa slays the demoness Pūtanā by sucking the life from her breast

The scene is shown in continuous narration. In the upper center the demoness Pūtanā, sent to slay Kṛṣṇa by his wicked uncle, Kaṃsa, approaches the divine child in the form of a beautiful woman and asks to give him suck. When Kṛṣṇa is given to her (right foreground), he clamps his mouth on her breast and sucks furiously. As her life ebbs away she assumes her true, hideous form, until she becomes an enormous grotesque (bottom left foreground), her huge breasts formed like overstuffed bolsters. The cowherd women, startled by the event, lift the infant Kṛṣṇa from the corpse. To die at the hands of a god is to achieve instant salvation, and so Pūtanā is liberated from the cycle of birth and rebirth. When the cowherds dismember and burn her body, the village is filled with the fragrance of sandalwood. For the standard version of the story, see *Bāghavata Purāṇa* 10.6.1–44.

This leaf, washed with light color, is related in style to catalogue number 122, but is bolder in execution. The series to which this drawing belongs is related to a famous Kangra *Bhāgavata Purāṇa* series now dispersed (see cat. no. 118). Many of the drawings are in the Government Museum and Art Gallery, Chandigarh, and one is in the Indian Museum, Calcutta. See Randhawa 1960, figs. 2–5, 7–8, 10; and Goswamy and Dallapiccola, figs. 22, 26, 29–31, 33, 35, 36, 191. Randhawa 1960 publishes several of them: figs. 1, 6, 9, and pls. I–XX.

❀ 122 ❀

Leaf from a series of Nala-Damayantī drawings

KANGRA SCHOOL, ca. 1800

Image 8⅞ × 13¼ in. (226 × 335 mm); sheet 11⅛ × 15⅜ in. (282 × 391 mm)

A banquet for priests

The love story of Nala and Damayantī is of great popularity in India. Elsewhere in the world it is familiar to generations of Sanskrit students because the simple and elegant version of the tale incorporated into the *Mahābhārata* is a good introduction to the epic. But the series of paintings and drawings from which this example comes is based on another rendition of the story, the *Naiṣadhacarita* of Srīharṣa. This primed drawing illustrates a feast of *brāhmaṇas* after the marriage of the hero and heroine. As King Bhīma, Damayantī's father, and her brother, Dama, watch with approval from a low balcony, hungry priests feast in a palace courtyard. In the lower right a few latecomers wash their feet before joining the banquet. Another squats to wash his hands and cannot restrain himself from reaching up to touch the breast of the woman who offers him water. Fortunately she seems pleased by his attentions. At the upper far right an arcade shelters the priests' belongings.

At the top of the drawing is a number. It was originally 65, but another hand has changed it to 64. A few notations in *nāgarī* script in the lower margin read *brāhmana*, *samārādhana*, and *santapaṇa*. These captions seem to be later additions.

The diagonal placement of the courtyard and the lines of feasting priests recall the composition of Sūrpaṇakhā at her brother's court from the *Rāmāyaṇa* series of circa 1775 (cat. no. 117). In the earlier picture the arrangement is used to express vigorous forward action; here it suggests the bustle and activity of a large banquet as the viewer's eye is directed back and forth within an enclosed space.

This drawing is part of a series numbering forty-seven paintings and forty-eight drawings. The drawings are now dispersed. The Boston Museum of Fine Arts has twenty-nine, formerly in the collection of Ananda K. Coomaraswamy. See Coomaraswamy 1916, vol. 2, pl. LXII; and Coomaraswamy 1926, pls. 38–53. The drawings are published in their entirety in Eastman, where this leaf, formerly in the now-dispersed Pan-Asian Collection, is no. 14, p. 88. A variant version of the same scene is among the drawings in the Boston Museum of Fine Arts (17.2401). See Eastman, pp. 88–89, no. 15; and Coomaraswamy 1926, p. 108, pl. 43. The paintings are in the Amar Mahal Museum in Jammu, established by Dr. Karan Singh; see Goswamy 1975.

These paintings and drawings are closely related to another set of drawings in the National Museum of India, New Delhi (Goswamy 1975, figs. 16, 17, 40, 41, 43, 45, 48). In a carefully argued discussion, Goswamy disputes the common attribution of the Amar Mahal/Boston series to the state of Kangra, preferring instead an assignment to Basohli, where a refined Kangra idiom was practiced in the late eighteenth and nineteenth centuries (pp. 43–55). Goswamy's analysis highlights the problems of understanding Pahāṛī styles and the need for constant reassessment and revision. For a survey of the conventional view of the series, see W. G. Archer 1973, vol. 1, pp. 299–303.

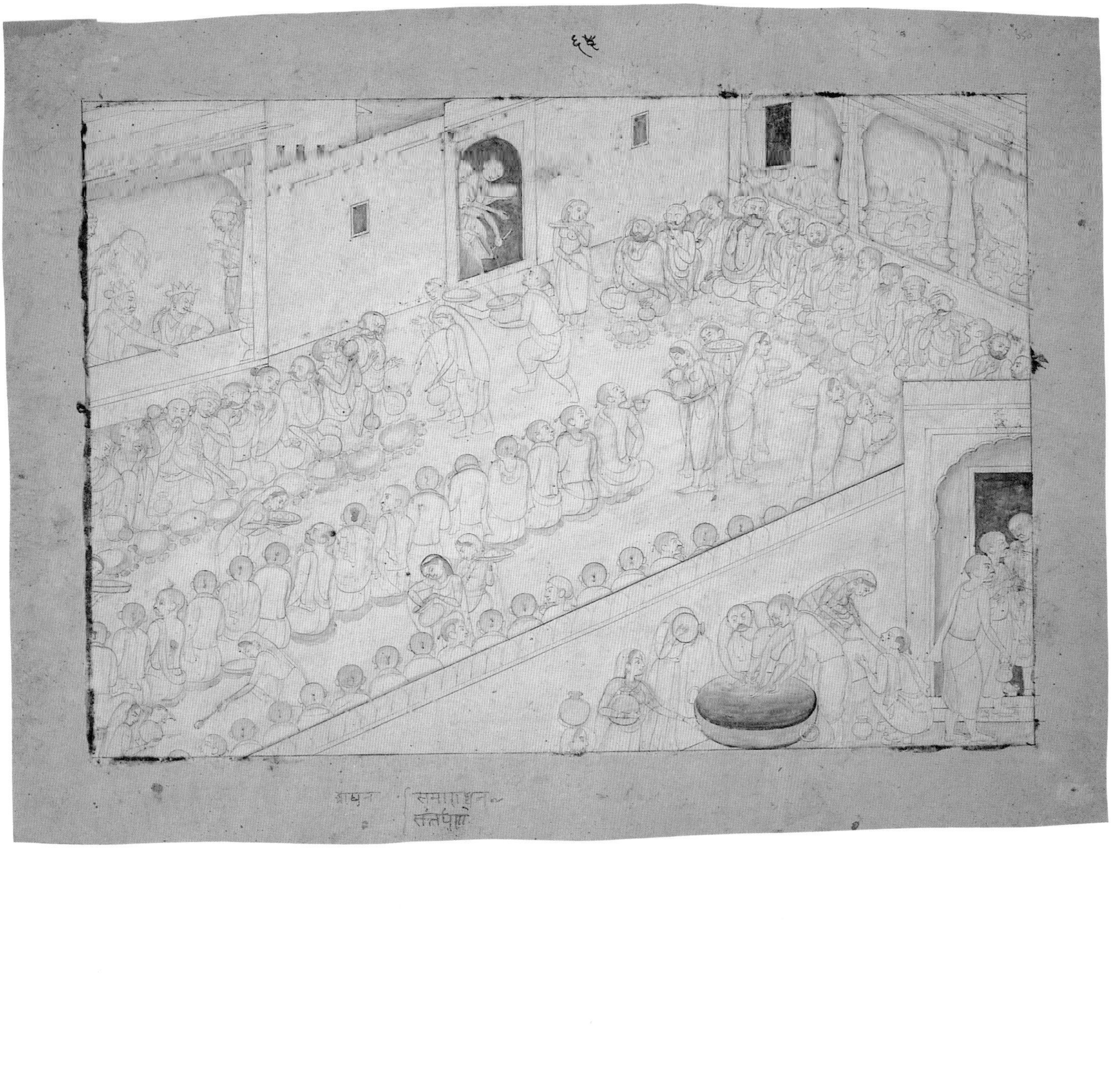

❀ 123 ❀

Leaf from a *Devī* series

Attributed to Sajanu

KANGRA SCHOOL AT MANDI, ca. 1800–1810

Image 11¼ × 7 in. (286 × 179 mm); sheet 13⅛ × 9¼ in. (334 × 236 mm)

The goddess Durgā enshrined

The multi-armed goddess Durgā is depicted in a shrine as she slays the buffalo demon (see cat. no. 62). Her skin is dark gray, like the lion and demon at her feet, suggesting an image made of stone. The goddess is dressed in rich clothing of red and gold. Another representation of her lion vehicle peeks from a niche in the superstructure of the pink temple. The temple is shown from more than one vantage point; the central shrine and entrance to the enclosure are rendered as if seen from the side, but the walled courtyard is shown from above. The artist employs these perspective shifts skillfully to achieve an elegantly abstracted view of a building that offers no visual obstruction in its revelation of the goddess it shelters. A smaller shrine to Śiva is in the lower right. Trees filled with birds are in the background. The streaked sky is gold, white, and blue. The main scene is set in an oval framed with floral arabesques and panels of birds.

The picture bears no ascription but it is possible to attribute it to Sajanu, a Mandi painter of the early nineteenth century whose style is very different from that associated with Mandi in the eighteenth century (see cat. nos. 108 and 109). He paints in the Kangra idiom, though the strong geometry of his work suggests that he may actually have learned his craft in Guler (see cat. no. 127 for a later example of Guler painting). He took special delight in elaborate borders such as the one on this picture. For a discussion of the artist and other works ascribed and attributed to him, see W. G. Archer 1973, vol. 1, pp. 360–67, vol. 2, pp. 273–81. It is possible that this picture belongs to a now-dispersed series of goddess paintings (see cat. nos. 87 and 88).

❀ 124 ❀

An album page

KANGRA, EARLY 19TH CENTURY

Image 10¾ × 8⅛ in. (273 × 207 mm); sheet 13¼ × 10⅜ in. (337 × 263 mm)

Lovers watch the approaching rains

The rainy season is a time for celebration in India, but it is also a difficult time for travel and can keep lovers apart. The couple portrayed here has been fortunate. They stand embracing as the heavy monsoon clouds break over distant hills. Lightning flashes in the angry sky, startling cranes into flight. An elegant peacock roosts on the eave of a white building, his head outstretched better to savor the coming rain. (A conceit of Indian literature is that peacocks dance in the forest to celebrate the beginning of the monsoon.) The lovers, their garments swaying in the wind, watch from a terrace. Maids near them carry a pipe, fans, and a covered dish, while in a downstairs room female musicians greet the rains and serenade the amorous pair. A pavilion awaits their lovemaking. A lotus pond and trees filled with birds are in the lower right. Parrots steal ripening mangoes from a tree laden with fruit; the stalk of a banana palm arches over with the weight of its load. In the distant hills cowherds hurry their animals to shelter. Nestled in a valley is a small town. The soft palette is dominated by grays and whites.

For similar compositions, see Randhawa 1962, frontis and figs. 75–77; fig. 63 depicts a similar scene, but there the heroine mourns the absence of her lover. See also Randhawa 1954, pl. 25.

❀ 125 ❀ 126 ❀

Two leaves from a *Gīta Govinda* series

KANGRA, ca. 1820–25

125. Leaf number 18. Kṛṣṇa lies alone in the forest pining for Rādhā

Image 9⅝ × 12½ in. (245 × 317 mm); sheet 11 × 14½ in. (279 × 369 mm)

The brightly colored forest-scape explodes with blossoming trees and shrubs. At the right Kṛṣṇa tosses alone on his forest bed, wishing that Rādhā were with him. In the center a maid passes through the dense forest on her way to Rādhā on the left, where she tells her of Kṛṣṇa's longing. Rādhā seems pleased with her power over Kṛṣṇa. Above her is the caption *rādhakā*. At top center is a woman before a princely figure. Over them is the caption *varāḍī rāgaṇī*, an indication of the appropriate musical mode for singing the text on the back. Perhaps we are to interpret the woman as a singer, just as often the author-narrator is included in an Indian painting. A pond filled with huge lotus flowers is in the foreground.

The leaf is numbered on the verso and bears the text of *Gīta Govinda* 5.1–6 with indications of the proper musical modes for the verses. Catalogue number 91 also illustrates a verse from *Gīta Govinda* 5.

126. Leaf number 40. Kṛṣṇa entreats Rādhā to make love

Image 9¼ × 12⅞ in. (235 × 327 mm); sheet 11⅛ × 14⅜ in. (282 × 365 mm)

It is night. Kṛṣṇa and Rādhā are isolated on their bed of leaves. She pulls near him in the darkness, bold because the night cloaks her passion. On the other side of a thicket two maids discuss the love of Rādhā and Kṛṣṇa. The dark sky is full of stars, but brighter still are the flowers that dot the arching forest shrubbery.

The leaf bears a number on the verso and verses numbered 1–3. These correspond to *Gīta Govinda* 12.10 and variant readings cited in Miller, pp. 123, 166, 203–4. The text vividly describes the physical state of the consummation of sexual desire.

This leaf falls near the end of the text, and so the series probably did not contain too many leaves over forty. It is published in French, pl. XXII, and in Khandalavala 1958, fig. 263.

The series to which these two leaves belong was in the ancestral collection of the maharaja of Lambagraon, a descendant of Saṃsāra Canda's brother. A large series, it is much harder in style and less unified in composition than late-eighteenth-century Kangra painting, but still visually pleasing. The streaky shading of the landscape observed earlier in the style is here even more apparent, the line coarser, and the colors less harmonious than those of the previous century (see cat. nos. 116–120). Nevertheless, the eye takes delight in the lazy profusion of flowering plants, and the frank eroticism of this series is not without charm.

The set is dispersed; for a discussion of its history and significance, see W. G. Archer 1973, vol. 1, pp. 307–8, vol. 2, p. 231. See also Archer and Binney, pp. 120–21, no. 92; and Pal 1978, pp. 204–5, no. 77. It is particularly interesting to compare these later illustrations with the pictures of the *Gīta Govinda* of circa 1780 (cat. no. 119).

❀ 127 ❀

Leaf of an unidentified series

GULER, ca. 1800–1820

Image 11¾ × 16¾ in. (299 × 426 mm); sheet 14¼ × 19¼ in. (362 × 489 mm)

The Five Celestial Sages on a pilgrimage in the Himalayas

This highly complex illustration comes from a large and still-unidentified narrative that chronicles the arduous Himalayan pilgrimage of five sages. The five are first shown in the lower right bathing and being shaved in preparation for worship at the Śiva shrine that dominates the right middle ground of the picture. The worshiping sages are observed from the left by a mountain man who tends his herd of goats. In the upper left the pilgrims bathe again in a cold mountain lake. One has submerged himself completely as his emaciated companions stand shivering. The five travel on at the top left. At top center a rustic couple make their way in the opposite direction with baskets strapped to their backs, their possessions in one and a child in the other. The same group of sages shown four times indicates that the use of continuous narration persisted in Indian painting even into the nineteenth century. The lightly painted illustration is dominated by an icy palette of whites and grays. Only a few other colors intrude, and even they are muted. The faceted rocks that fill the landscape intensify the feeling of cold isolation. Surely the sages cannot be far from Śiva's abode. The red margins are ruled with white.

For other leaves from this same series, see Pal 1978, pp. 194–95, no. 72; and Kramrisch, pp. 222–24, nos. P-52a, P-52b, P-52c. This leaf seems to fall between P-52b and P-52c in the narrative sequence. A slightly later picture from another version of the story that was painted elsewhere in the Hills is published in W. G. Archer 1973, vol. 1, p. 173, vol. 2, p. 126, no. 5.

॥६॥

INSCRIPTIONS

Because of the significance of the texts and inscriptions on the backs of Indian miniature paintings, and the difficulty of access to them, a selected group from the collection is reproduced here.

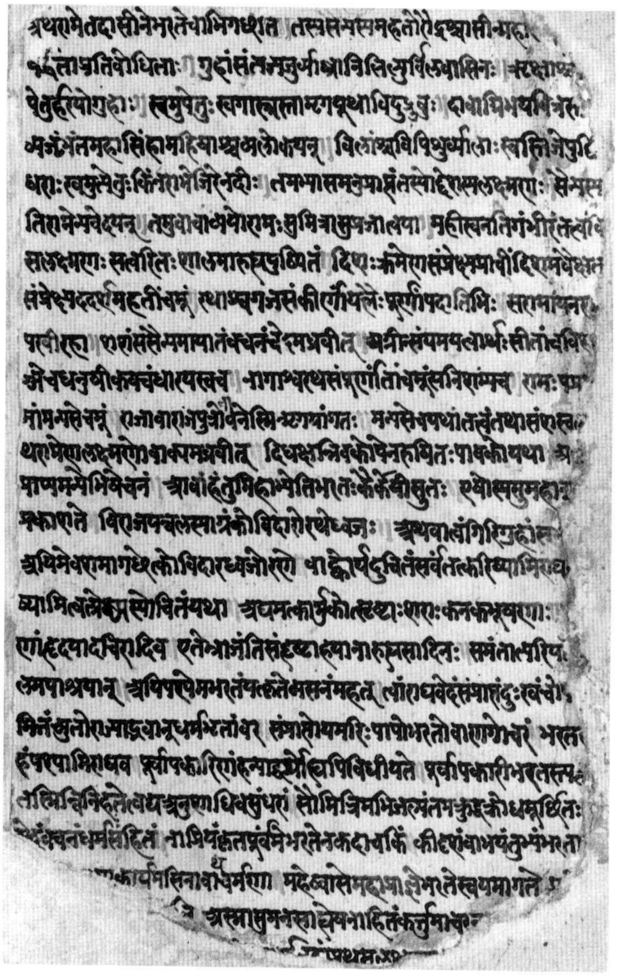

Catalogue no. 15

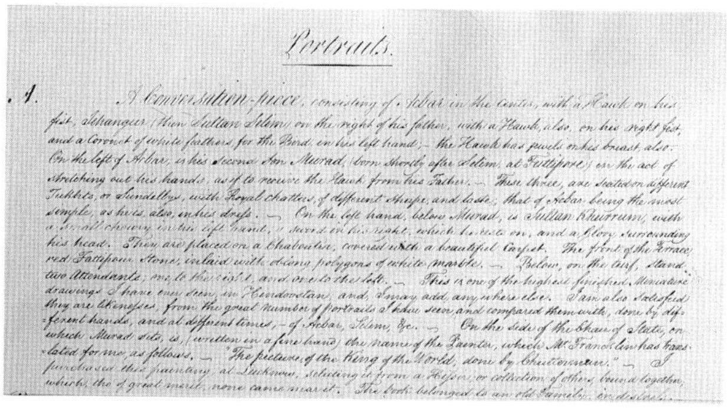

Portraits.

1. A Conversation-piece, consisting of Acbar in the center, with a Hawk on his fist, Jehangeer (then Sultan Selim) on the right of his father, with a Hawk, also, on his right fist, and a Coronet of white feathers for the Bird, in his left hand; — the Hawk has jewels on his breast, also. On the left of Acbar, is his second Son Murad, (born shortly after Selim, at Futtypore) in the act of stretching out his hands, as if to receive the Hawk from his Father. — These three, are seated on different Tukhts, or Sundellys, with Royal Chatters, of different shape, and taste; that of Acbar being the most simple, as his, also, in his dress. — On the left hand, below Murad, is Sultan Khurrum, with [illegible] in his left hand, a sword in his right, which he rests on, and a Glory surrounding his head. They are placed on a Chabootra, covered with a beautiful Carpet. The front of the Terrace, red Fattepour Stone, inlaid with oblong polygons of white marble. — Below, on the turf, stand two Attendants, one to the right, and one to the left. — This is one of the highest finished Miniature drawings I have ever seen, in Hindoostan, and, I may add, any where else. I am also satisfied they are likenesses, from the great number of portraits I have seen, and compared them with, done by different hands, and at different times, — of Acbar, Selim, &c. — On the side of the Chair of State, on which Murad sits, is, (written in a fine hand) the name of the Painter, which Mr Francklin has translated for me, as follows. — "The picture of the King of the World, done by Chutterman." — I purchased this painting at Lucknow, selecting it from a [illegible], or collection of others bound together, which tho' of great merit, none came near it. The book belonged to an old Family in distress...

Catalogue no. 23

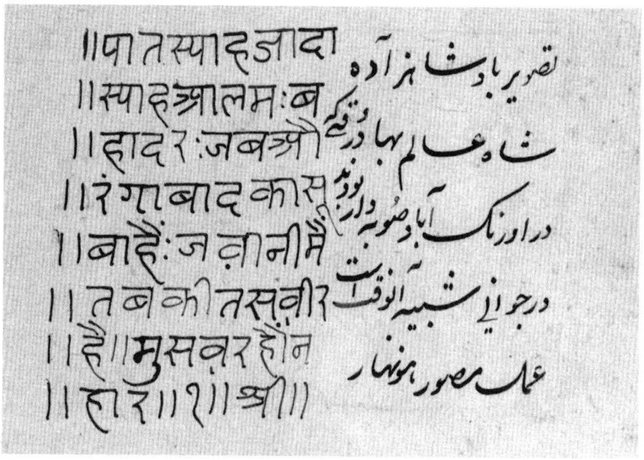

॥पातस्याहजादा
॥स्याहआलमःब
॥हादरःजबऔ
॥रंगाबादकास
॥बाहैःजवानीमैं
॥तबकीतसवीर
॥है॥मुसवरहोन
॥हार॥१॥श्री॥

تصویر بادشاهزاده
شاه عالم بهادر که
در اورنگ آباد صوبه دار بودند
در جوانی شبیه آن وقت
عمل مصور هونهار

Catalogue no. 28

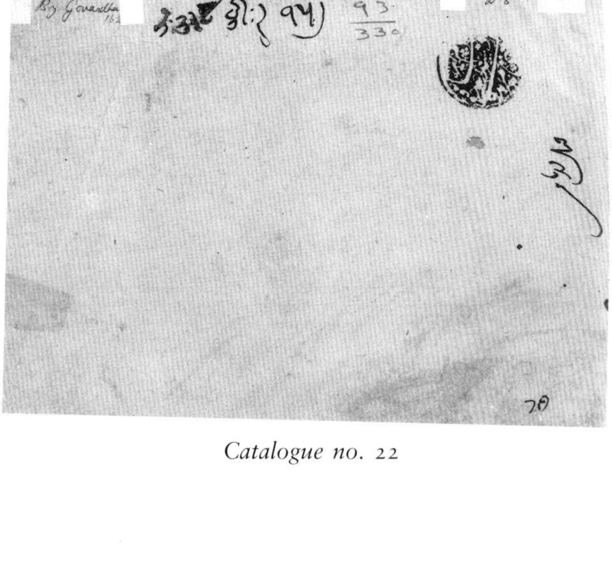

Catalogue no. 22

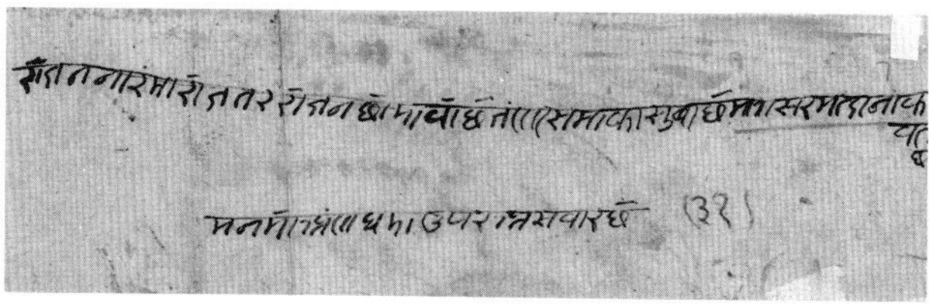

Catalogue no. 56

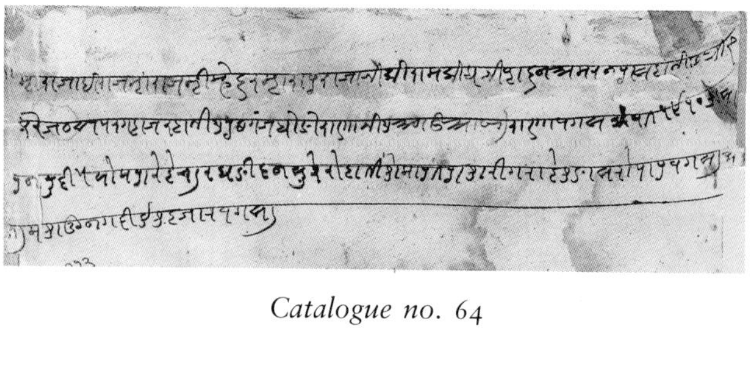

Catalogue no. 64

Catalogue no. 70

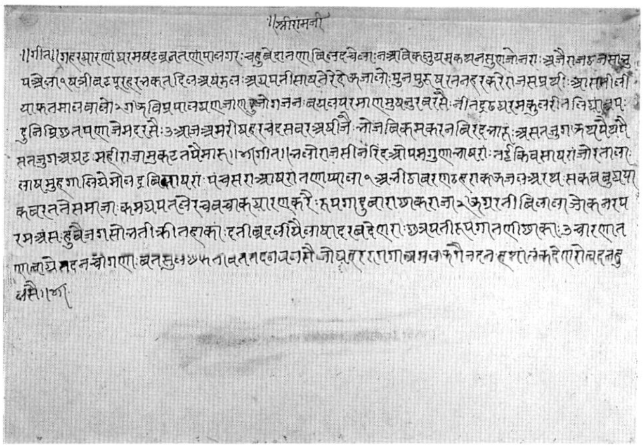

Catalogue no. 80

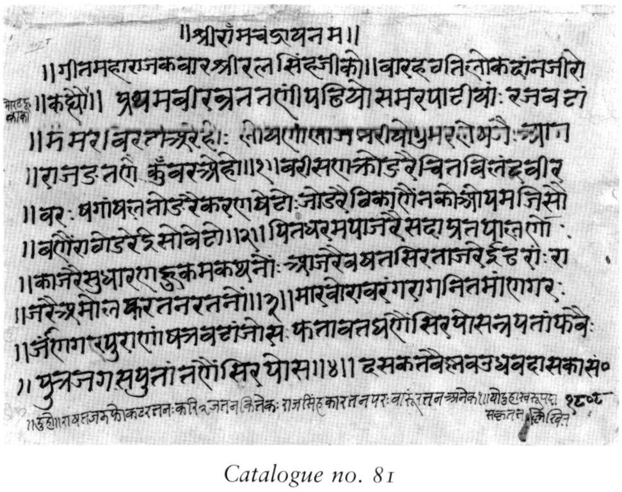

Catalogue no. 81

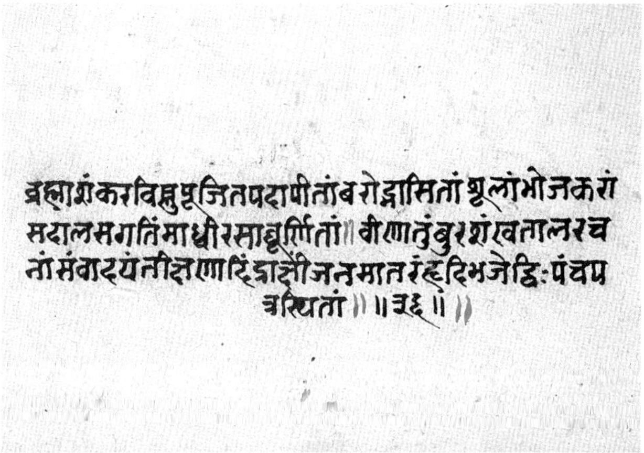

Catalogue no. 87

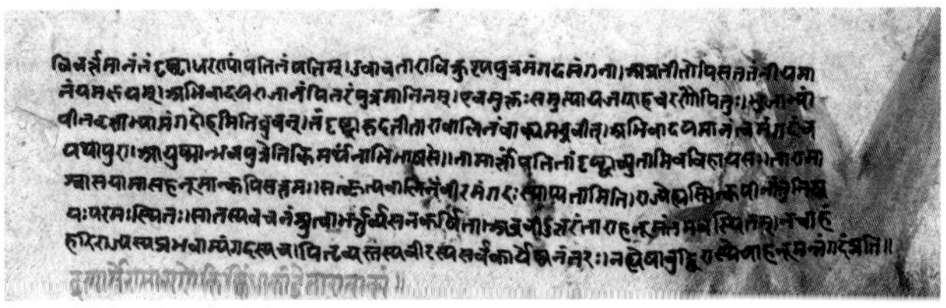

Catalogue no. 102

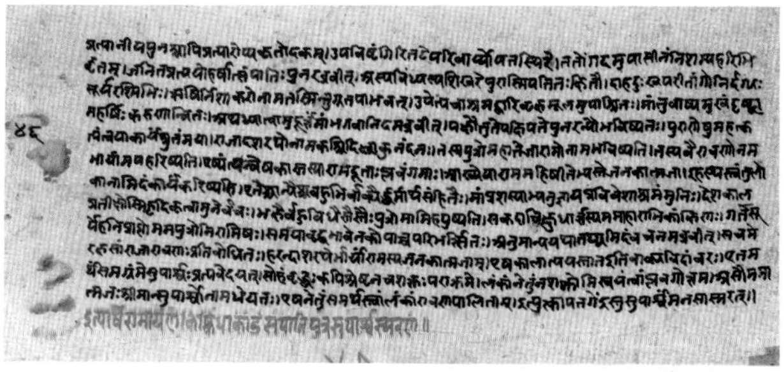

Catalogue no. 103

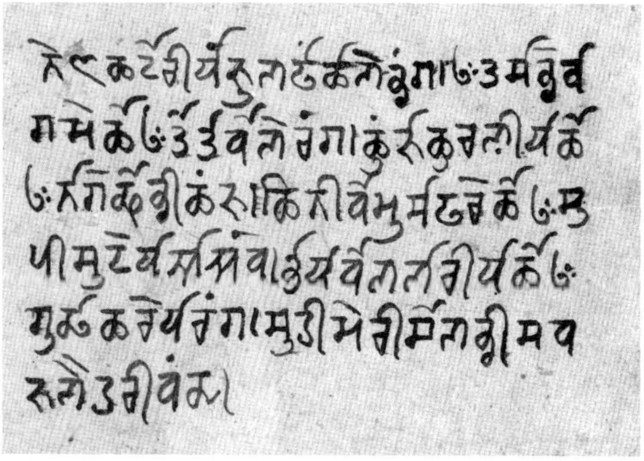

Catalogue no. 110

BIBLIOGRAPHY

AIJAZUDDIN — Aijazuddin, F. S. *Pahari Paintings and Sikh Portraits in the Lahore Museum*. London/New York: Sotheby Parke Bernet, 1977.

Akbarnama — *The Akbarnama of Abu-L-Fazl*. Translated by H. Beveridge. Biblioteca Indica. 3 vols. Calcutta: Asiatic Society of Bengal, 1897–99.

ANDHARE — Andhare, Shridhar. "The *Dhola-Maru* MS of the National Museum: A Consideration in Style and Date." *Chhavi* 2 (1981), pp. 298–300.

ANDHARE AND SINGH — Andhare, Shridhar, and Ravat Nahar Singh. *Deogarh Painting*. New Delhi: Lalit Kalā Akademi, 1977.

ARCHER, M. 1972 — Archer, Mildred. *Company Drawings in the India Office Library*. London: H. M. Stationery Office, 1972.

1979 — Archer, Mildred. *India and British Portraiture, 1770–1825*. London/New York: Sotheby Parke Bernet, 1979.

ARCHER, W. G. 1956 — Archer, W. G. *Indian Painting*. London: B. T. Batsford, 1956.

1958 — Archer, W. G. *Central Indian Painting*. London: Faber and Faber, 1958.

1959 — Archer, W. G. *Indian Painting in Bundi and Kotah*. Victoria and Albert Museum Monograph, no. 13. London: H. M. Stationery Office, 1959.

1960 — Archer, W. G. *Indian Miniatures*. Greenwich, Conn.: New York Graphic Society, 1960.

1973 — Archer, W. G. *Indian Paintings from the Punjab Hills: A Survey and History of Pahari Miniature Painting*. Foreword by Sherman Lee. 2 vols. London and New York: Sotheby Parke Bernet, 1973.

1976 — Archer, W. G. *Visions of Courtly India: The Archer Collection of Pahari Miniatures*. Exhibition catalogue. Washington, D.C.: International Exhibitions Foundation, 1976.

ARCHER AND BINNEY — *Rajput Miniatures from the Collection of Edwin Binney, 3rd*. Introduction by W. G. Archer, catalogue entries by Edwin Binney, 3rd. Exhibition catalogue. Portland, Oreg.: Portland Art Museum, 1968.

ARCHER AND LIGHTBOWN — Archer, Mildred, and Ronald Lightbown. *India Observed: India as Viewed by British Artists, 1760–1860*. Exhibition catalogue. London: Victoria and Albert Museum in Association with Trefoil Books, 1982.

ASHTON — Ashton, Leigh, ed. *The Art of India and Pakistan*. "Sculpture" by K. de B. Codrington, "Bronzes and Textiles" by John Irwin, "Painting" by Basil Gray. Commemorative catalogue of exhibition held at the Royal Academy of Arts, 1947–48. London: Faber and Faber, 1950.

Bābar-nāma — *See* Beveridge.

BAHADUR — Bahadur, K. P., trans. *The Rasikapriyā of Keshavadāsa*. Delhi, Patna, and Varanasi: Motilal Banarsidass, 1972.

BEACH 1970–71 — Beach, Milo Cleveland. "Painting at Devgarh." *Archives of Asian Art*, vol. 24 (1970–71), pp. 23–25.

1974 — Beach, Milo Cleveland. *Rajput Painting at Bundi and Kota*. Ascona: Artibus Asiae, 1974.

1978 — Beach, Milo Cleveland. *The Grand Mogul: Imperial Painting in India, 1600–1660*. With contributions by Stuart Cary Welch and Glenn D. Lowry. Exhibition catalogue. Williamstown, Mass.: Sterling and Francine Clark Institute, 1978.

1981 — Beach, Milo Cleveland. *The Imperial Image: Paintings for the Mughal Court*. Exhibition catalogue. Washington, D.C.: Freer Gallery of Art, 1981.

Beatty — Arnold, Sir Thomas W. *The Library of A. Chester Beatty: A Catalogue of the Indian Miniatures*. Revised and edited by J. V. S. Wilkinson. 3 vols. Oxford and London: Privately printed, 1936.

BEVERIDGE — Beveridge, Annette Susanna, trans. *The Bābur-nāma in English*. 2 vols. London, Luzac, 1921. Reprint. New Delhi: Oriental Books Reprint Corporation, 1970.

Bhāgavata Purāṇa — *See* Tagare.

Bihārī Satasaī — *Bihārī Satasaī*. Edited and translated into modern Hindi by Nemīcanda Jaina. Jaipur: Padama Buka Kampant, 1968.

BINNEY 1973	Binney, Edwin, 3rd. *Indian Miniature Painting: From the Collection of Edwin Binney, 3rd. I, The Mughal and Deccani Schools.* Exhibition catalogue. Portland, Oreg.: Portland Art Museum, 1973.
1979	Binney, Edwin, 3rd. *Panorama de la miniatura de la India: Miniaturas de la colección de Edwin Binney III.* Monterey, Mex.: Fonapas, El Colegio de Mexico, and Promocion de las Artes, 1979.
BINYON AND ARNOLD	Binyon, Laurence, and Thomas W. Arnold. *The Court Painters of the Grand Moguls.* New York: Oxford University Press, 1921.
BINYON, WILKINSON, AND GRAY	Binyon, Laurence, J. V. S. Wilkinson, and Basil Gray. *Persian Miniature Painting. Including a Critical and Descriptive Catalogue of the Miniatures Exhibited at Burlington House January–March 1931.* London: Oxford University Press, 1933.
BIRDWOOD	Birdwood, Sir George C. M. *The Industrial Arts of India.* Part 1. London: Chapman and Hall, 1880.
BROWN	Brown, Percy. *Indian Painting under the Mughals, A.D. 1550 to A.D. 1750.* Oxford: Clarendon Press, 1924.
CHANDRA 1957–59	Chandra, Pramod. "A Series of Ramayana Paintings of the Popular Mughal School." *Bulletin of the Prince of Wales Museum of Western India,* vol. 6 (1957–59), pp. 64–70.
1960	Chandra, Pramod. "Usted Salivahana and the Development of Popular Mughal Art." *Lalit Kalā,* no. 8 (October 1960), pp. 25–46.
1971	Chandra, Pramod. "Indian Painting." In *Indian Miniature Painting: The Collection of Earnest C. and Jane Werner Watson.* Exhibition catalogue. Madison, Wis.: Elvehjem Art Center, 1971.
1976	*Ṭūṭī-nāma: Tales of a Parrot. . . . Complete Colour Facsimile Edition in Original Size of the Manuscript in Possession of the Cleveland Museum of Art.* Vol. 1, *Commentarium: The Ṭūṭī-nāmah of the Cleveland Museum of Art and the Origins of Mughal Painting.* Text by Pramod Chandra, foreword by Sherman E. Lee. Vol. 2, *Facsimile.* Codices selecti phototypice impressi, vol. 55. Graz: Akademische Druck- und Verlagsanstalt, 1976.
1983	Chandra, Pramod. *On the Study of Indian Art.* Cambridge: Harvard University Press, 1983.
CHANDRA AND EHNBOM	Chandra, Pramod, and Daniel J. Ehnbom. *The Cleveland Tuti-nama Manuscript and the Origins of Mughal Painting.* Catalogue of exhibition held at the Cleveland Museum of Art, 1976, and the David and Alfred Smart Gallery, University of Chicago, 1977. Chicago: University of Chicago Press, 1977.
CHÂTELAIN	Châtelain, Henri Abraham. *Atlas historique. . . .* Amsterdam: Frères Châtelain, 1719.
CHRISTIE'S 1978	*Important Indian Miniatures.* Sale. Christie's, London, July 6, 1978.
1979	*Important Islamic and Indian Manuscripts and Miniatures. The Properties of the Late Vera Amherst Hale Pratt and Others.* Sale. Christie's, London, April 19, 1979.
COLNAGHI	*Indian Painting: Mughal and Rajput and a Sultanate Manuscript.* Exhibition catalogue. London: P. & D. Colnaghi, 1978.
COOMARASWAMY 1910	Coomaraswamy, Ananda K. *Indian Drawings.* London: Printed for the India Society, 1910.
1912	Coomaraswamy, Ananda K. "Rājput Paintings." *Burlington Magazine,* vol. 20, no. 108 (March 1912), pp. 315–24.
1916	Coomaraswamy, Ananda K. *Rajput Painting.* 2 vols. London: Oxford University Press, 1916.
1926	Coomaraswamy, Ananda K. *Catalogue of the Indian Collections in the Museum of Fine Arts, Boston.* Part 5, *Rājput Painting.* Boston: Museum of Fine Arts, 1926.
CZUMA	Czuma, Stanislaw. *Indian Art from the George P. Bickford Collection.* Exhibition catalogue. Cleveland: Cleveland Museum of Art, 1975.
DAHMEN-DALLAPICCOLA	Dahmen-Dallapiccola, Anna Libera. *Rāgamālā-Miniaturen von 1475 bis 1700.* Wiesbaden: O. Harrassowitz, 1975.
DICKINSON AND KHANDALAVALA	Dickinson, Eric, and Karl Khandalavala. *Kishangarh Painting.* New Delhi: Lalit Kalā Akademi, 1959.
DOSHI	Doshi, Saryu. "An Illustrated Manuscript from Aurangabad Dated 1650 A.D." *Lalit Kalā,* no. 15 (1972), pp. 19–28, pls. 11–13.

EASTMAN
Eastman, Alvan Clark. *The Nala-Damayantī Drawings*. Boston: Museum of Fine Arts, 1959.

EBELING
Ebeling, Klaus. *Ragamala Painting*. Basel, Paris, New Delhi: Ravi Kumar, 1973.

EHNBOM 1982
Ehnbom, Daniel J. "Three Miniatures from a Bhagavata Purana Series." In *Two Thousand Years of Indian Art*. Exhibition catalogue. London: Spink & Son, 1982, pp. 17–18, 94–95.

IN PRESS
Ehnbom, Daniel J. *An Analysis and Reconstruction of the Dispersed Bhāgavata Purāṇa from the Caurapancāśikā Group*. Zurich: Rietberg Museum, in press.

FALK AND ARCHER
Falk, Toby, and Mildred Archer. *Indian Miniatures in the India Office Library*. London: Sotheby Parke Bernet, 1981.

FINDLY
Findly, Ellison Banks. *From the Courts of India: Indian Miniatures from the Collection of the Worcester Art Museum*. Exhibition catalogue. Worcester, Mass.: Worcester Art Museum, 1981.

FRENCH
French, J. C. *Himalayan Art*. London: Oxford University Press, 1931.

GANGOLY
Gangoly, O. C. *Critical Catalogue of Miniature Paintings in the Baroda Museum*. Baroda: B. L. Mankad, 1961.

GARCIN DE TASSEY
Garcin de Tassey, J. *Histoire de la littérature hindoui et hindustani*. 2 vols. Paris, 1839–47.

Gīta Govinda
See Miller.

GLÜCK
Glück, Heinrich. *Die indischen Miniaturen des Haemzae-Romanes im Österreichischen Museum für Kunst und Industrie im Wien und in anderen Sammlungen*. Zurich: Amalthea, 1925.

GODARD
Godard, Yetta. "Les Marges du Muraḳḳa Gulshan." *Athar-é Irān*, vol. 1 (1936), pp. 11–33.

GOETZ 1924
Goetz, Hermann. "Kostüm und Mode an den indischen Fürstenhöfen in der Groszmoghul-Zeit (16. bis 19. Jahrhundert)." *Jahrbuch der asiatischen Kunst*, vol. 1 (1924), pp. 67–101.

1950
Goetz, Hermann. *The Art and Architecture of Bikaner State*. Oxford: B. Cassirer, 1950.

GOSWAMY 1968
Goswamy, B. N. "Pahari Painting: The Family as the Basis of Style." *Marg*, vol. 24, no. 4 (September 1968), pp. 17–62.

1975
Pahari Paintings of the Nala-Damayanti Theme in the Collection of Dr. Karan Singh. Essay and notes by B. N. Goswamy. New Delhi: National Museum, 1975.

GOSWAMY AND DALLAPICCOLA
Goswamy, B. N., and A. L. Dallapiccola. *Krishna, The Divine Lover*. Boston: David R. Godine, 1982.

GRAY
Gray, Basil, ed. *The Arts of India*. Ithaca, N.Y.: Cornell University Press, 1981.

GUPTA
Gupta, P. L. *Candāyana*. Bombay: Hindi Grantha Ratnakara, 1964.

Hamza-nāma
Hamza-nāma: Vollständige Wiedergabe der bekannten Blätter der Handschriften aus dem Beständen aller erreichbaren Sammlungen. 2 vols. Codices selecti phototypice impressi, vol. 52. Graz: Akademische Druck- und Verlagsanstalt, 1974–.

HAVELL
Havell, Ernest Binfield. *Indian Sculpture and Painting*. London: J. Murray, 1908.

Heeramaneck Collection
The Arts of India and Nepal: The Nasli and Alice Heeramaneck Collection. Exhibition catalogue. Boston: Museum of Fine Arts, 1966.

HENDLEY 1883
Hendley, Thomas H. *Memorials of the Jeypore Exhibition 1883*. 4 vols. London, 1883.

1897
Hendley, T. H. *The Rulers of India and Chiefs of Rajputana*. London: W. Griggs, 1897.

HOLLIS
Hollis, Howard. "Portrait of a Nobleman." *Bulletin of the Cleveland Museum of Art*, vol. 33, no. 7 (September 1946), pp. 180–81, 185.

HUTCHINS
Hutchins, Francis G. *Young Krishna*. West Franklin, N.H.: Amarta Press, 1980.

Image of Man
In the Image of Man. The Indian Perception of the Universe through 2000 Years of Painting and Sculpture. Catalogue of an exhibition held at the Hayward Gallery. London: Weidenfeld and Nicolson in Association with the Arts Council of Great Britain, 1982.

Indian Heritage
The Indian Heritage: Court Life and Arts under Mughal Rule. Exhibition catalogue.

London: Victoria and Albert Museum, 1982.

JACQUEMONT — Jacquemont, Victor. *Letters from India; Describing a journey in the British dominions of India, Tibet, Lahore, and Cashmere, during the years 1828, 1829, 1830, 1831*. Translated from the French. 2 vols. London: E. Churton, 1834.

Kathāsaritsāgara — *See* Penzer.

KEŚAVADĀSA — Keśavadāsa. *Rasikapriyā*. New Delhi: National Museum of India, 1962.

KHANDALAVALA 1951 — Khandalavala, Karl. "Leaves from Rajasthan." *Marg*, vol. 4, no. 3 (1951), pp. 2–24, 49–56.

1958 — Khandalavala, Karl. *Pahari Miniature Painting*. Bombay: New Book Company, 1958.

KHANDALAVALA AND CHANDRA 1965 — Khandalavala, Karl, and Moti Chandra. *Miniatures and Sculptures from the Collection of the Late Sir Cowasji Jehangir, Bart.* Bombay: Prince of Wales Museum of Western India, 1965.

1969 — Khandalavala, Karl, and Moti Chandra. *New Documents of Indian Painting: A Reappraisal*. Bombay: Prince of Wales Museum of Western India, 1969.

KHANDALAVALA, CHANDRA, AND CHANDRA — Khandalavala, Karl, Moti Chandra, and Pramod Chandra. *Miniature Painting: A Catalogue of the Exhibition of the Sri Motichand Khajanchi Collection*. New Delhi: Lalit Kalā Akademi, 1960.

KRAMRISCH — Kramrisch, Stella. *Manifestations of Shiva*. Exhibition catalogue. Philadelphia: Philadelphia Museum of Art, 1981.

Kṛishṇa — *Kṛishṇa*. Exhibition catalogue. New Delhi: National Museum of India, 1982.

KRISHNA — Krishna, Anand. *Malwa Painting*. Varanasi: Bharat Kala Bhavan, 1963.

KRISHNADASA — Krishnadasa, Rai. *Mughal Miniatures*. New Delhi: Lalit Kalā Akademi, 1955.

LAURIN ET AL. — Laurin, René, et al. *Arts d'Asie*. Exhibition catalogue. Paris: Hôtel Drouot, 1979.

LEACH — Leach, Linda York. "Later Mughal Painting." In *The Arts of India*, edited by Basil Gray, pp. 141–58. Ithaca, N.Y.: Cornell University Press, 1981.

LEE — *Rajput Painting*. With an introductory essay and catalogue notes by Sherman E. Lee. Catalogue by George Montgomery. Exhibition catalogue. New York: Asia House, 1960.

LEWIS — *Paintings and Drawings of Persia and India. . . . From the Collection of John Frederick Lewis*. Exhibition catalogue. Philadelphia: Pennsylvania Academy of the Fine Arts, 1924.

LOSTY 1982 — Losty, Jeremiah P. *The Art of the Book in India*. Exhibition catalogue. London: British Library, 1982.

1983 — Losty, J. P. "Two Mughal Manuscripts Acquired by OMPB." *India Office Library and Records and Oriental Manuscripts and Printed Books Newsletter*, vol. 30 (November 1983), pp. 13–14.

Mahābhārata — *The Mahābhārata*. 27 vols. Poona: Bhandarkar Oriental Research Institute, 1927–72.
See also Roy

MANUCCI — Manucci, Niccolao. *Storia do mogor. Or Mogul India 1653–1708*. Translated with introduction and notes by William Irvine. Royal Asiatic Society, Indian Texts Series, I. 4 vols. London: John Murray, 1906–8.

MARTIN — Martin, F. R. *The Miniature Painting and Painters of Persia, India, and Turkey, from the Eighth to the Eighteenth Century*. London: B. Quaritch, 1912.

MCINERNEY — McInerney, Terence. *Indian Painting: 1525–1825*. Exhibition catalogue. London: David Carritt, 1982.

MCNEAR — McNear, Everett, and Ann McNear. *Persian and Indian Miniatures from the Collection of Everett and Ann McNear*. Exhibition catalogue. Chicago: Art Institute of Chicago, 1974.

MEHTA — Mehta, Nānālāl Chamanlāl. *Studies in Indian Painting*. Bombay: D. B. Taraprevala, 1926.

MILLER — Miller, Barbara Stoler, ed. and trans. *Love Song of the Dark Lord: Jayadeva's Gītagovinda*. New York: Columbia University Press, 1977.

MITTAL 1963 — Mittal, Jagdish. "Deccani Paintings at the Samasthans of Wanaparthy, Gadwal, and Shorapur." *Marg*, vol. 26, no. 2 (March 1963), pp. 57–64.

1969 — Mittal, Jagdish. *Andhra Paintings of the*

Ramayana. Hyderabad: Lalit Kalā Akademi, 1969.

MITTER — Mitter, Partha. *Much Maligned Monsters: History of European Reactions to Indian Art.* Oxford: Clarendon Press, 1977.

OHRI 1967 — Ohri, V. C. "Laharu and Mahesh: The Miniature Painters at Chamba in the Mid Eighteenth Century A.D." *Lalit Kalā*, no. 13 (1967), p. 30.

1974 — Ohri, V. C. "Kangra Painting of Pre-Sansār Chand Period." *Lalit Kalā*, no. 17 (1974), p. 43.

OPRESCU — Oprescu, George. *Oriental Art in Rumania.* Bucharest: Meridiane Publishing House, 1963.

PAL 1967a — Pal, Pratapaditya. "A *Kalāpustaka* from Nepal." *Bulletin of the American Academy of Benares*, vol. 1 (November 1967), pp. 23–33.

1967b — Pal, Pratapaditya. *Rāgamālā Paintings in the Museum of Fine Arts, Boston.* Exhibition catalogue. Boston: Museum of Fine Arts, 1967.

1976 — Pal, Pratapaditya. *The Flute and the Brush: Indian Paintings from the William Theo Brown and Paul Wonner Collection.* Exhibition catalogue. Newport Beach, Calif.: Newport Harbor Art Museum, 1976.

1978 — Pal, Pratapaditya. *The Classical Tradition in Rajput Painting, from the Paul F. Walter Collection.* Exhibition catalogue. New York: Pierpont Morgan Library/Gallery Association of New York State, 1978.

PARKS — [Parks, Fanny.] *Wanderings of a Pilgrim in Search of the Picturesque.* 2 vols. London: Pelham Richardson, 1850.

PENZER — Somadeva Bhatta. *The Ocean of Story, Being C. H. Tawney's Translation of Somadeva's Kathā Sarit Sāgara.* Edited with an introduction and terminal essay by N. M. Penzer. 10 vols. London: Privately printed, 1924–28. Reprint. UNESCO Collection of Representative Works, Indian Series. Delhi, Patna, and Varanasi: Motilal Banarsidass, 1968.

Polsky Collections — *Indian Paintings from the Polsky Collections.* Exhibition catalogue. Princeton: University Art Museum, 1982.

Rāmāyaṇa — *See Vālmīki.*

RANDHAWA 1954 — Randhawa, M. S. *Kangra Valley Painting.* Delhi: Publications Division, Ministry of Information and Broadcasting, Govt. of India, 1954. Reprint. New Delhi, 1972.

1960 — Randhawa, M. S. *Kangra Paintings of the Bhāgavata Purāṇa.* New Delhi: National Museum of India, 1960.

1962 — Randhawa, M. S. *Kangra Paintings on Love.* New Delhi: National Museum, 1962.

1963 — Randhawa, M. S. *Kangra Paintings of the Gīta Govinda.* Introduction by W. G. Archer. New Delhi: National Museum, 1963.

1966 — Randhawa, M. S. *Kangra Paintings of the Bihārī Sat Saī.* New Delhi: National Museum, 1966.

Rasikapriyā — *See* Bahadur.

ROBINSON — Robinson, B. W., ed. *Islamic Painting and the Arts of the Book. The Keir Collection.* With an introduction by Ivan Stchoukine and contributions by B. W. Robinson, Ernst J. Grube, G. M. Meredith-Owens, and R. W. Skelton. London: Faber and Faber, 1976.

ROY — *The Mahabharata of Krishna-Dwaipayana Vyasa.* Translated into English prose from the original Sanskrit text by Pratap Chandra Roy. 2d ed. 12 vols. Calcutta: D. Bose, 1919–54.

SEYLLER — Seyller, John. "Model and Copy: The Illustration of Three *Razmnāma* Manuscripts." *Archives of Asian Art*, vol. 38. In press.

SHARMA — Sharma, O. P. *Indian Miniature Painting.* Exhibition catalogue. Brussels: Bibliothèque Royale Albert Ier, 1974.

SIMSAR 1937 — *Oriental Manuscripts of the John Frederick Lewis Collection in the Free Library of Philadelphia.* A descriptive catalogue by Muhammed Ahmed Simsar. Philadelphia: Free Library, 1937.

1978 — Nakhshabi, Ziya' u'd-Din. *Tales of a Parrot: The Cleveland Museum of Art's Ṭūṭī-Nāma.* Translated and edited by Muhammed A. Simsar. Cleveland: Cleveland Museum of Art/Graz: Akademische Druck- und Verlagsanstalt, 1978.

SIVARAMAMURTI 1968 — Sivaramamurti, C. *South Indian Paintings.* New Delhi: National Museum, 1968.

1977 — Sivaramamurti, Calambur. *The Art of India*. New York: Harry N. Abrams, 1977.

SKELTON 1956 — Skelton, Robert. "Murshidabad Painting." *Marg*, vol. 10, no. 1 (December 1956), pp. 10–22.

1957 — Skelton, Robert. "The Mughal Artist Farokh Beg." *Ars Orientalis*, vol. 2 (1957), pp. 393–411.

1961 — Skelton, Robert. *Indian Miniatures from the XVth to XIXth Centuries*. Foreword by W. G. Archer. Exhibition catalogue. Venice: Published for Fondazione Giorgio Cini by Neri Pozza, 1961.

1969 — Skelton, Robert. "Two Mughal Lion Hunts." In *Victoria and Albert Museum Yearbook, Number One*, pp. 33–48. London: Phaidon, 1969.

1970 — Skelton, Robert. "Mughal Paintings from [a] Harivaṃśa Manuscript." In *Victoria and Albert Museum Yearbook, Number Two*, pp. 41–54. London: Phaidon, 1970.

1976a — Skelton, Robert. "Facets of Indian Painting." *Apollo*, vol. 104, no. 176 (October 1976), pp. 266–73. (Reprinted in *Treasures from the Collection of Frits Lugt at Institut Néerlandais, Paris*. London: Apollo, 1976.)

1976b — Skelton, Robert. "Indian Painting of the Mughal Period." In *Islamic Painting and the Arts of the Book: The Keir Collection*, edited by B. W. Robinson, pp. 233–74. London: Faber and Faber, 1976.

1981 — Skelton, Robert. "Shaykh Phūl and the Origins of Bundi Painting." *Chhavi 2* (1981), pp. 123–39.

SMART 1973 — Smart, Ellen. "Four Illustrated Mughal Babur-nama Manuscripts." *Art and Archeology Research Papers*, vol. 3 (1973), pp. 54–58.

1978 — Smart, Ellen S. "Six Folios from a Dispersed Manuscript of the Babarnama." In *Indian Painting*, pp. 111–32. Exhibition catalogue. London: P. & D. Colnaghi, 1978.

SMITH — Smith, Vincent A. *A History of Fine Art in India and Ceylon: From the Earliest Times to the Present Day*. Oxford: Clarendon Press, 1911.

SÖRENSON — Sörenson, Sören. *An Index to Names in the Mahābhārata*. London: Williams and Norgate, 1904–25.

SPINK & SON 1976 — *Painting for the Royal Courts of India*. Exhibition catalogue. London: Spink & Son, 1976.

1980 — *Islamic Art from India*. Exhibition catalogue. London: Spink & Son, 1980.

1982 — *Two Thousand Years of Indian Art*. Exhibition catalogue. London: Spink & Son, 1982.

STCHOUKINE — Stchoukine, Ivan. *La Peinture indienne à l'époque des Grands Moghols*. Paris: Librairie Ernest Leroux, 1929.

SULEIMAN — Suleiman, Hamid. *Miniatiury k Babur-Name*. Tashkent: "Fan," 1970.

TAGARE — Tagare, Ganesh Vasudeo, trans. *The Bhāgavata Purāṇa*. Delhi, Varanasi, and Patna: Motilal Banarsidass, 1978.

TANDAN 1980 — Tandan, Raj. *The Ragamala Paintings from Basohli*. New Delhi: Lalit Kalā Akademi, 1980.

1982 — Tandan, Raj Kumar. *Indian Miniature Painting*. Bangalore: Natesan, 1982.

TOD — Tod, James. *Annals and Antiquities of Rajast'han, or the Central and Western Rajpoot States of India*. 2 vols. London, 1829–32.

TOOTH AND SONS — *Indian Paintings from the Seventeenth to Nineteenth Centuries*. Exhibition catalogue. London: Arthur Tooth and Sons, 1975.

TOPSFIELD 1980 — Topsfield, Andrew. *Paintings from Rajasthan in the National Gallery of Victoria*. Melbourne: National Gallery of Victoria, 1980.

1981a — Topsfield, Andrew. "Painting for the Rajput Courts." In *The Arts of India*, edited by Basil Gray, pp. 159–76. Ithaca, N.Y.: Cornell University Press, 1981.

1981b — Topsfield, Andrew. "Sāhibdīn's *Gīta-Govinda* Illustrations." *Chhavi 2* (1981), pp. 231–38.

Tūtī-nāma — *See* Simsar 1978.

Tūzuk — *The Tūzuk-i-Jahāngīrī: or Memoirs of Jahāngīr*. Translated by Alexander Rogers and edited by Henry Beveridge. 2 vols. London: Royal Asiatic Society, 1909–14.

Reprint. Delhi: Munshiram Manoharlal, 1968.

Vālmīki — *The Vālmīki Rāmāyaṇa*. 7 vols. Baroda: Oriental Institute, 1960–75.

WALDSCHMIDT AND WALDSCHMIDT 1967 — Waldschmidt, Ernst, and Rose Leonore Waldschmidt. *Miniatures of Musical Inspiration in the Collection of the Berlin Museum of Indian Art: Pictures from the Western Himalaya Promontory*. Wiesbaden: O. Harrassowitz, 1967.

1975 — Waldschmidt, Ernst, and Rose Leonore Waldschmidt. *Miniatures of Musical Inspiration in the Collection of the Berlin Museum of Indian Art*. Part 2, *Ragamala Miniatures from Northern India and the Deccan*. Wiesbaden: O. Harrassowitz, 1975.

WEBSTER 1973 — Webster, Mary. "The Mystery of the Lucknow Cock-Fight, Zoffany in India, I," *Country Life*, vol. 153 (1973), pp. 588–89.

1976 — Webster, Mary. *Johann Zoffany 1733–1810*. Exhibition catalogue. London: National Portrait Gallery, 1976.

WELCH, A. — Welch, Anthony. *Calligraphy in the Arts of the Muslim World*. Exhibition catalogue. Austin: University of Texas Press in Cooperation with the Asia Society, New York, 1979.

WELCH, S. C. 1961 — Welch, Stuart Cary. "The Paintings of Basāwan." *Lalit Kalā*, no. 10 (October 1961), pp. 7–17.

1964 — Welch, Stuart Cary. *The Art of Mughal India*. Exhibition catalogue. New York: Asia Society, 1964; distributed by Harry N. Abrams.

1973 — Welch, Stuart Cary. *A Flower from Every Meadow: Indian Paintings from American Collections*. With contributions by Mark Zebrowski. Exhibition catalogue. New York: Asia Society, 1973; distributed by New York Graphic Society.

1976 — Welch, Stuart Cary. *Indian Drawings and Painted Sketches, Sixteenth through Nineteenth Centuries*. Exhibition catalogue. New York: Asia Society, 1976.

1978 — Welch, Stuart Cary. *Room for Wonder: Indian Painting during the British Period 1760–1880*. Exhibition catalogue. New York: American Federation of Arts, 1978.

1985 — Welch, Stuart Cary. *India!* Exhibition catalogue. New York: Metropolitan Museum of Art, 1985.

WELCH AND BEACH — Welch, Stuart Cary, and Milo Cleveland Beach. *Gods, Thrones, and Peacocks. Northern Indian Painting from Two Traditions: Fifteenth to Nineteenth Centuries*. Exhibition catalogue. New York: Asia Society, 1965; distributed by Harry N. Abrams.

WELCH AND WELCH — Welch, Anthony, and Stuart Cary Welch. *Arts of the Islamic Book: The Collection of Prince Sadruddin Khan*. Exhibition catalogue. Ithaca, N.Y.: Published for the Asia Society by Cornell University Press, 1982.

ZEBROWSKI — Zebrowski, Mark. *Deccani Painting*. Berkeley: University of California Press, 1983.

INDEX

Page references printed in *italics* refer to illustrations.